WOMEN IN
MODERN DRAMA

WOMEN IN
MODERN DRAMA

Freud, Feminism, and European
Theater at the Turn of the Century

by GAIL FINNEY

Cornell University Press

Ithaca and London

First published 1989 by Cornell University Press.

International Standard Book Number 0-8014-2284-1
Library of Congress Catalog Card Number 88-47924

Printed in the United States of America

Librarians: Library of Congress cataloging information appears on the last page of the book.

The paper in this book is acid-free and meets the guidelines for permanence and durability of the Committee on Production Guidelines for Book Longevity of the Council on Library Resources.

10-4-90

For my grandmother,
Mercedes Cambeilh,
and sisters,
Carol Dougherty and Jill Lawson

Contents

Preface

Turn-of-the-century literature is strikingly diverse. Its variety is indicated by the various "isms" used to describe it—naturalism, aestheticism, symbolism, impressionism, neoromanticism. The drama of the time is no exception. While such naturalist writers as Shaw and Synge strive for the utmost verisimilitude in their rendering of speech and milieu and often feature proletarian characters, aestheticist playwrights such as Wilde and Hofmannsthal present us with aristocratic dandies speaking cultivated phrases in highly stylized settings, and Ibsen, Strindberg, and Hauptmann work in both the naturalist and the symbolist modes. Common to all these literary modes, however, is an interest in female psychology and sexuality. Women characters in turn-of-the-century drama are varied and complex. From femme fatale to New Woman, from childlike waif to mature housewife, from hysteric to feminist, from barmaid to grande dame—women figures now populate the stage in larger numbers and with greater power than at any previous point in the nineteenth century.

The prominence of female characters in the drama of the period had everything to do with the situation of women at the turn of the century, a time when the first feminist movement was challenging the traditional view that women are fundamentally different from and subordinate to men. This view is nowhere better represented than in the writings of Freud. His theories of femininity occupy one end of a spectrum of turn-of-the-century attitudes toward women, the other end being occupied by feminism. This spectrum of conflicting beliefs serves to illuminate a series of female figures created by dramatists of the day and thus helps us to assess the ambivalent attitudes of these writers toward the women's movement.

Of major importance for this book's development was my participation in the Harvard Faculty Seminar on Feminist Literary Theory during its inaugural year, 1984–1985. My thanks go in particular to the members of the Planning Committee, Marianne Hirsch, Alice Jardine, and Susan Winnett, who devoted considerable time and energy to launching and directing the seminar. I am also grateful for financial support from the National Endowment for the Humanities and the Clark Fund of Harvard University.

A version of Chapter 4 has appeared in *Women in Theatre*, vol. 11 of *Themes in Drama*, ed. James M. Redmond (Cambridge: Cambridge Univ. Press, 1989), and is included here with the permission of the editor and publisher.

I express my sincere appreciation to the friends and colleagues who offered thoughtful comments on portions of the manuscript: Dorrit Cohn, Laurie Edson, Karl Guthke, Deborah Harter, John Hoberman, Alfred Hoelzel, Barry Jacobs, Simon Karlinsky, Peter Klein, Birgitta Knuttgen, Stephen Mitchell, and Deborah Nord. Further thanks go to Bernhard Kendler of Cornell University Press for the efficiency and good sense with which he oversaw every phase of the book's production, and to Martha Linke and Barbara Salazar for the acuity with which they edited the manuscript.

Finally, I am deeply indebted, for their support and friendship throughout the period in which this book was conceived and written, to James G. Basker and Caroline Newman.

GAIL FINNEY

Davis, California

WOMEN IN
MODERN DRAMA

Woman's Place at the Turn of the Century: Emancipation or Hysterization?

The late 1870s mark the beginning of a remarkably rich period in the history of European theater, a period in which roles for women were abundant. Rather than being confronted with the standard heroines of nineteenth-century farce and melodrama, turn-of-the-century theatergoers were treated to Shaw's Major Barbara and Candida, Synge's Pegeen Mike, Strindberg's Laura and Miss Julie, Wilde's Salomé, Ibsen's Nora Helmer and Hedda Gabler, Wedekind's Lulu, and a wealth of other individualized and memorable female characters. Insofar as the drama is by definition the most public and social of all literary genres, the reasons for this sudden flowering of stage heroines can be found in the immense upheavals in the condition of women at the turn of the century, changes by which no dramatist of the day could remain unaffected. These developments must be seen, however, against the background of women's situation in earlier nineteenth-century Europe.

Because the story of women's oppression in the last century has been told often, I will rehearse it only briefly here. Foremost

I

among the frustrations of women's lives was their condemnation
to trivial occupations or idleness. In his autobiography Edward
Carpenter, turn-of-the-century socialist and feminist, offers a
description of his family life that can be seen as representative of
Victorian middle- and upper-class society in England and elsewhere:

> There were six or seven servants in the house, and my six sisters
> had absolutely nothing to do except dabble in paints and music
> . . . and wander aimlessly from room to room to see if by any
> chance "anything was going on." Dusting, cooking, sewing, darn-
> ing—all light household duties were already forestalled; there
> was no private garden, and if there had been it would have been
> "unladylike" to do anything in it; *every* girl could not find an
> absorbing interest in sol-fa or water-colours; athletics were not
> invented; every aspiration and outlet, except in the direction of
> dress and dancing, was blocked; and marriage, with the growing
> scarcity of men, was becoming every day less likely, or easy to
> compass. More than once girls of whom I least expected it told me
> that their lives were miserable "with nothing on earth to do."[1]

It is hardly surprising that women were not permitted to undertake challenging tasks in this period: Victorian physicians and
anthropologists believed that female physiological functions diverted roughly 20 percent of women's creative energy from
brain activity; that the frontal lobes of the female brain were
lighter and less developed than male lobes; and that women
were therefore less intelligent than men.[2]

Married women were scarcely better off than the single wom-
en described by Carpenter. As industrialism grew throughout
Europe during the nineteenth century, men came more and

[1]Edward Carpenter, *My Days and Dreams* (London: Allen & Unwin, 1916), pp.
31–32.
[2]Elaine Showalter, "Feminist Criticism in the Wilderness," 1981; rpt. in *The
New Feminist Criticism: Essays on Women, Literature, and Theory,* ed. Showalter (New
York: Pantheon, 1985), p. 250. This view was shared by such nineteenth-century
German thinkers as Eduard von Hartmann; see vol. II of his *Philosophy of the
Unconscious* (1869), trans. William C. Coupland, 2d ed. (New York: Harcourt,
Brace, 1931), p. 67.

more to regard the home as a peaceful haven and moral refuge
from the increasing pressures of capitalist society. That such a
view strengthened the confinement of women to the domestic
sphere is nowhere better demonstrated than in Ruskin's essay
"Of Queens' Gardens" (1865), that consummate expression of
nineteenth-century chivalry and sentimentality:

> The man, in his rough work in open world, must encounter all
> peril and trial:—to him, therefore, the failure, the offence, the
> inevitable error: often he must be wounded, or subdued, often
> misled, and *always* hardened. But he guards the woman from all
> this; within his house, as ruled by her, unless she herself has
> sought it, need enter no danger, no temptation, no cause of error
> or offence. This is the true nature of home—it is the place of
> Peace; the shelter, not only from all injury, but from all terror,
> doubt, and division.[3]

Woman's place in the home—as mother—was further assured
by the lack of reliable methods of contraception. It was, in short,
the female's duty to live for others; the Victorian social critic
William R. Greg speaks for his male contemporaries throughout
Europe when he characterizes as "redundant" those women who
choose to do otherwise, women "who, in place of completing,
sweetening, and embellishing the existence of others, are compelled to lead an independent and incomplete existence of their
own."[4]

Women were at a similar disadvantage in matters of sex. Propriety dictated that middle-class women remain ignorant about
sex until marriage; as might be expected, the consequences were
often disastrous. The comments of the popular and influential
Victorian physician Dr. William Acton typify the orthodoxy of
the age: "I should say that the majority of women (happily for
them) are not very much troubled with sexual feeling of any
kind. . . . As a general rule, a modest woman seldom desires any

[3]John Ruskin, "Of Queens' Gardens," in his *Sesame and Lilies* (New York:
Wiley, 1865), pp. 90–91.
[4]William R. Greg, "Why Are Women Redundant?" in his *Literary and Social
Judgments* (Boston: Osgood, 1873), p. 276.

sexual gratification for herself. She submits to her husband, but only to please him; and, but for the desire of maternity, would far rather be relieved from his attentions."[5] With such opinions holding sway, it is difficult to imagine that women in nineteenth-century Europe were sexually satisfied.[6] Nowhere was the double standard more apparent than in the matter of divorce. The British Divorce Act of 1857 decreed that a husband could divorce his wife on the grounds of adultery alone, while a woman was required to prove her husband guilty of rape, sodomy or bestiality, or adultery *in conjunction* with incest, bigamy, cruelty, or desertion.[7] Appropriately, the phrase "suffer and be still," coined by a popular writer of mid-nineteenth-century etiquette books to summarize a woman's "highest duty," has been used as the title of a book on women in the Victorian age.[8]

In view of the inequities they endured, it is little wonder that many women were moved to react against their lot. I would like here to concentrate on two such reactions, both reaching their peak at the turn of the century, the one outer-directed, the other inner-directed: the first feminist movement, often called "old feminism" to distinguish it from the new movement that began in the 1960s, and hysteria. In keeping with the primary motivation behind both the old and the new women's movements, throughout this book "feminism" as a historical or sociological term refers to the drive for equal rights for the sexes. The term has a somewhat different meaning when used in connection

---

[5]William Acton, *The Functions and Disorders of the Reproductive Organs* (1857), cited in Steven Marcus, *The Other Victorians: A Study of Sexuality and Pornography in Mid-Nineteenth-Century England* (New York: Basic Books, 1974), p. 31.

[6]Peter Gay seeks to revise such conceptions of Victorian sexuality, but focuses for the most part on the United States. As he himself points out, it is impossible to prove that the sexually uninhibited couples he portrays represent the rule rather than the exception; Gay, *Education of the Senses*, vol. I of *The Bourgeois Experience: Victoria to Freud* (New York: Oxford Univ. Press, 1984).

[7]Richard J. Evans, *The Feminists: Women's Emancipation Movements in Europe, America, and Australasia, 1840–1920* (London: Croom Helm, 1977), p. 63.

[8]The phrase is found in Mrs. Sarah S. Ellis, *The Daughters of England* (1845); see *Suffer and Be Still: Women in the Victorian Age*, ed. Martha Vicinus (Bloomington: Indiana Univ. Press, 1972), p. x.

with literary criticism or psychological theory, as I will explain later.

Although the term "feminism" did not appear in print until 1895, the roots of the feminist movement lie in the eighteenth century, where two main influences can be distinguished: the Enlightenment notion that everyone is equally endowed with reason and that women should therefore have the same rights to education as men, and the emphasis of the bourgeois revolutions on equality and on individual rights and liberties.[9] The movement was further fueled in the nineteenth century by the liberal Protestant belief that individuals are responsible for their own salvation, as well as by the rise of the middle classes and, concomitantly, of an increasing number of professions that excluded women. While nineteenth-century feminism officially began in the United States with the first Women's Rights Convention in Seneca Falls, New York, in 1848, some of the movement's earliest and most influential advocates were Europeans. Even the briefest treatment of the history of feminism is incomplete, for example, without mention of Mary Wollstonecraft's startlingly modern *Vindication of the Rights of Woman* (1792), which attacks the socialization of women into pleasing "toys" and pleads for their right to a serious education; in the same year

9My brief survey of old feminism draws primarily on Evans, *Feminists;* Patricia Stubbs, *Women and Fiction: Feminism and the Novel, 1880–1920* (1979; London: Methuen, 1981); *Feminism: The Essential Historical Writings,* ed. Miriam Schneir (New York: Vintage, 1972); and *The Feminist Papers: From Adams to Beauvoir,* ed. Alice S. Rossi (New York: Bantam, 1973). On facets of European feminism see also Olive Banks, *Faces of Feminism: A Study of Feminism as a Social Movement* (Oxford: Robertson, 1981); Richard J. Evans, *The Feminist Movement in Germany, 1894–1933* (London: Sage, 1976); Andrew Rosen, *Rise Up, Women! The Militant Campaign of the Women's Social and Political Union, 1903–1914* (London: Routledge & Kegan Paul, 1974); Werner Thönnessen, *The Emancipation of Women: The Rise and Decline of the Women's Movement in German Social Democracy, 1863–1933,* trans. Joris de Bres (London: Pluto, 1973); Herrad Schenk, *Die feministische Herausforderung: 150 Jahre Frauenbewegung in Deutschland,* 2d ed. (Munich: Beck, 1981); Sylvia Pankhurst, *The Suffragette Movement: An Intimate Account of Persons and Ideals* (1931; London: Virago, 1977); and Ray (Rachel C.) Strachey, *The Cause: A Short History of the Women's Movement in Great Britain* (1928; Bath: Chivers, 1974).

Theodor von Hippel published a comparable work in Germany, *Über die bürgerliche Verbesserung der Weiber (On Improving the Status of Women)*. Similarly, John Stuart Mill's *Subjection of Women* (1869) deplores the fact that women have been socially conditioned to live for others and deny themselves, to shut themselves off from productive occupations, and, worst of all, to assent in their own subjection. Often called the "feminist bible," the essay was soon translated into many languages and served as a catalyst for feminist movements throughout the world.

The advances achieved by the women's movement in the 1960s and '70s make it easy to forget that many of the goals women have been struggling to attain during the last twenty years had already been fought for during the nineteenth century: the improvement of women's education at both the secondary and university levels, access for women to medicine and the other professions, the right of married women to own property and to retain it after divorce or separation, equal pay for equal work, and safe, reliable methods of birth control. Common to all these causes was the goal of equality with men. Although some suffragists believed in innate sexual differences, arguing, for example, that women were uniquely suited to certain careers, their primary goal was nonetheless equal rights for both sexes. Even moral reforms such as the temperance campaign and the battle against prostitution were motivated by a desire for equality, albeit with female standards as the norm—by the hope that men would rise to the moral behavior of women.[10] Progress was made in many of these areas. In England and in a number of continental nations, women began in the middle decades of the century to enter established universities, to found their own colleges, and, somewhat later, to attend medical

[10]Its stress on equality marks a significant difference between old feminism and certain branches of contemporary feminism, especially in France, where a number of prominent feminist writers emphasize the existence of specifically feminine styles of thinking and writing. See *New French Feminisms: An Anthology*, ed. Elaine Marks and Isabelle de Courtivron (1980; New York: Schocken, 1981), and works listed in the bibliography under "French Women Writers and *l'Écriture féminine*" in Showalter, *New Feminist Criticism*, pp. 390–392.

schools; Married Women's Property Acts were passed from the
1870s on.

Political reforms came more slowly. It was the issue of female
suffrage—"the cause," as it was called—that mobilized and united feminist movements worldwide. The drive for the vote took
on militant and occasionally even violent dimensions. Probably
the best-known incident occurred in the early 1900s in England,
where women suffragists under the leadership of Emmeline
Pankhurst were sent to prison because they disrupted political
meetings, staged mass marches, and smashed shop windows,
their imprisonment beginning a cycle of hunger strikes, force-
feeding, release, and reimprisonment. Inspired by the push for
suffrage, European feminism achieved its greatest strength in
the forty years around the turn of the century and lapsed into a
period of hibernation after 1920, since by then the vote had
been granted to women in England and in most of those countries on the Continent where feminist activity had been greatest.

The suffragist was not the only figure to whom women's oppression in the nineteenth century gave birth. A second was the
female hysteric. Hysteria was of course not a new ailment—it
was recognized even in the days of Hippocrates. Yet by all accounts, the number of hysterical women patients rose dramatically during the Victorian era.[11] This increase can be seen as the
culmination of the wave of female illness that occurred in the
last century, often reaching alarming proportions. Barbara
Ehrenreich and Deirdre English document the trend: "In the
mid- and late nineteenth century a curious epidemic seemed to
be sweeping through the middle- and upper-class female population both in the United States and England [and, one might
add, other European countries as well]. Diaries and journals

[11]Charles Bernheimer, Introduction to *In Dora's Case: Freud—Hysteria—Feminism*, ed. Bernheimer and Claire Kahane (New York: Columbia Univ. Press,
1985), p. 5. See also Elaine Showalter, *The Female Malady: Women, Madness, and
English Culture, 1830–1980* (New York: Pantheon, 1985), for a fascinating discussion of the Victorian association of hysteria and insanity with women in
particular.

from the time give us hundreds of examples of women slipping into hopeless invalidism."[12] Sickness was, quite simply, one of the few ways to avoid the reproductive and domestic duties so closely bound up with women's sphere at the time. In the course of the century doctors came increasingly to believe that women were inherently weak, dependent, and sickly—natural patients. Hysteria, which tended to come and go in fits and starts and to manifest itself in symptoms ranging from shortness of breath, chronic coughing or sneezing, loss of voice, and eating disorders to temporary paralysis or loss of sensation in various parts of the body, was a more complex issue, since, lacking an organic basis, it did not respond to medical treatment.

Where feminism is rebellious, emancipatory, and—in its potential to change the world outside—constructive, hysteria is compliant, imprisoning, and self-destructive. Toril Moi's claim with respect to Hélène Cixous's and Catherine Clément's *Jeune née (The Newly Born Woman)* is illuminating: "Hysteria is not, *pace* Hélène Cixous, the incarnation of the revolt of women forced to silence but rather a declaration of defeat, the realization that there is no other way out. Hysteria is, as Catherine Clément perceives, a cry for help when defeat becomes real, when the woman sees that she is efficiently gagged and chained to her feminine role."[13]

Both responses to female oppression—hysteria and feminism—are successively embodied in Bertha Pappenheim. She is better known as Anna O., the name given to her by the prominent Viennese neurologist Josef Breuer in his case history of his treatment of her in the early 1880s. A highly intelligent girl with an unusually lively imagination, she suffered a hysterical collapse while devoting herself full-time to nursing her tubercular

[12]Barbara Ehrenreich and Deirdre English, *For Her Own Good: 150 Years of the Experts' Advice to Women* (Garden City: Anchor, 1978), p.103.
[13]Toril Moi, "Representation of Patriarchy: Sexuality and Epistemology in Freud's Dora," in *In Dora's Case*, p. 192. As Maria Ramas notes ("Freud's Dora, Dora's Hysteria," in *In Dora's Case*, p. 179n), recent feminist discussions of hysteria tend to stress its element of compliance.

father. Anna's hysterical symptoms, which included hallucinations, alternating periods of overexcitement and somnolence, and an inability to speak her native language, were alleviated by what she herself dubbed the "talking cure" or "chimney-sweeping," the process of telling Breuer about her fantasies under self-induced hypnosis.[14] Breuer then eliminated her symptoms temporarily by hypnotizing her and encouraging her to recall the occasions on which they had first appeared. Bertha Pappenheim later left Vienna for Germany, where she became the country's first social worker and an active campaigner for women's rights. She sought to further the feminist cause, for example, by translating Wollstonecraft's *Vindication of the Rights of Woman* into German and by writing a play titled *Women's Rights*.

Consideration of Bertha Pappenheim as the inventor of the cathartic method of therapy brings us to psychoanalysis, one male reaction to the hysteria brought on by women's oppression. For although the founder of psychoanalysis never met Anna O. and learned about her only through his friend and patron Breuer, she was the hysteric whom Freud most often named and discussed, and her case was profoundly useful to him in his own treatment of hysterics in Vienna after his return from Paris, where he studied hysteria under Charcot in the mid-1880s. Indeed, it was Freud's clinical experience with female hysterics that gave birth to psychoanalysis, since the cathartic techniques of hypnosis, suggestion, and free association led him to the discovery of the unconscious mind and thus of repression, the cornerstone of the new science.

[14]Josef Breuer, "Fräulein Anna O.," in Breuer and Sigmund Freud, *Studies on Hysteria* (*Studien über Hysterie*, 1895), vol. II of *The Standard Edition of the Complete Psychological Works of Sigmund Freud*, trans. and ed. James Strachey et al. (London: Hogarth, 1955), p. 30. (This edition is hereafter cited as *SE*.) For a psychoanalytic feminist reading of Anna's speech problems which discusses in greater depth her complicated relationship with Breuer, see Dianne Hunter, "Hysteria, Psychoanalysis, and Feminism: The Case of Anna O.," in *The (M)other Tongue: Essays in Feminist Psychoanalytic Interpretation*, ed. Shirley Nelson Garner, Claire Kahane, and Madelon Sprengnether (Ithaca: Cornell Univ. Press, 1985), pp. 89–115.

Freud's eventual belief that the nature of hysterical repression
is psychosexual—that hysteria is the expression of secret sexual
desires—is closely bound up with his patriarchal conceptions of
female sexuality. This connection is nowhere clearer than in his
famous case study of "Dora," whose hysterical symptoms he attributes to the repression of her desires for her father, for Herr
K. (whose wife, Frau K., is having an affair with Dora's father),
and, at the deepest level, for Frau K.—when in fact the primary
cause of Dora's hysteria is her role as a pawn in their game, a
role determined by her position as a woman in turn-of-the-century Europe.[15] The debate that Freud sparked about femininity
and female sexuality has been crucial to the history of psychoanalysis.[16] In his *Three Essays on the Theory of Sexuality* (1905), for
instance, he attributes women's greater susceptibility to hysteria
to their sexuality: "The fact that women change their leading
erotogenic zone in this way [from clitoris to vagina], together
with the wave of repression at puberty, which, as it were, puts
aside their childish masculinity, are the chief determinants of
the greater proneness of women to neurosis and especially to
hysteria. These determinants, therefore, are intimately related
to the essence of femininity."[17] Freud makes an equally revealing statement about the relationship between femininity and
psychoanalysis in his paper "Femininity" (1933): "The wish to
get the longed-for penis eventually in spite of everything may
contribute to the motives that drive a mature woman to analysis,
and what she may reasonably expect from analysis—a capacity,
for instance, to carry on an intellectual profession—may often
be recognized as a sublimated modification of this repressed
wish."[18]

[15]Freud, "Fragment of an Analysis of a Case of Hysteria" ("Bruchstück einer
Hysterie-Analyse," 1905), *SE*, VII, 7–122. For a collection of interpretations of
this controversial case, see *In Dora's Case* and the works listed in its bibliography.
[16]Cf. *Feminine Sexuality: Jacques Lacan and the "école freudienne,"* trans. Jacqueline Rose, ed. Rose and Juliet Mitchell (1982; New York: Norton, 1985), pp.
27–28.
[17]Freud, *Three Essays on the Theory of Sexuality* (*Drei Abhandlungen zur Sexualtheorie*), *SE*, VII, 221.
[18]Freud, "Femininity" ("Die Weiblichkeit"), *SE*, XXII, 125.

Freud's theories of female sexuality, which were elaborated in these and other essays, will be more fully explored in Part I. For our purposes at this point, it is sufficient to stress the crucial place of Freudian psychoanalysis in what Michel Foucault calls the "hysterization" of women. Reflecting his ongoing interest in the relationship between knowledge and power, the first volume of his *History of Sexuality* attempts to overturn received ideas about sexual repression by arguing that for the last two hundred years institutions of power have not thwarted but rather have encouraged a discourse of sexuality, though one fraught with taboos and prohibitions. According to Foucault, this "deployment of sexuality," which intensified during the nineteenth century, was brought about by four strategies or mechanisms of knowledge and power centering on sex: the hysterization of the female body, the pedagogization of children's sex, the socialization of procreative behavior, and the psychiatrization of perverse pleasure.[19] The first of these processes is key, since the idle woman, Foucault observes, was the first figure to be invested with sexuality. His definition of hysterization makes clear that its import was to tie women to their reproductive function, for hysterization is

a threefold process whereby the feminine body was analyzed— qualified and disqualified—as being thoroughly saturated with sexuality; whereby it was integrated into the sphere of medical practices, by reason of a pathology intrinsic to it; whereby, finally, it was placed in organic communication with the social body (whose regulated fecundity it was supposed to ensure), the family space (of which it had to be a substantial and functional element), and the life of children (which it produced and had to guarantee, by virtue of a biologico-moral responsibility lasting through the entire period of the children's education): the Mother, with her negative image of "nervous woman," constituted the most visible form of this hysterization. [104]

[19]Michel Foucault, *The History of Sexuality*, vol. I, *An Introduction*, trans. Robert Hurley (New York: Vintage, 1978), pp. 104–105. Subsequent page references appear in the text. See also "The History of Sexuality," in Foucault, *Power/ Knowledge: Selected Interviews and Other Writings, 1972–1977*, trans. Colin Gordon et al. (Sussex: Harvester, 1980), pp. 183–193.

It is not difficult to recognize Freudian psychoanalysis—the institutionalization of sexual confession—as a powerful instrument of hysterization.

Lest such a statement seem reductive, it should be noted that Freud came increasingly to believe in the original psychological bisexuality of both men and women and that psychoanalysis, when used to deal with what he viewed as unhealthy sexual repression in both sexes, was potentially liberating. In the main, however, both his new science and his concomitant theories of female sexuality stressed sexual *difference*. This emphasis is epitomized in his attacks on feminism per se, such as his remark in differentiating girls from boys as regards the passing of the Oedipus complex: "Here the feminist demand for equal rights for the sexes does not take us far, for the morphological distinction is bound to find expression in differences of psychical development. 'Anatomy is Destiny', to vary a saying of Napoleon's."[20] Similarly, referring to Mill's *Subjection of Women*, which Freud himself had translated into German in 1880, he criticizes the author for neglecting the inborn distinction between men and women, "the most significant one that exists."[21]

That this emphasis on sexual difference as a reaction against feminism was not limited to psychoanalysis is evident in an observation, couched as a supposition, made by Virginia Woolf in *A Room of One's Own* (1929):

> No age can ever have been as stridently sex-conscious as our own; those innumerable books by men about women in the British Museum are a proof of it. The Suffrage campaign was no doubt to blame. It must have roused in men an extraordinary desire for self-assertion; it must have made them lay an emphasis upon their sex and its characteristics which they would not have troubled to think about had they not been challenged. And when one is chal-

---

[20]Freud, "The Dissolution of the Oedipus Complex" ("Der Untergang des Ödipuskomplexes," 1924), *SE*, XIX, 178.

[21]Quoted by Ernest Jones, *The Life and Work of Sigmund Freud*, ed. and abr. Lionel Trilling and Steven Marcus (New York: Basic Books, 1961), p. 118.

lenged, even by a few women in black bonnets, one retaliates, if one has never been challenged before, rather excessively.[22]

By contrast, male contemporaries such as Edward Carpenter and the German socialist August Bebel, in their attention to women's need for autonomy, move, like their female counterparts in the feminist movement, in the direction of equality, of *sameness.*

To return now to the drama, we can see how the historical conjunction, itself dramatic, of these major developments involving women and affecting men helps to explain the presence of so many memorable female characters on the turn-of-the-century stage. This double spectrum—of women's responses to their oppression (feminism and hysteria) and of men's reactions to these responses (feminism and hysterization)—produced a field of conflicting currents of thought which inevitably left their mark on dramatists of the day. Caught up in these contrary forces, male dramatists were often deeply ambivalent toward women, and the versions of womanhood they created for the theater are correspondingly ambiguous. It is against the background of this force field that I examine the portrayals of a variety of female characters created by male playwrights between 1880 and 1920, the period embracing both the culmination of the first feminist movement and the origins of Freud's theories of female sexuality.

In pointing up the ambiguities in these characters I proceed in terms of analogy rather than influence, with Freudian theories of femininity and female sexuality offering a paradigmatic analogue for the dramatic depiction of female difference, often resisted by a character's own impulse toward emancipation and equality. My purpose here is to present Freud not as a culprit but simply as one of the most emphatic voices of turn-of-the-century patriarchal society. (Indeed, the role of turn-of-the-cen-

[22]Virginia Woolf, *A Room of One's Own* (1929; New York: Harcourt Brace, 1957), p. 103.

tury "culprit hysterizer" is much more aptly assigned to Otto
Weininger, the Viennese philosopher who in his notorious best-
seller *Geschlecht und Charakter* [1903] [*Sex and Character*] distinguishes woman from man by defining her as lacking in soul, will,
and morality.)²³ I regard Freud, in other words, neither as an
"evil man, and one of women's greatest enemies," nor as a "bril-
liant dreamer, who was either blind to the conditions around
him or did not look beyond those conditions"—the two poles
spanned by most American feminist views of Freud.²⁴

For both Freud and feminism the family is the main object of
attention, in the one case as the locus of psychic dynamics and in
the other as the microcosm of a society in need of change. Accordingly, family relationships provide my structure of orientation. After examining Schnitzler's *La Ronde* as a reflection of the

²³Otto Weininger, *Sex and Character*, (London: Heinemann, 1906), esp. pp.
186–213. Weininger's book was only one of a number of works written around
the turn of the century which, like Freud's, focused on sexuality as the subject of
scientific or quasi-scientific investigation. Others were Gustav Naumann's
Geschlecht und Kunst (Sex and art), August Francé's *Liebesleben der Pflanzen* (The
love life of plants), Ernst Wolzogen's *Dritte Geschlecht* (*The Third Sex*), Marie
Stopes's *Married Love*, articles by Laura Marholm in the journal *Freie Bühne für
modernes Leben*, and studies of sexuality by Havelock Ellis and Richard Krafft-
Ebing. Cf. Marilyn Scott-Jones, "Laura Marholm and the Question of Female
'Nature,'" in *Beyond the Eternal Feminine: Critical Essays on Women and German
Literature*, ed. Susan L. Cocalis and Kay Goodman (Stuttgart: Heinz, 1982), p.
214.
²⁴These formulations are Jane Gallop's, in *The Daughter's Seduction: Feminism
and Psychoanalysis* (Ithaca: Cornell Univ. Press, 1982), p. 1. The first pole is
probably best represented by Kate Millett's *Sexual Politics* (New York: Ballantine,
1969), pp. 249–287. For a critique of traditional feminist views on Freud see
Juliet Mitchell, *Psychoanalysis and Feminism* (New York: Vintage, 1974), who takes
his early feminist critics to task for having denied his theories of the unconscious
and of infantile sexuality and argues, as I do here, that feminists should not
reject these theories but use them to understand the operations of patriarchal
systems. On Freud and feminism see also, e.g., *(M)other Tongue*, pp. 15–115; the
following articles in *The Future of Difference*, ed. Hester Eisenstein and Alice
Jardine (1980; New Brunswick: Rutgers Univ. Press, 1985): Christiane Mak-
ward, "To Be or Not to Be . . . a Feminist Speaker," esp. pp. 102–104, and Jane
Gallop and Carolyn Burke, "Psychoanalysis and Feminism in France," pp. 106–
121; and Helen B. Lewis, "Is Freud an Enemy of Women's Liberation? Some
Historical Considerations," in *The Psychology of Today's Woman: New Psychoanalytic
Visions*, ed. Toni Bernay and Dorothy W. Cantor (Hillsdale, N.J.: Analytic Press,
1986), pp. 7–35.

limited range of social opportunities open to women at the turn
of the century, I explore women's two major roles within the
family, daughter and mother/wife. By concentrating successively on pairs of plays that offer representative variations of each
role type, I endeavor to point out the ambiguities of gender
identity and familial relationship which so often characterize
female figures in turn-of-the-century drama. From a consideration of the femme fatale stereotype of the "sterile" daughter in
Wilde's *Salomé* and Wedekind's Lulu plays, *Earth-Spirit* and *Pandora's Box*, I move to the problematics of the daughter whose
emotional life is subjugated to her father's will in Synge's *Playboy
of the Western World* and Hauptmann's *Rose Bernd*. Ibsen's *Hedda
Gabler* and Hofmannsthal's *Woman without a Shadow* present two
versions, the one tragic and the other deceptively conciliatory, of
the woman who resists maternity. The final chapters investigate
the complexities of maternal power, both beneficent and malevolent, as envisioned by Shaw in *Candida* and by Strindberg in *The
Father*. (I do not deal with Chekhov because the problems from
which his characters suffer are existential and transcend gender
boundaries, affecting men and women alike.) No doubt other
plays could have been selected, but in every instance I attempted
to choose the text most illustrative and representative of the
respective role variation. In each case I discuss the stage history
and reception of the drama in question and treat the play
against the background of relevant aspects of the author's
oeuvre as a whole. My investigation of images of women in these
works leads to a consideration of such interconnected concerns
as the sexual threat of the femme fatale, the father-daughter
relationship, the dynamics of hysteria, and the implications of
motherhood—issues perennially of interest to dramatists, but
particularly so at the turn of the century, when traditional views
of women collided directly with the feminist struggle for equal
rights.

   To uncover the ambiguities of gender identity and family relationship in female characters on the turn-of-the century stage,
I employ the tools of both psychoanalytic and feminist criticism

and draw in addition on the provocative body of work that has resulted from the marriage of the two. My aim in using psychoanalytic approaches can be summarized by Shoshana Felman's programmatic call for mutuality in the relationship between psychoanalysis and literature:

> The notion of *application* would be replaced by the radically different notion of *implication:* bringing analytical questions to bear upon literary questions, *involving* psychoanalysis in the scene of literary analysis, the interpreter's role would here be, not to *apply* to the text an acquired science, a preconceived knowledge, but to act as a go-between, to *generate implications* between literature and psychoanalysis—to explore, bring to light and articulate the various (indirect) ways in which the two domains do indeed *implicate each other,* each one finding itself enlightened, informed, but also affected, displaced, by the other.[25]

With the exception of work on Shakespeare, feminist critics have done little in the area of drama. The genre with which women have traditionally been most involved—as readers, writers, and critics—is the novel, the type of literature most concerned with interpersonal relations, with private, emotional experience, with, in other words, what has traditionally been woman's sphere. In an illuminating article Nancy Reinhardt suggests reasons for the virtual exclusion of women from the theater for so long.[26] As a form of entertainment that extends back to classical Greece, she notes, drama has been the most traditional and conservative of all the arts; as a public and social institution, theater has been male-dominated. In Europe, women were prohibited from appearing in Greek tragedy and comedy, most of medieval religious drama, Jesuit theater, morality plays, and Elizabethan drama. Moreover, women did not attend the theater in large numbers until the nineteenth and twentieth

[25]Shoshana Felman, "To Open the Question," in *Literature and Psychoanalysis. The Question of Reading: Otherwise,* ed. Felman (1977; Baltimore: Johns Hopkins Univ. Press, 1982), pp. 8–9.
[26]Nancy S. Reinhardt, "New Directions for Feminist Criticism in Theatre and the Related Arts," *Soundings,* 64 (1981), 361–387.

centuries, since the theater was not a place to which women had free access. This situation had much to do with the popular image of actresses as scarlet women, a view traceable to three major factors: the Puritan disapproval of entertainment, the belief that it was improper for women to display themselves in the theater, and the fact that the aristocracy had tended to select its mistresses from the stage.[27] During the nineteenth century, however, the respectability of the theater as a profession increased for both men and women, and the wealth of demanding female parts in turn-of-the-century European drama brought fame to Ellen Terry, Elizabeth Robins, Sarah Bernhardt, Eleonora Duse, Mrs. Patrick Campbell, Florence Farr, Louise Dumont, and others.[28]

As far as the relative paucity of female playwrights is concerned, one may look to Voltaire for an answer of sorts: when asked why no woman had ever written a decent tragedy, he responded that "the composition of a tragedy requires *testicles*."[29] In recent years French feminist theorists have explored the general predominance of men's writing over women's from a rather less deterministic perspective than Voltaire's. Influenced by La-

[27]Julie Holledge, *Innocent Flowers: Women in the Edwardian Theatre* (London: Virago, 1981), p. 7.

[28]For recent work on actresses in the Victorian and Edwardian eras see, in addition to Holledge, Mary Heath, "A Crisis in the Life of the Actress: Ibsen in England" (diss., Univ. of Massachusetts at Amherst, 1985), which discusses Robins, Campbell, Farr, and others; Rachel Brownstein, "Representing the Self: Arnold and Brontë on Rachel," *Browning Institute Studies*, 13 (1985), 1–24 (Brownstein is also working on a book on the image and myth of Rachel, to be published by Knopf); Nina Auerbach, "Ellen Terry's Victorian Marriage," in Auerbach, *Romantic Imprisonment: Women and Other Glorified Outcasts* (New York: Columbia Univ. Press, 1986), pp. 268–291, and *Ellen Terry: Player in Her Time* (New York: Norton, 1987); Joanne E. Gates, "'Sometimes Suppressed and Sometimes Embroidered': The Life and Writing of Elizabeth Robins, 1862–1952" (diss., Univ. of Massachusetts at Amherst, 1987), and "Elizabeth Robins: From *A Dark Lantern* to *The Convert*—A Study of Her Fictional Style and Feminist Viewpoint," *Massachusetts Studies in English*, 6 (1978), 25–40; and Jane Marcus, "Art and Anger" (on works by Elizabeth Robins and Virginia Woolf), *Feminist Studies*, 4 (1978), 69–98.

[29]*The Oxford Dictionary of Quotations*, 3d ed. (Oxford: Oxford Univ. Press, 1979), p. 561, quoted in Reinhardt, "New Directions," p. 373.

can's relegation of language to a "symbolic" order that is inherently patriarchal, they associate the feminine with gaps in speech, with the unsayable or unrepresentable. For Cixous, writing has been "run by a libidinal and cultural—hence political, typically masculine—economy" where the female is repressed and mystified, where woman "has never *her* turn to speak."[30] Similarly, Xavière Gauthier writes that when women attempt to express their "femaleness" through phallocentric language, the result of this contradiction is often silence.[31]

When women have written, it is not primarily to the drama that they have been drawn. The writer of a drama typically envisions his or her work translated to the stage and regards an unproduced play as incomplete. Yet one of the most visible manifestations of the oppression of women at the turn of the century was their exclusion from the professions of directing and producing. Julie Holledge observes that in the nineteenth century, women writers preferred to limit themselves to novels, which could be written in the privacy of their own homes, rather than fight to get plays produced by actor-managers for whom spectacle was more important than language.[32] Holledge goes on to discuss plays subsequently written by turn-of-the-century actresses themselves as members of the Actresses' Franchise League. For the most part these works, intended to promote the cause of female suffrage, did not survive their era. Yet the last twenty years have seen a rebirth of women's theater, which might be said to be coming into its own.[33] As one might expect,

[30]Hélène Cixous, "The Laugh of the Medusa," in *New French Feminisms*, p. 249.
[31]Xavière Gauthier, "Is There Such a Thing as Women's Writing?" in *New French Feminisms*, pp. 161–164.
[32]Holledge, *Innocent Flowers*, p. 43.
[33]For discussions of this new theater, see Janet Brown, *Feminist Drama: Definition and Critical Analysis* (Metuchen, N.J.: Scarecrow Press, 1979); Dinah L. Leavitt, *Feminist Theatre Groups* (Jefferson, N.C.: McFarland, 1980); Michelene Wandor, *Understudies: Theatre and Sexual Politics* (London: Methuen, 1981), revised and expanded as *Carry On, Understudies* (1986); *Women in Theatre: Compassion and Hope*, ed. Karen Malpede (New York: Drama Book Publishers, 1983), pp. 231–265; Helene Keyssar, *Feminist Theatre: An Introduction to Plays of Contemporary*

however, a lack of women playwrights has meant a relative lack of women drama critics.

This book is an effort to begin filling the gap in feminist criticism of non-Shakespearian drama and thus to help bring women's participation in drama criticism up to the level of their current involvement in acting and playwriting. For my definition of a "feminist" approach to reading drama is closely tied to the assumption of a woman's perspective on the text (regardless of the actual sex of the reader). This approach is grounded in the feminist adaptation of two concepts important in reader-response criticism: the "implied reader" and the "horizon of expectations." As developed by Wolfgang Iser, the term "implied reader"—the counterpart to Wayne Booth's "implied author"— "incorporates both the prestructuring of the potential meaning by the text, and the reader's actualization of this potential through the reading process. It refers to the active nature of this process—which will vary historically from one age to another."[34] Iser's reference to historical variation in the reading process evokes an association with his colleague Hans Robert Jauss's concept of the horizon of expectations of a given literary text, or

---

British and American Women (London: Macmillan, 1984); *Women and Theatre: Calling the Shots,* ed. Susan Todd (London: Faber & Faber, 1984); Jeannette L. Savona, "French Feminism and Theatre: An Introduction," *Modern Drama,* 27 (1984), 540–545; *Women in Theatre,* special issue of *Drama: The Quarterly Theatre Review,* no. 152 (1984); Clare Coss, Sondra Segal, and Roberta Sklar, "Separation and Survival: Mothers, Daughters, Sisters—The Women's Experimental Theater," in *Future of Difference,* pp. 193–235; *Staging Gender,* special issue of *Theatre Journal,* 37 (1985); Jane Moss, "Le Corps spectaculaire: Le Théâtre au féminin," *Modern Language Studies,* 16 (Fall 1986), 54–60; and Sue-Ellen Case, *Feminism and Theatre* (New York: Methuen, 1988). For twentieth-century plays by women, see, e.g., *Plays by and about Women,* ed. Victoria Sullivan and James Hatch (New York: Random House, 1973); *Was geschah, nachdem Nora ihren Mann verlassen hatte? 8 Hörspiele von Elfriede Jelinek et al.,* ed. Helga Geyer-Ryan (Munich: Deutscher Taschenbuch, 1982); and *Plays by Women,* ed. Michelene Wandor and Mary Remnant (London: Methuen, 1982–86).

[34]Wolfgang Iser, *The Implied Reader: Patterns of Communication in Prose Fiction from Bunyan to Beckett* (Baltimore: Johns Hopkins Univ. Press, 1974), p. xii. On the "implied author" see Wayne C. Booth, *The Rhetoric of Fiction* (Chicago: Univ. of Chicago Press, 1961), esp. p. 138.

the culturally determined cluster of expectations brought to the
text by a hypothetical reader at a particular moment in history.[35]
In suggesting the possibility "of *different* horizons of expectation co–existing among different publics in any one society,"[36]
Susan Suleiman intimates the possibility of a feminist adaptation
of these principles of reader-oriented literary criticism—an
approach that would consider the ways in which gender and
gender-typing can influence the reading patterns of men and
women. Jonathan Culler has taken a systematic look at the phenomenon of "reading as a woman," defining the process as "to
avoid reading as a man, to identify the specific defenses and
distortions of male readings and provide correctives"; feminist
criticism, he writes, "employs the hypothesis of a woman reader
to provide leverage for displacing the dominant male critical
vision and revealing its misprisions."[37] Such reading often involves reading the text against itself, as it was not meant to be
read—*resisting* it. One of the most extensive examples of this
type of work is Judith Fetterley's *Resisting Reader: A Feminist
Approach to American Fiction,* which seeks to counteract the conventional "immasculation" of feminine readers, or the way in
which "women are taught to think as men, to identify with a
male point of view, and to accept as normal and legitimate a
male system of values."[38] Putting into practice Adrienne Rich's
concept of re-vision—"'the act of looking back, of seeing with
fresh eyes, of entering an old text from a new critical direction'"
(xxii)—Fetterley reexamines canonical texts of American literature to disclose the designs on and thinking toward women implicit in them.

[35]Hans Robert Jauss, "Literary History as a Challenge to Literary Theory," in
Jauss, *Toward an Aesthetic of Reception,* trans. Timothy Bahti (Minneapolis: Univ.
of Minnesota Press, 1982), pp. 3–45.
[36]Susan R. Suleiman, "Introduction: Varieties of Audience–Oriented Criticism," in *The Reader in the Text: Essays on Audience and Interpretation,* ed. Suleiman
and Inge Crosman (Princeton: Princeton Univ. Press, 1980), p. 37.
[37]Jonathan Culler, *On Deconstruction: Theory and Criticism after Structuralism*
(Ithaca: Cornell Univ. Press, 1982), pp. 54, 57.
[38]Judith Fetterley, *The Resisting Reader: A Feminist Approach to American Fiction*
(Bloomington: Indiana Univ. Press, 1978), p. xx.

In the chapters that follow I attempt a similar reexamination of turn-of-the-century European drama. I endeavor to shed new light on a selected group of canonical male-authored texts by viewing them through a feminist lens, one that reveals the attitudes and ideologies shaping their depiction of female characters. Ideally, these works will emerge both familiar and illumined.

PART I

Freud's Double?

1 Female Sexuality and Schnitzler's *La Ronde*

> I will make a confession which for my sake I must ask you to
> keep to yourself and share with neither friends nor strangers.
> I have tormented myself with the question why in all these
> years I have never attempted to make your acquaintance and
> to have a talk with you. . . . The answer contains the confession
> which strikes me as too intimate. I think I have avoided you
> from a kind of reluctance to meet my double [aus einer Art
> von Doppelgängerscheu].

This often cited confession forms the center of Freud's third
letter to Arthur Schnitzler, written in 1922 to congratulate the
author on the occasion of his sixtieth birthday.[1] By this time
Schnitzler's dramas and prose works had won him international
renown as the sharp-eyed critic of fin-de-siècle Viennese society;
indeed, until the late 1930s he was more famous than Freud.
Freud's "reluctance" to meet Schnitzler stemmed from his conception of the double, which he had adopted from Otto Rank
and described in his paper "The Uncanny" in 1919. During the
stage of primary narcissism which dominates the minds of children and primitive adults, Freud writes, the idea of the double

[1]*Letters of Sigmund Freud,* ed. Ernst L. Freud, trans. Tania and James Stern
(New York: Basic Books, 1960), p. 339. Schnitzler had begun their correspon-
dence on the occasion of Freud's fiftieth birthday in 1906. For the original
versions of Freud's letters to Schnitzler, see Sigmund Freud, "Briefe an Arthur
Schnitzler," ed. Heinrich Schnitzler, *Neue Rundschau,* 66 (1955), 95–106.
Schnitzler's letters to Freud have been lost.

operates as an insurance against the destruction of the ego; once this stage has passed, however, the double reverses its character and becomes the uncanny harbinger of death, and confrontation with one's double causes identity confusion.[2]

But Freud overcame his reservations about Schnitzler. The birthday letter of May 1922 prompted Schnitzler to suggest that they meet at last, and Freud responded with a dinner invitation. The following August, Schnitzler visited Freud in Berchtesgaden, where he was vacationing. Yet although they continued to exchange their publications, between 1922 and Schnitzler's death in 1931 they saw each other only five more times: three times by accident and on two occasions when Schnitzler visited Freud in a sanatorium located down the street from Schnitzler's house.

Freud had good reason to see himself mirrored in Schnitzler. The parallels between the two men begin on the biographical level: Freud was only six years older than Schnitzler; both were products of the same milieu, Vienna at the height of the Hapsburg monarchy; both were educated, upper-middle-class, nonpracticing Jews; they traveled in the same circles and Freud was well acquainted with Schnitzler's brother Julius, a surgeon. Perhaps most important, both Freud and Schnitzler were doctors with an interest in psychiatry, although Schnitzler eventually chose to specialize in laryngology, the same field in which his father had distinguished himself.

Schnitzler's first exposure to Freud dates from 1886, when he attended and reported on a meeting at which Freud spoke on male hysteria. That same year Schnitzler worked under the neurologist Theodor Meynert, just as Freud had done a few years before. In Meynert's psychiatric clinic Schnitzler learned hypnosis, with which he carried out sensational experiments in his father's polyclinic. Schnitzler's most extensive medical treatise was a discussion of the treatment of hysterical voicelessness through hypnosis and suggestion, and in the late 1880s and

---

[2]Freud, "The Uncanny" ("Das Unheimliche"), *SE*, XVII, 234–235.

early 1890s he reviewed several of Freud's translations of psychiatric works by Charcot and Bernheim. Hypnosis appears in two of his dramas, where it is used to express characteristically Schnitzlerian ideas. In one of the one-act plays included in *Anatol* (1893; dates following plays refer to year of publication), which launched Schnitzler's career as a playwright, the title character hypnotizes his lover in order to learn whether she is truly faithful to him but is then afraid to ask her the question, preferring his illusions to certainty. *Paracelsus* (1898), in which the noted Renaissance doctor discovers a married woman's secret sexual fantasies through hypnosis, astonished Freud with its knowledge about "these things"[3]—the conscious and unconscious desires that complicate married life.

Schnitzler's writing increasingly took precedence over his activities as a physician, especially after the death of his father, who had from the beginning been the motivating force behind his medical career. Throughout, Schnitzler's works reflect his fascination with the dynamics of the human psyche; it is no accident that he was the first writer in the German language to use the technique of the autonomous interior monologue (in the novella *Leutnant Gustl*, 1901). He makes frequent use of dreams in his prose writings, notably in *Traumnovelle* (1928) (*Rhapsody: A Dream Novel*). And many of his works, such as the novella *Fräulein Else* (1924), are akin to case studies in their minute exploration of psychologically troubled characters.

In light of Schnitzler's preoccupations, it is little wonder that the renaissance in Schnitzler scholarship in recent decades has in large measure consisted of efforts to detail the affinities between the Viennese writer and the founder of psychoanalysis. Thus we find attempts to demonstrate that Schnitzler anticipated Freud's most important ideas and categorizations of the psychoses in

[3]Quoted in Ernest Jones, *The Life and Work of Sigmund Freud*, ed. and abr. Lionel Trilling and Steven Marcus (New York: Basic Books, 1961), p. 225. Freud also refers to *Paracelsus*, with reference to resistance, in a footnote to his case study of Dora; see "Fragment of an Analysis of a Case of Hysteria" ("Bruchstück einer Hysterie-Analyse," 1905), *SE*, VII, 44n.

Schnitzler's oeuvre.[4] But critics of such attempts hold that there
is little point in arguing about whether Freud or Schnitzler was
the first to make this or that discovery,[5] particularly since Freud
himself repeatedly observed that many of the insights he gained
through analysis and experimentation were not original with
him but were known to creative writers. Moreover, "Freudian"
interpretations of Schnitzler's works, of which there have been a
considerable number, overlook or underestimate Schitzler's expressed reservations about psychoanalysis. Although Schnitzler
claimed in an interview, "In some respects I am the double of
Professor Freud,"[6] he could never overcome his sense that there
was something monomaniacal about Freud's way of thinking
and that psychoanalysis, dominated by "fixed ideas,"[7] tended to
overinterpret. It seems plausible to conclude that the differences

[4]E.g., Frederick J. Beharriell, "Schnitzler's Anticipation of Freud's Dream
Theory," *Monatshefte*, 45 (1953), 81–89, and "Freud's 'Double': Arthur Schnitzler," *Journal of the American Psychological Association*, 10 (1962), 722–730 (these
essays are revised and combined in Beharriell, "Schnitzler: Freud's Doppelgänger," *Literatur und Kritik*, 19 [1967], 546–555); Robert O. Weiss, "The Psychoses in the Works of Arthur Schnitzler," *German Quarterly*, 41 (1968), 377–400.
    [5]See, e.g., Hartmut Scheible, *Arthur Schnitzler und die Aufklärung* (Munich:
Fink, 1977), pp. 47–48. In "Arthur Schnitzler und Sigmund Freud: Aus den
Anfängen des Doppelgängers," *Germanisch-Romanische Monatsschrift*, 24 (1974),
193–223, Bernd Urban, in describing Schnitzler's medical knowledge and experience in the early days of research on hysteria in order to demystify what Freud
saw as Schnitzler's "intuition" of his ideas, also invokes Freud's disavowal of his
originality.
    [6]George S. Viereck, "The World of Arthur Schnitzler," in Viereck, *Glimpses of
the Great* (London: Duckworth, 1930), p. 333.
    [7]Commenting on a study of his works up to *Anatol* by Freud's student Theodor
Reik, one of the first to draw parallels between Schnitzler and Freud, Schnitzler
writes that it is "not uninteresting" but that it "lapses into the fixed psychoanalytic
ideas toward the end"; Arthur Schnitzler, diary entry of 27 June 1912, *Tagebuch,
1909–1912*, ed. Werner Welzig et al. (Vienna: Österreichische Akademie der
Wissenschaften, 1981), p. 339. (Unless I have noted otherwise, all translations
are my own.) Ernest Jones, with whom Schnitzler also argued about these matters, mentions that he had particular difficulty accepting Freud's ideas of incest
and infantile sexuality (Jones, *Life and Work of Sigmund Freud*, p. 435). Michael
Worbs follows a survey of Freudian configurations in Schnitzler's works with a
discussion of Schnitzler's criticisms of psychoanalysis; see Worbs, *Nervenkunst:
Literatur und Psychoanalyse im Wien der Jahrhundertwende* (Frankfurt: Europäische
Verlagsanstalt, 1983), pp. 225–258.

between the two men were as responsible as the similarities for the infrequency of their personal contact. Schnitzler's ambivalence is perfectly captured in a diary entry made on the day he arrived in Berchtesgaden to visit Freud in 1922: "His entire being attracted me again, and I feel a certain desire to talk with him about the various chasms in my works (and in my life)—but I think I'd prefer not to."[8] Schnitzler's ambivalent attitude toward Freud's thinking is probably nowhere clearer than in the writer's views on female sexuality. Both sex and women play such a prominent role in his oeuvre that the importance of this issue for Schnitzler can scarcely be overestimated.[9] One of the works most useful in exploring his conception of female sexuality is *Reigen* (1903) (*The Round Dance*), probably best known outside Austria and Germany through Max Ophüls's romanticized film version of 1950, *La Ronde*.[10] (Since the appearance of Ophüls's film, the

[8]This quotation of 16 August 1922 from the unpublished diaries is cited in Urban, "Arthur Schnitzler und Sigmund Freud," p. 223. In addition to Urban and Scheible, scholars who have warned against a facile identification of Freud and Schnitzler include Henri F. Ellenberger, who in *The Discovery of the Unconscious: The History and Evolution of Dynamic Psychiatry* (New York: Basic Books, 1970) writes that Schnitzler, in contrast to Freud, emphasized the importance of role-playing in hypnosis and hysteria, the unreliability of memory, the thematic rather than the symbolic element in dreams, and the self-deceptive rather than the aggressive component in the origin of war (pp. 471–474); and Wolfgang Nehring, "Schnitzler, Freud's Alter Ego?" *Modern Austrian Literature*, 10, nos. 3 and 4 (1977), 179–194, who observes that Schnitzler focuses on individuals in a particular society, whereas Freud's findings are universal; that unlike Freudian analysis, Schnitzler's diagnoses do not lead to self-awareness; and that whereas Freud strives to detect the genesis of neuroses, Schnitzler analyzes psychological phenomena only as they appear in the present.

[9]In "Schnitzler's Frauen und Mädchen," *Diskussion Deutsch*, 13 (1982), 507–517, Renate Möhrmann points out the abundance and variety of female figures in Schnitzler's works, a feature particularly striking in his dramas, since the unusually high proportion of female characters has caused difficulties in producing his plays (507).

[10]On the film's transformations of the play see, e.g., Anna Kuhn, "The Romantization of Arthur Schnitzler: Max Ophuls' Adaptations of *Liebelei* and *Reigen*," in *Probleme der Moderne: Studien zur deutschen Literatur von Nietzsche bis Brecht. Festschrift für Walter Sokel*, ed. Benjamin Bennett et al. (Tübingen: Niemeyer, 1983), pp. 83–99.

French title has taken precedence, even in English translations, and I will use that title here.) Schnitzler's drama quite literally revolves around sex: nine of its ten dialogues frame an act of sexual intercourse, conveyed by a row of dashes in the text and, in early productions, by a lowering and raising of the curtain on stage; in each case one of the partners has appeared in the previous scene and the other appears in the following scene— *A-B, B-C, C-D,* and so on. Character *A*'s reappearance in the last scene completes the "round" and creates the impression that the cycle will be repeated endlessly. The play's innovative structure, unique not only in Schnitzler's oeuvre but in the drama of the time, is the perfect vehicle for its message—so daring in its day—about the universality of sexual desire. In its relentless portrayal of sexuality *La Ronde* stands as a summation of many of the themes that preoccupied Schnitzler: marriage and adultery, the roles and linguistic games men and women play with each other, the tension between reality and illusion and, concomitantly, between honesty and deception, both self-deception and deception of others.

The production history of *La Ronde* reveals just how shocking its subject matter was. "Dear Pornographer": thus the salutation of a tongue-in-cheek letter from Hofmannsthal and Richard Beer-Hofmann to Schnitzler advising him, in the face of Fischer's refusal to publish the play, to take care in his selection of a publisher for his "piece of dirt" (*Schmutzwerk*) and to demand a lot of money in advance, since the book would surely be confiscated by the censors.[11] Their prediction was realized in 1904, the year after the play's publication. Although unauthorized versions of *La Ronde* were occasionally performed outside Austria and Germany during the first decades of the century, the first full production in German did not take place until 1920, in Berlin. Within a year its cast and director were tried for obscen-

[11]Hofmannsthal and Beer-Hofmann to Schnitzler, 15 February 1903, in Hugo von Hofmannsthal/Arthur Schnitzler, *Briefwechsel,* ed. Therese Nickl and Heinrich Schnitzler (Frankfurt: Fischer, 1964), pp. 167–168.

ity, but acquitted. In every German city in which the play was performed, riots and demonstrations erupted, many of them anti-Semitic; theater patrons came armed with rotten eggs and stink bombs. But nowhere was the scandal greater than in Vienna, the setting of the drama and thus the "scene of the crime." Here the controversy even led to fights in parliament, suggesting that a statement made about Vienna in 1981, fifty years after Schnitzler's death, was true at the turn of the century as well: "Hardly any other city is as unhesitatingly tolerant of sexual freedom as Vienna—as long as one condition is met: that it is never talked about."[12] In 1922 Schnitzler, thoroughly fed up with the whole affair, forbade any further productions of his much-maligned drama. Fifty years after his death, however, his son Heinrich lifted the ban, and since then directors have attempted to make up for the play's long period of dormancy.

The scandalous quality of *La Ronde* lay at least in part in the fact that it spares no social class. The play's use of nameless, paradigmatic types, spanning all levels of society from prostitute to count, has often been noted. Yet these characters represent not only social types but also gender types—"the parlourmaid," "the young gentleman," "the actress," and so forth. A close look at the play in terms of Freudian categories reveals the degree to which its characters strain against the confines of these gender stereotypes.[13] As we shall see, Schnitzler often sets up conventional masculine-feminine dichotomies only in order to problematize and undermine them. I should emphasize that I am not interested in determining Freud's influence on Schnitzler or,

---

[12]Ernest Bornemann, Profil no. 18, 1981, quoted in Renate Wagner, *Arthur Schnitzler: Eine Biographie* (Vienna: Molden, 1981), p. 338. For a full account of the play's scandal-ridden production history see Wagner, pp. 325–338, and Ludwig Marcuse, *Obscene: The History of an Indignation*, trans. Karen Gershon (London: MacGibbon & Kee, 1965), pp. 165–214.

[13]See Barbara Gutt, *Emanzipation bei Arthur Schnitzler* (Berlin: Spiess, 1978), for a survey of female types in Schnitzler's works in general. For the most part Gutt focuses on describing and illustrating these types rather than on the attempts of the women characters to break out of them. On character types in Schnitzler's dramas see also Jürg Scheuzger, *Das Spiel mit Typen und Typenkonstellationen in den Dramen Arthur Schnitzlers* (Zurich: Juris, 1975).

since Freud's writings on femininity postdate *La Ronde*, in demonstrating the degree to which Schnitzler anticipated Freud. Rather, my intention is to use Freud's thinking as a lens through which to examine the play's treatment of the kinds of roles and stereotypes assigned to women in turn-of-the-century Vienna. Because of the range of types encompassed by *La Ronde*, close study of this work should also prove illuminating for the dramas discussed in subsequent parts of this book.

As I mentioned in the Introduction, the issue of female sexuality has been crucial to the history of psychoanalysis, though its fate has been a turbulent one. Steven Marcus calls the discussion of female sexuality since Freud a "tragicomedy"; in Kate Millett's words, the question has been a "scientific football or a swamp of superstitious misinformation."[14] No one was more perplexed about the subject than Freud. One finds expressions of his uncertainty from his first writings on the topic to his last—from his statement in *Three Essays on the Theory of Sexuality* (1905) that the erotic life of women "is still veiled in an impenetrable obscurity" to his characterization of the nature of femininity as a "riddle" in "Femininity" (1933).[15] Surely one of his most frequently quoted utterances is that in which he described to Marie Bonaparte "the great question that has never been answered and which I have not yet been able to answer, despite my thirty years of research into the feminine soul": "What does a woman want?" ("Was will das Weib?").[16] And yet he did construct a theory of

[14]Steven Marcus, introduction to Freud, *Three Essays on the Theory of Sexuality*, trans. and ed. James Strachey (New York: Basic Books, 1975), p. xxxviii; Kate Millett, *Sexual Politics* (New York: Ballantine, 1969), p. 164. For psychoanalytic views of female sexuality since Freud see, e.g., *Female Sexuality: New Psychoanalytic Views*, ed. Janine Chasseguet-Smirgel (London: Virago, 1981); *Women and Analysis: Dialogues on Psychoanalytic Views of Femininity*, ed. Jean Strouse (New York: Grossman, 1974); Harold P. Blum, *Female Psychology: Contemporary Psychoanalytic Views* (New York: International Universities Press, 1977); and Zenia O. Fliegel, "Half a Century Later: Current Status of Freud's Controversial Views on Women," *Psychoanalytic Review*, 69 (1982), 7–28.

[15]Freud, *Three Essays on the Theory of Sexuality* (*Drei Abhandlungen zur Sexualtheorie*), *SE*, VII, 151, and "Femininity" ("Die Weiblichkeit"), in *New Introductory Lectures on Psycho-Analysis, SE*, XXII, 113.

[16]Quoted by Jones, *Life and Work of Sigmund Freud*, p. 377.

female sexuality, and one whose ramifications were far-reaching. An understanding of this theory necessitates a brief rehearsal of his conception of the early development of sexuality. In his essays on infantile sexuality (notably the *Three Essays* and "The Infantile Genital Organization," 1923) Freud postulates the concept of sexual monism: child sexuality for both sexes is masculine, since both girls and boys recognize only the male genital organ. (He was to persist throughout in viewing libido as masculine, as he indicates in, for example, "Femininity," 131.) From the child's point of view the clitoris is simply a substitute for the penis; "the little girl is a little man" ("Femininity," 118). Thus Freud labels the phase following the oral and anal phases the phallic phase in both sexes. In both sexes the girl's lack of a penis leads to a castration complex, since children believe that the girl had a penis and lost it. But the castration complex manifests itself differently in the two sexes, and these distinctions are closely bound up with differences in the Oedipus complex in boys and girls, outlined in "The Dissolution of the Oedipus Complex" (1924) and elsewhere. For Freud the Oedipus complex, which has been described as "a shibboleth on which psychoanalysis stood or fell,"[17] was the central phenomenon of the sexual period in early childhood. After the boy discovers that the girl lacks what he has, Freud hypothesizes, he comes to dread the possibility of castration, perhaps as a punishment for masturbation brought on by his oedipal desires for his mother. His castration complex leads him to repress these desires and to begin internalizing his father's authority, thus forming the kernel of his superego, which will maintain the prohibition against incest.

The situation is different with girls. Whereas in boys the Oedipus complex is terminated by the castration complex, the girl's Oedipus complex is produced by the castration complex. Accepting her castration as having already occurred, she comes

[17]Juliet Mitchell, "On Freud and the Distinction between the Sexes," in *Women and Analysis*, p. 33.

to envy the boy his penis: "She has seen it and knows that she is without it and wants to have it."[18] Yet she gradually replaces her wish for a penis by her wish for a child, and with this purpose in mind she rejects her mother, the primary object of her pre-oedipal affection, and takes her father as a love object. At this culminating stage of her Oedipus complex, the girl's relationship with her mother is colored by jealousy: "The girl has turned into a little woman" ("Some Psychical Consequences of the Anatomical Distinction between the Sexes," 256). Freud emphasizes that these two desires—to possess a penis and to bear a child—are crucial in helping to prepare the woman's nature for its subsequent sex role. Significantly, because her castration has already taken place, the girl has less reason to move beyond the Oedipus complex than the boy. The two results are that women may remain until a late age strongly dependent on a paternal object or on their actual father, and that their superego does not become as well developed, as "inexorable," as it does in men; thus women show less sense of justice than men and are more influenced in their judgments by feelings of affection, envy, or hostility. In "Female Sexuality" Freud sums up the significance of this difference in the development of child sexuality as follows: "We should probably not be wrong in saying that it is this difference in the reciprocal relation between the Oedipus and the castration complex which gives its special stamp to the character of females as social beings."[19] Perhaps most important, according to this theory that takes the male as the norm and defines the female in terms of a lack, the castration complex leads both sexes to disparage woman, the castrated being.

   To repeat, this summary of Freud's conception of the early development of sexuality is not intended as an indictment but rather, interpreted metaphorically, as representative of the atti-

[18]Freud, "Some Psychical Consequences of the Anatomical Distinction between the Sexes" ("Einige psychische Folgen des anatomischen Geschlechtsunterschieds," 1925), SE, XIX, 252.
[19]Freud, "Female Sexuality" ("Über die weibliche Sexualität," 1931), SE, XXI, 230.

tudes of his social order. What about Schnitzler, who belonged
to precisely the same social order? Did he take a different
stance? We may best answer this question by interweaving more
specific considerations of Freud's writings on women into a close
analysis of the text of *La Ronde*.

Inherent in Freud's definition of libido as masculine is his
attribution of a less pronounced sex drive to women. He never
gave up his belief, expressed as early as *Three Essays*, that "the
tendency to sexual repression seems in general to be greater [in
girls than in boys]" (219), and in "The Taboo of Virginity" (1918)
he writes of the "general female tendency to take a defensive line
[toward sex]."[20] He simply does not regard female sexuality as
an active, independent drive. What seems to Freud to be more
important to women than sex is love; as he states in "Anxiety and
Instinctual Life" (1933), the fear of castration found in men is
replaced in the female sex by a fear of loss of love.[21] Concomitant with these views is his often repeated association of masculine sexuality with activity and feminine sexuality with passivity. Indeed, he notes that the contrast between masculinity
and femininity must frequently be replaced in psychoanalysis by
that between activity and passivity (*Three Essays*, 160). Although
he occasionally qualifies this equation,[22] he clearly believes in its
essential validity, since many of his most important claims are
based on this dichotomy (such as his definition of libido as masculine), and in one of the last works to be published during his
lifetime he refers to the male's "struggle against his passive or
feminine attitude."[23]

Turning now to Schnitzler, we find that such dichotomies do
not hold up under scrutiny, although at first glance they may
seem to. In two scenes— those between the young gentleman

[20]Freud, "The Taboo of Virginity" ("Das Tabu der Virginität"), *SE*, XI, 201.

[21]Freud, "Anxiety and Instinctual Life" ("Angst und Triebleben"), in *New
Introductory Lectures on Psycho-Analysis*, *SE*, XXII, 87.

[22]E.g., in "Instincts and their Vicissitudes" ("Triebe und Triebschicksale,"
1915), *SE*, XIV, 134, and "Femininity," 115–116.

[23]Freud, "Analysis Terminable and Interminable" ("Die endliche und die un-
endliche Analyse," 1937), *SE*, XXIII, 250.

and the young wife and between the "sweet girl" (süßes Mädel) or grisette and the poet—men rip women's clothes in their haste to get on with things. Similarly, the male characters are often in a hurry to get away from their partners once the sexual act is over—thus the soldier with both the prostitute and the parlourmaid, the young gentleman with the parlourmaid, and the husband with the sweet girl, whose observation that he is "different" after their intimacies[24] sums up this phenomenon. By contrast, the reaction of the parlourmaid with the soldier and of the sweet girl with the husband following intercourse is to ask their partners whether they care for them. These conventional gender roles are not maintained, however; in the scenes between the young gentleman and the young wife and between the sweet girl and the poet it is the men who express concern about the women's love for them afterward and the women who are in a hurry to get home, and in the play's final scene even the count seems to wish he meant something more to the prostitute than the other men she has been with. And several of the female characters are anything but passive in their sexual relations. The prostitute approaches the soldier even though she claims not to want any money from him, hence falling out of her social role; the parlourmaid's interest in the young gentleman is evident in the way she primps before taking him the glass of water he requests; the young wife goes to her rendezvous with the young gentleman in full awareness of what awaits her; and, most obviously, the actress initiates sex with both the poet and the count.

A similar pattern emerges in *La Ronde* in connection with a characteristic Freud often associates with women, shame. In *Three Essays* he observes that the development of the inhibitions of sexuality, such as shame, takes place in little girls "earlier and in the face of less resistance than in boys" (219), and in a frequently cited passage in "Femininity" he writes: "Shame, which is

---

[24]Schnitzler, *La Ronde*, trans. Sue Davies and John Barton (Harmondsworth: Penguin, 1982), scene vi, p. 37. Subsequent quotations are from this edition and are identified in the text by scene and page number.

considered to be a feminine characteristic *par excellence* but is far more a matter of convention than might be supposed, has as its purpose, we believe, concealment of genital deficiency" (132). He then goes on to describe women's invention of plaiting and weaving—one of their few contributions to civilization, he notes—as an unconscious imitation of the interwoven hair that conceals their genitals. In commenting on this passage Sarah Kofman points out the ambiguous nature of Freud's conception of feminine shame as "both a *conventional* virtue (more or less linked to cultural repression) and a *natural* one, since, in her invention of weaving, woman was only 'imitating' nature."[25] Moreover, Kofman adds, this "natural/conventional artifice" serves to excite and charm men: "Feminine modesty is thus a trick of nature that allows the human species to perpetuate itself" (49).

Kofman's observations are illuminating apropos of *La Ronde*, which unmasks the contradictions of traditional conceptions of shame such as those expounded by Freud and shows it to be a supposedly natural but in fact artificial convention that serves to enhance seduction. The parlourmaid's embarrassment as the young gentleman opens her blouse and kisses her breasts in broad daylight, heightened when she learns that he has seen her undressed in her room at night, does not deter him but rather intensifies the desire of both. Similarly, the fact that the young wife comes to the young gentleman's flat "heavily veiled" (iv, 12) and her insistence that if she becomes conscious of what she is doing she will "sink into the earth with shame" (iv, 16) are simply part of her game of seduction, just as her feeble protestations in the drawing room that "it is so light here" (iv, 17) only move the young gentleman to lead her into the bedroom. Indeed, the implicit comparison of the young wife to a popular contemporary actress suggests that she is merely playing a role expected of

[25]Sarah Kofman, *The Enigma of Woman: Woman in Freud's Writings*, trans. Catherine Porter (Ithaca: Cornell Univ. Press, 1985), p. 49. Subsequent page references appear in the text.

her: when the young gentleman is taken aback to discover that
she is not wearing a corset, she responds that the actress never
wears one either. Neither she nor the sweet girl (with the poet)
can bear to have their partners look on while they get dressed,
although they have just had sex with them. Schnitzler takes his
unmasking of shame one step further, however; he does not
limit it to women: in the scene between the actress and the count
it is the count who is reluctant to engage in love in the daytime.
The actress has a simple solution: "Close your eyes if it's too light
for you" (ix, 59).

The blurring of conventional sex-typed distinctions in *La
Ronde* complements a pattern in the play which might be labeled
"one-upwomanship," a pattern in which female characters repeatedly get the better of male characters whose views on wom-
en are very similar to Freud's. One of the best illustrations of this
pattern is the bedroom scene between the young wife and her
husband, who is a perfect embodiment of patriarchal values. His
attitude toward his wife, whom he addresses as "my child," is
intimated right from the beginning of the scene, when he urges
her not to read anymore that evening since it will "ruin her eyes"
(all quotations from the play in this paragraph are from scene v).
For him, male and female spheres of activity are clearly separate, as his adaptation of lines from Schiller's "Das Lied von der
Glocke" ("The Song of the Bell") at the end of the scene demonstrates: "One can't always be a good lover. One has to keep going
out into a hostile world. One must fight and one must strive."
Nowhere are the differences between men and women clearer
to him than in the area of premarital and extramarital sexual
experience, as we learn from his explanations to his wife.
Whereas women like herself come to their husbands pure and
relatively ignorant about love, he tells her, men are forced before marriage to rely on those "poor creatures" who sell themselves. (This distinction is of course class-bound; both the husband and the poet question the sweet girl about her previous
lovers.) Similarly, whereas the husband forbids his wife to associate with adulterous women—women whose lives are full of "lies,

trickery, deceit and danger"—he admits that he was once involved with a married woman.

   In his belief in a double standard Schnitzler's husband typifies
the "civilized sexual morality" described by Freud in "'Civilized'
Sexual Morality and Modern Nervous Illness" (1908). The main
intention of this essay, whose claim that civilization is founded
on the suppression of instincts anticipates *Civilization and Its Discontents* (1930), is to lament the debilitating effects of a social
code that prohibits sexual intercourse outside of monogamous
marriage. As a corollary Freud calls attention to the "double
code of morality" that tolerates lapses in the male but condemns
them in the female. He points out that this double code is but-
tressed by women's education, which employs drastic measures
to keep them ignorant of sex until marriage. Freud goes on to
link women's ignorance in sexual matters and their intellectual
inferiority in general:

> [Women's] upbringing forbids their concerning themselves intel-
> lectually with sexual problems though they nevertheless feel ex-
> tremely curious about them, and frightens them by condemning
> such curiosity as unwomanly and a sign of a sinful disposition. In
> this way they are scared away from *any* form of thinking, and
> knowledge loses its value for them. . . . I think that the un-
> doubted intellectual inferiority of so many women can . . . be
> traced back to the inhibition of thought necessitated by sexual
> suppression.[26]

Despite his criticism of the conditions that foster the "double
code," Freud offers no alternatives or proposals for reform, and
he obviously does not believe that civilization can or should be
done away with.[27] Later statements on the issue show him to be

[26]Freud, "'Civilized' Sexual Morality and Modern Nervous Illness" ("Die
'kulturelle' Sexualmoral und die moderne Nervosität"), *SE*, IX, 198–199.

[27]Cf. Peter Heller, "Freud as a Phenomenon of the *Fin de Siècle*," in *Arthur
Schnitzler and His Age: Intellectual and Artistic Currents*, ed. Petrus W. Tax and
Richard H. Lawson (Bonn: Bouvier, 1984), pp. 4, 7. See pp. 4–7 of Heller's essay
for a detailed reading of "'Civilized' Sexual Morality and Modern Nervous Illness."

even closer to the position represented by the husband in *La Ronde*. In *Civilization and Its Discontents,* for example, he writes, "Women represent the interests of the family and of sexual life. The work of civilization has become increasingly the business of men, it confronts them with ever more difficult tasks and compels them to carry out instinctual sublimations of which women are little capable";[28] similarly, in "Femininity" he regards women as "weaker in their social interests and as having less capacity for sublimating their instincts than men" (134).

Taking a close look at the fifth scene of *La Ronde* against this background, we find that the traditional moral code embodied by the husband does not have the last word but that his wife acts as a kind of satiric "corrective" at every juncture. Her fascination with his premarital sex life and with the life of prostitutes already shows her transcending the double standard that did not allow middle-class women to express such interests. Similarly, when her husband feigns pity for the lot of prostitutes, she responds that she does not find such pity appropriate, since she thinks they must lead quite a pleasant life. When he reminds her that these women are destined to fall lower and lower, she observes, "It sounds rather pleasant." And when he struggles to describe the existence of adulterous women, she supplies the word "pleasure." As we might expect, her husband is shocked by these formulations. His attitude is encapsulated by his reaction to her veiled threat to withhold sex if he does not answer a pressing question she has: "You do have a way of talking . . . please remember, you're a mother . . . that our little girl is asleep in there . . ." (Schnitzler's ellipses). This response anticipates his anger in the next scene at the sweet girl's suggestion that his wife is as unfaithful as he is. He simply cannot accept the thought that a respectable woman possesses the same kind of sexual desire as a man.

The most graphic manifestation of this attitude is the hus-

<hr/>

[28]Freud, *Civilization and Its Discontents (Das Unbehagen in der Kultur), SE,* XXI, 103.

band's practice of alternating periods of platonic "friendship" with "honeymoons" in his marriage, thereby rendering his wife newly pure in his mind before each honeymoon. One such instance is depicted in this scene, in which the couple's sexual encounter follows closely on the husband's statement that "one can only love what is true and pure" and his exclaimed wish that he had known his wife as a child. His reliance on the fantasy of renewed virginal purity in his wife is illuminated by Freud's diagnosis in "The Taboo of Virginity," which describes the demand in civilized societies for virginity in women at marriage as a "logical continuation of the right to exclusive possession of a woman, which forms the essence of monogamy" (193). Freud adds that a woman's experience of losing her virginity "creates a state of bondage in the woman which guarantees that possession of her shall continue undisturbed and makes her able to resist new impressions and enticements from outside" (193). In light of the young wife's adultery, it is hardly necessary to point out the extent to which such attitudes are ironized in Schnitzler's play.

The husband's inability to reconcile sexuality with motherhood and his overall idealization of his wife reflect a further tendency that Freud considered characteristically male, the need to overvalue the love object. In "On the Universal Tendency to Debasement in the Sphere of Love" (1912) he theorizes that this need grows out of incestuous fixations that cause men to make unconscious associations between the women they love and their mothers and/or sisters. But because the incest taboo prohibits sexual relations with such women, the tendency to overvalue the *love* object produces a counterpart need in men to debase the *sexual* object in their estimation in order to maintain potency. That the union between love and sexual fulfillment realized in the bedroom scene between the husband and his wife in Schnitzler's play is a rarity for them is evident in her wistful remarks about the encounter.

This dissociation of love and sensuality seems perfectly exemplified in *La Ronde* in the scene between the young wife and

the young gentleman, whose explanation for his impotence with
her is "I must love you too much" (iv, 18). As support for this
position he brings in Stendhal's *De l'amour*, which, he tells her,
relates tales of cavalry officers who suffered a similar misfortune
during their first encounters with the women they most loved.
Yet a closer look at both this scene and Stendhal's book suggests
that the reason for the young gentleman's failure may not be an
excess of love. Just a few lines before the couple's unsatisfactory
encounter, the following exchange occurs:

> (*He undoes her shoes and kisses her feet. She has slipped into bed.*)
> Wife: Oh, it's cold.
> Gentleman: Soon, it'll get warm.
> Wife (*laughing quietly*): You think so?
> Gentleman (*unpleasantly disturbed, to himself*): She shouldn't have
> said that. [iv, 17]

What "disturbs" the gentleman here is the sexuality manifested
by the wife's question and accompanying laughter.[29] In her
open acknowledgment of her sexuality she strains against the
confines of the conventional role that her society assigns to
middle-class women and continues the process of subordination
prefigured on the gestural level when the gentleman removed
her shoes and kissed her feet. Hence we see that his sexual
performance in fact suffers not because of an overvaluation of
her, as the Freudian diagnosis would have it, but for precisely
the opposite reason.

A further explanation for the gentleman's difficulties is supplied by the chapter in *De l'amour* which he refers to but does not
name, "Des Fiasco" ("Concerning Fiascos"), a kind of miniature
treatise on impotence. Here Stendhal writes that if a first rendezvous is expected and eagerly awaited, a man often suffers a
"fiasco through imagination." The gentleman's eager anticipation of his tryst in *La Ronde* is evident in his careful preparations

[29]Martin Swales's association of laughter with sexual excitement in the scene
between the soldier and the parlourmaid is applicable to this scene as well; see
Swales, *Arthur Schnitzler: A Critical Study* (Oxford: Clarendon, 1971), p. 237.

before the wife's arrival at the flat he has rented: spraying the rooms and bedpillows with violet perfume; making sure the blinds are closed; removing a tortoiseshell comb—a remnant of a former rendezvous—from a drawer in the bedside table; laying out cognac, candies, and dishes; combing his hair and moustache. The factor of surprise accounts for the gentleman's success in his second attempt with the wife, which occurs unexpectedly, just after she has announced her intention to leave in five minutes.[30] Because *De l'amour* is so clearly relevant to this scene, it is not inappropriate to compare Stendhal's text to the gentleman's retelling of it. The comparison reveals that the gentleman alters Stendhal's story of the lieutenant who could do nothing but kiss his beloved and weep for joy during his first three nights with her: whereas Stendhal makes no mention of the woman's tears, in the gentleman's narration both she and the lieutenant weep— a version much more in keeping with his traditional notions of what is fitting behavior for women. That this alteration is more than a picayune detail is evident in the wife's reaction; she not only finds it hard to believe that the woman cried along with the man, she goes on to object, "But there are surely a lot who don't weep at all" (iv, 19). She brings these sentiments to a head a few lines later with her sarcastic response to the gentleman's exclamation that he is happy: "But you don't need to cry as well"— a remark that enrages the gentleman in its veiled reference to his impotence and her resulting dissatisfaction. The young wife's skeptical reaction to the gentleman's romanticized tale, indicating her pragmatic approach to sex, once again calls into question the conventional gender roles sanctioned by her society and epitomized in Freudian doctrine.

[30]Lotte S. Couch's claim, paralleling Freudian doctrine, that the young gentleman fails with the young wife because they belong to the same class does not explain his successful second attempt; see Couch, "Der Reigen: Schnitzler und Sigmund Freud," *Österreich in Geschichte und Literatur*, 16 (1972), 221–222. Her article points out a number of similarities between Freud and Schnitzler manifested in *La Ronde* but does not take note of the ways in which the play problematizes such parallels.

The Freudian theory that men dissociate love and sexuality and tend as a consequence to choose sexual objects who are ethically or socially inferior to them would seem to be borne out by the entire framework of *La Ronde:* in every case where there is a class difference between partners, it is the man who belongs to the higher class. Yet the female figures in these scenes also problematize the hierarchical thinking at the foundation of Freud's views on sexuality. The degree to which the prostitute transcends stereotyped conceptions of her role, announced as we have seen in her offer of free services to the soldier, is heightened in the scene in which she reveals to the count that she is on the job at the same early hour every day, like any conscientious employee. The parlourmaid's position makes her appear to be the quintessential incorporation of the association between femininity and servitude implicit in Freud's writings.[31] But when her sexual encounter with the young gentleman is interrupted by the doorbell and he irritably says that it probably rang earlier and they didn't notice it, she responds, "Oh, I've been listening all the time" (iii, 11), thus considerably undermining any impression of devoted subservience we may have formed. Her final gesture in the scene—stealing a cigar from the young gentleman's smoking table after he has left the room—caps off the commentary.

A similar pattern emerges in the scenes focusing on the sweet girl, an example of the famous character type that became inextricably bound up with Schnitzler's name early in his career. Based on an actual type—the girl from the petty bourgeois suburbs of Vienna—the *süßes Mädel* was first "defined" by the playboy Anatol in one of the one-act plays in the *Anatol* cycle, *Weihnachtseinkäufe* (*Christmas Shopping*): "She's not fascinatingly beautiful . . . she's not particularly elegant—and she's not at all clever. . . . But she has the soft appeal of a spring evening . . .

[31]Cf. Maria Ramas, who in "Freud's Dora, Dora's Hysteria," in *In Dora's Case: Freud—Hysteria—Feminism*, ed. Charles Bernheimer and Claire Kahane (New York: Columbia Univ. Press, 1985), argues that for Freud, "femininity was linked with service specifically with regard to sexuality" (174), that indeed for him "servitude was a metaphor for femininity" (176).

and the grace of a bewitched princess . . . and the spirit of a girl
who knows how to love!"[32] Both the husband and the poet seem
to have a similar image of this type of girl, to judge from their
condescending treatment of the sweet girl in *La Ronde*. Again
and again, however, she thwarts their expectations. The husband is repeatedly taken aback by her worldliness, for instance,
especially by the fact that she guesses from his behavior that he is
married. And when he tells her that he would like to see her on a
regular basis but that he has to be able to trust her since he cannot be around to watch out for her, she retorts, "Oh, I can look
after myself" (vi, 39), a remark that emphasizes the independence he finds so difficult to reconcile with his idea of what a girl
like her should be.

The poet takes an even more patronizing tone with the sweet
girl. A caricature of the fin-de-siècle aesthete, he is not interested in hearing about her domestic responsibilities—which as
Schnitzler was aware were only too real for girls of this class[33]—
but prefers to beautify everything, including what he perceives
as her stupidity: "Of course you're stupid. But that's why I love
you. Oh, it's so beautiful when women are stupid" (vii, 41). Following their sexual encounter he stands over her with a candle,
declaiming: "You are beautiful, you are beauty, you are perhaps
even nature itself. You are 'sacred simplicity'" (vii, 44). His rap-
tures are ended, however, when she cries out that he is dripping
wax on her. Thus his condescending aestheticism is satirically—

[32]Schnitzler, *Anatol*, trans. Frank Marcus (London: Methuen, 1982), p. 19
(Schnitzler's ellipses). On a more pragmatic note, W. G. Sebald adds another
dimension to the "sweetness" of the sweet girl by pointing out that she was more
likely to be sexually hygienic and thus free of venereal disease than prostitutes;
Sebald, "Die Mädchen aus der Feenwelt: Bemerkungen zu Liebe und Prostitution mit Bezügen zu Raimund, Schnitzler und Horvath," *Neophilologus*, 67
(1983), 112–114. The prevalence of venereal disease in Schnitzler's milieu is
evident in the remarks of Theodor Reik, who relates that one of his physician
friends speculated about the "tragicomedy" that would have resulted if even one
of the characters in *La Ronde* had had gonorrhea; see Reik, *Arthur Schnitzler als
Psycholog* (Minden, Westphalia: Bruns, 1913), pp. 79–80.
[33]See e.g., the descriptions in his autobiography of the harsh living and working conditions suffered by Jeanette Heger, a girl from this background with
whom he had a brief relationship; Schnitzler, *Jugend in Wien* (Vienna: Molden,
1968), pp. 307–308.

and symbolically—deflated on the gestural level, the level on which so much happens in this play, dealing as it does with matters that are "not to be spoken of."

The poet is put in his place much more directly by the actress, who is his intellectual superior. When he tries his patronizing, beautifying phrases on her, often repeating exactly the same expressions he used with the sweet girl in the previous scene, she simply dismisses them as "rubbish" and tells him he is talking "like a complete idiot" (viii, 49). Her pragmatism in sexual matters contrasts sharply with his feigned romanticism; when he leaves her room in the inn briefly, she sarcastically warns him not to start something with the waitress, and she shows her greater sexual awareness in her revelation that a mutual friend of theirs is homosexual, something the poet has had no inkling of.

The actress merits a closer look for a number of reasons. As we have seen, all the characters in *La Ronde* are role-players. In contrast to Freud's association of secretiveness and insincerity with women (*Three Essays*, 151), Schnitzler presents men and women alike as partners in a round of deception. (This notion is by no means limited in Schnitzler's oeuvre to *La Ronde*, as is evident in the last line spoken by the title character in Schnitzler's *Paracelsus:* "We are always playing; he who knows this is wise.") Hence the actress in *La Ronde*, a role-player by profession, is in a sense the most "authentic" character in the play. She is also the most narcissistic, bragging about her acting abilities to both the poet and the count and reminding them that many other men would like to be in their place. She emerges, in fact, as a virtual parody of Freud's conception of the narcissistic woman, in his opinion "the type of female most frequently met with, which is probably the purest and truest one."[34] Such a type

---

[34]Freud, "On Narcissism: An Introduction" ("Zur Einführung des Narzißmus," 1914), *SE*, XIV, 88. To repeat, I am obviously not suggesting that Schnitzler parodied Freud, since "On Narcissism" appeared after *La Ronde* was written, but rather that Schnitzler's depiction of the actress can be seen as a parody of female narcissism as Freud was later to describe it.

results, he writes, when at the onset of puberty a girl's primary narcissism is intensified, so that her ability to form outward attachments is impaired. Especially common in attractive women, secondary narcissism manifests itself in a self-contented coolness toward men, who tend to be fascinated by such women precisely because of their inaccessibility and self-sufficiency. Freud compares this fascination with the charm exerted by children, cats and larger beasts of prey, great criminals, and humorists, all of whom "compel our interest by the narcissistic consistency with which they manage to keep away from their ego anything that would diminish it" ("On Narcissism," 89). Exemplifying such a personality type in the extreme, the actress mocks both the poet and the count at every turn, tells the poet at one point that he is nothing but a "whim" for her (viii, 52), and insists to both the poet and the count that she hates people and has nothing to do with them—all of which serves to heighten the fascination she seems to possess for both lovers. Similarly, she elicits in both men complaints about her enigmatic nature, a trait Freud singles out as the reverse side of the narcissistic woman's charm.

Such a conception of femininity is unusual in Freud, whose entire theory of sexual development, as we have seen, rests on the definition of women as lacking that which men have, a lack that leads to their denigration by both sexes. Kofman argues that "On Narcissism" opened up a new and frightening path in Freud's thinking in its attribution of self-sufficiency to women and that he overcame this difficulty by defining excessive narcissism as pathological: "It is as if Freud . . . 'knew,' dream-fashion, that women were 'great criminals' but nevertheless strove, by bringing about such a reversal as occurs in dreams, to pass them off as hysterics" (*Enigma*, 66). Not so Schnitzler: one might say that in his depiction of the actress he travels down the path that Freud does not take. She not only strains against conventional female roles, as do the other women characters in *La Ronde*, she adopts male roles, in effect switching places with various male figures in the play. She addresses the poet as "my child," the designation that he and the husband have used with other female figures, and she calls the poet patronizing names, as he has done with the sweet girl; her assurance to the count that her bedroom door will not open from the outside echoes the husband's assurances to the sweet girl in their *chambre séparée*. Most notably, it is the actress who is on the offensive sexually. It is her idea to go to the country inn with the poet, and she sends him away from her room only in order to call him back again when she is undressed and in bed. After the count kisses her hand, she astonishes him by kissing his in return. Having appropriated the power associated with the male role—a transferal symbolized by her request that he remove his saber—she succeeds by gradations in getting him into her bed despite his protestations against making love in the daytime. The description of his final submission—"The Count resists no longer" (ix, 59)—is reminiscent of similar phrases used earlier in the play in connection with female figures. And in a final reversal of traditional role conceptions, Schnitzler suggests that the actress's sexual capacity is greater than the count's: whereas she wants to see him again that evening, he would prefer to wait until two days later.

The count's manifest fear of the actress is elucidated by a passage from "The Taboo of Virginity" in which Freud attempts to explain the primitive custom demanding that defloration of the bride be carried out before marriage and by someone other than the husband-to-be:

> Wherever primitive man has set up a taboo he fears some danger and it cannot be disputed that a generalized dread of women is expressed in all these rules of avoidance. Perhaps this dread is based on the fact that woman is different from man, for ever incomprehensible and mysterious, strange and therefore apparently hostile. The man is afraid of being weakened by the woman, infected with her femininity and of then showing himself incapable. The effect which coitus has of discharging tensions and causing flaccidity may be the prototype of what the man fears; and realization of the influence which the woman gains over him through sexual intercourse, the consideration she thereby forces from him, may justify the extension of this fear. In all this there is

nothing obsolete, nothing which is not still alive among ourselves.
[198–199]

Perhaps this suspicion of the primitive, untamed nature of female sexuality is at the bottom of Freud's famous statement that "the sexual life of adult women is a 'dark continent' for psychology."[35] As we have seen, however, it is not in Freud but in his contemporary Schnitzler that we find an exploration of the powerful and liberating potential that lay within this "dark continent."

Not surprisingly, although Schnitzler did not take a stand on the women's movement per se, he was enthusiastically received by a number of feminist groups.[36] And yet any claim about the emancipatory quality of *La Ronde* must be qualified in at least two respects. First, on an existential plane, it is with good reason that this play has often been seen as a modern variation on the medieval dance of death, which represented Death as leveling class distinctions by dancing with all social types from poorest to richest. Schnitzler's play, in which sex is the great leveler, is a kind of round dance of dead souls in which men and women alike objectify each other in their easy progression from one partner to the next. The impersonal, even anonymous quality of their intimacies is emphasized by the repetition of the same or similar lines in different scenes, by the observation made by several characters that their partners remind them of someone else, and by the fact that they are frequently unable to see each other's faces. And numerous references to transience and death reveal the deepest motivating force behind these frenzied sexual encounters. Second, on a social plane, it must be kept in mind that *La Ronde* is above all a portrayal of its time. Indeed,

---

[35]Freud, *The Question of Lay Analysis (Die Frage der Laienanalyse*, 1926), *SE*, XX, 212. Freud uses the English "dark continent" in the original. Sander L. Gilman describes it as a "phrase with which [Freud] tied female sexuality to the image of contemporary colonialism and thus to the exoticism and pathology of the Other"; Gilman, *Difference and Pathology: Stereotypes of Sexuality, Race, and Madness* (Ithaca: Cornell Univ. Press, 1985), p. 107.

[36]See Gutt, *Emanzipation bei Arthur Schnitzler*, pp. 157–168.

Schnitzler himself described the work as a "series of scenes which . . . if dug up again in a few hundred years would provide a unique illumination of an aspect of our culture."[37] As a portrait of Viennese society under the Hapsburg monarchy, the play can only go so far in presenting emancipatory possibilities for women. Although it clearly problematizes conventional masculine-feminine distinctions in its depiction of female characters transcending traditional conceptions of their role in the bedroom, these characters nevertheless remain limited to marginal positions in society: the status of the prostitute and the parlourmaid requires little comment; the actress, though a professional, practices an occupation that her society does not respect; and the sweet girl can expect little more than a modest version of the domestic confinement experienced by the young wife.

In its wide-ranging portrayal of sexual desire *La Ronde* covers the spectrum of all the female character types we will examine in the rest of this book: we will encounter the prostitute again in Wedekind's Lulu; the working-class girl in Synge's Pegeen Mike, Hauptmann's Rose Bernd, and Hofmannsthal's Dyer's Wife; the performer in Lulu and in Wilde's Salomé; the middle-class wife and mother or would-be mother in Ibsen's Hedda Gabler, Shaw's Candida, and Strindberg's Laura. But insofar as Schnitzler's female figures belong to a patriarchal society, they are, metaphorically speaking, all daughters. The next four chapters will focus on the dynamics of actual father–daughter relationships as presented by the drama of the time.

[37]Schnitzler to Olga Waissnix, 26 February 1897, in Schnitzler/Waissnix, *Liebe, die starb vor der Zeit: Ein Briefwechsel*, ed. Therese Nickl and Heinrich Schnitzler (Vienna: Molden, 1970), p. 317.

PART II

Demythologizing the Femme Fatale, or The Daughter's Education

The femme fatale is as old as literature. As long as men have sung or written about women, they have created alluring and yet disturbing embodiments of the dangers of female sexual power over them. The lineage of the femme fatale may be traced back to Helen of Troy, whose beautiful face launched ten years of war and destruction. In her wake have followed a procession of sirens and gorgeous witches, vamps and *belles dames sans merci* who have animated literature and art throughout the ages. But the fatal woman comes into her own particularly during the second half of the nineteenth century, when she becomes a type as pervasive as the Byronic hero during the first half of the century. First named, described, and catalogued by Mario Praz in *The Romantic Agony*, the fatal woman of this period is born with Gautier's Cleopatra (*Une Nuit de Cléopâtre*, 1845), who kills her lovers the morning after, and reappears in works by

Baudelaire, Flaubert, Swinburne, D'Annunzio, and others.[1] Indeed, she has been viewed as perhaps the favorite theme of
decadent writers, in whose works she appears as a manifestation
of decadent antifeminism.[2]

The typical femme fatale of the nineteenth century is cold,
arrogant, and inaccessible, yet irresistible; defiant of social convention; mysterious, enigmatic, and exotic, often Middle Eastern or North African; charming yet cruel, sometimes to the
point of perversity and even sadism; she frequently takes the
form of the *allumeuse* (literally, "a woman who ignites"), who
excites men's desire without satisfying it. But the essential, defining quality of her nature, combining as it does beauty and death,
is its two-sidedness. It is thus not difficult to recognize why the
type of the femme fatale flourished in the latter nineteenth century: erotically fascinating yet dangerous, the fatal woman is the
figure of an overcompensating reaction both to the sexual re-
pressiveness of the era and to the waves of hysteria and feminism it produced.[3]

Two of the most ancient types of the femme fatale appear
in turn-of-the-century incarnations, one in Oscar Wilde's re-
creation of the biblical figure Salomé, who demanded from Herod the head of John the Baptist in return for her dance, the

[1]Mario Praz, *The Romantic Agony*, trans. Angus Davidson (1933; Cleveland:
World-Meridian, 1956), pp. 187–286. See also H. R. Hays, *The Dangerous Sex:
The Myth of Feminine Evil* (New York: Putnam's, 1964), and Virginia M. Allen,
The Femme Fatale: Erotic Icon (Troy, N.Y.: Whitson, 1983).

[2]See, e.g., Jean Pierrot, *The Decadent Imagination, 1880–1900*, trans. Derek
Coltman (Chicago: Univ. of Chicago Press, 1981), p. 38.

[3]Cf. Bram Dijkstra's *Idols of Perversity: Fantasies of Feminine Evil in Fin-de-Siècle
Culture* (New York: Oxford Univ. Press, 1986), which presents a wealth of examples of evil women in literature and painting in arguing that turn-of-the-century
misogyny is in part a reaction against feminism.The idealized counterpart of the
femme fatale is the "femme fragile," a type that, like the femme fatale, is common throughout nineteenth-century literature but becomes especially prevalent
around 1900. In contrast to the femme fatale, the "femme fragile" is typically
childlike, delicate, ethereal, passive, and spiritualized nearly to a state of holi-
ness. See Ariane Thomalla, *Die "femme fragile": Ein literarischer Frauentypus der
Jahrhundertwende* (Düsseldorf: Bertelsmann, 1972), and Hans Hinterhäuser, *Fin
de Siècle: Gestalten und Mythen* (Munich: Fink, 1977), pp. 107–145.

other in Frank Wedekind's modern version of Pandora, classical mythology's equivalent of Eve. In taking a closer look at these two characters, we will explore the social origins of each "fatal woman" and will thereby problematize the conventional interpretation of the theme as the outgrowth of a uniformly misogynistic impulse.

2 The (Wo)Man in the Moon: Wilde's *Salomé*

As a symbol of luxury, opulence, and fatal female sensuality, "l'agent omniprésent du mal et du mâle,"[1] the figure of Salomé fascinated painters from Cranach to Moreau. Literary portraits also abound, and in the course of literary history interest in Salomé has peaked at three times in particular: during the Roman decadence; in the Middle Ages, when the Crusades inspired an increased veneration of John the Baptist; and, most notably, during the postromantic era.[2] The last of these periods was inaugurated with Heine's *Atta Troll* (1843), a political satire in which Herodias (often confused or merged with her daughter Salomé) is one of three femmes fatales to appear to the narrator in a kind of phantasmagoria. The myth of Salomé was subsequently treated by Mallarmé, Flaubert, Evan John, Jean Lorrain, Arthur William G. O'Shaughnessy, Jules Laforgue, Arsène Houssaye, Apollinaire, and many others. As this list indicates, the theme was especially favored by French symbolist and decadent writers, for whom Salomé was the quintessential femme fatale; her popularity among them was so great that Maurice Krafft claimed in 1912 to have enumerated 2,789 French poets

---

[1]Gilbert Laurens, "Salomé et l'agonie romantique," in *Recherches en Sciences des Textes: Hommage à Pierre Albouy* (Grenoble: Presses Universitaires de Grenoble, 1977), p. 77.

[2]Helen Grace Zagona, *The Legend of Salome and the Principle of Art for Art's Sake* (Geneva: Droz, 1960), p. 22.

55

who had celebrated the dancer.[3] The Salomé traditions in painting and literature come together in one of the most memorable
depictions of the theme, Huysmans's *A rebours* (1884) (*Against
Nature*), where Des Esseintes describes the transporting effects
on him of two of Gustave Moreau's paintings, *The Apparition* and
Salomé Dancing before Herod. To the mind of Des Esseintes, Salomé has become in Moreau "the symbolic incarnation of un-
dying Lust, the Goddess of immortal Hysteria, the accursed
Beauty exalted above all other beauties by the catalepsy that
hardens her flesh and steels her muscles, the monstrous Beast,
indifferent, irresponsible, insensible, poisoning, like the Helen
of ancient myth, everything that approaches her, everything
that sees her, everything that she touches."[4]

Huysmans's treatment of Salomé was one of the primary influences on Wilde's one-act play *Salomé* (published in French in
1893, in English in 1894), which may be regarded as the culmination of the turn-of-the-century preoccupation with the myth.
Written in French (and corrected by friends of Wilde), in Paris,
and in a lyrical, symbolist mode that contrasts sharply with the
tone of his social comedies of upper-class English life, this drama
seems much more a part of the French literary tradition than the
English. In fact Wilde was thoroughly familiar with French literature and saw it as his task in the late 1880s and early 1890s to
introduce it to the British reading public and plead its cause, and
he became one of the major theoreticians of French decadence.
In a letter to Edmond de Goncourt written in 1891, just as he
was completing *Salomé*, Wilde proclaimed, "French by sympathy,
I am Irish by race, and the English have condemned me to speak
the language of Shakespeare."[5]

Wilde's allegiance to France was strengthened by the produc-

---

[3]Michel Décaudin, "Un Mythe 'fin de siècle': Salomé," *Comparative Literature
Studies*, 4 (1967), 109.
[4]Joris-Karl Huysmans, *Against Nature*, trans. Robert Baldick (Harmondsworth: Penguin, 1959), p. 66.
[5]Wilde to Goncourt, 17 December 1891, in *Selected Letters of Oscar Wilde*, ed.
Rupert Hart-Davis (Oxford: Oxford Univ. Press, 1979), p. 100.

tion history of *Salomé,* which he originally intended to put on at
the Palace Theatre in London, in French, with Sarah Bernhardt
in the title role. His enthusiasm was high, since he considered
Bernhardt "undoubtedly the greatest artist on any stage," with
"the most beautiful voice in the world"; he was later recorded as
saying, "The three women I have most admired are Queen Victoria, Sarah Bernhardt, and Lillie Langtry. I would have married any one of them with pleasure."[6] Rehearsals of *Salomé* had
already begun at the Palace in 1892 when the Examiner of Plays
for the Lord Chamberlain, a Mr. Pigott, refused to grant the
work a license because it contained biblical material, thus in-
fringing on a law established at the time of the Protestant Refor-
mation to prohibit Catholic mystery plays. Wilde's rage at Pigott,
whom Shaw described as a "walking compendium of vulgar in-
sular prejudice,"[7] was so intense that he threatened to renounce
his British citizenship and leave for France, where he felt his art
could be appreciated. Although he did not carry out the threat—
unfortunately for him, as things turned out—he increasingly
viewed France as his spiritual home and spent the last years of
his life there. Appropriately, the first public performance of
Salomé took place in Paris, at Lugné-Poe's Théâtre de l'Oeuvre in
1896. Wilde, in Reading Gaol at the time, was deeply grateful,
and attributed the subsequent improvement in his treatment as
a prisoner to this event.

Reactions to *Salomé* in Europe and the United States were
mixed. They are perhaps best summed up by the American
writer Edgar Saltus's characterization of the play as a thing that
"could have been conceived only by genius wedded to insanity."[8]
The drama was particularly popular in Germany, especially after the debut in Dresden in 1905 of Richard Strauss's opera

[6]H. Montgomery Hyde, *Oscar Wilde: A Biography* (New York: Farrar, Straus &
Giroux, 1975), pp. 140, 40.
[7]George Bernard Shaw, vol. I of *Our Theatres in the Nineties* (New York: Wise,
1931), p. 51.
[8]Quoted in *Oscar Wilde: The Critical Heritage,* ed. Karl E. Beckson (New York:
Barnes & Noble, 1970), p. 132.

Salome, the libretto of which was an abridged translation of Wilde's text. The musical qualities of the play had been foreseen by both Wilde and Lord Alfred Douglas, who translated it into English. In our own time the opera, which according to a music critic present at its first performance at the New York Metropolitan "left the listeners staring at each other with starting eyeballs and wrecked nerves,"[9] has largely eclipsed the play in popularity.

An understanding of Wilde's interpretation of the femme fatale necessitates a look at his variations on the Salomé myth, for his most striking innovation is in the presentation of Salomé herself. In the Bible and in Flaubert's *Hérodias* Salomé is merely the passive instrument of Herodias's revenge on John the Baptist, who has condemned Herodias's marriage to her former husband's half brother Herod as incestuous; indeed in the Gospels of Matthew and Mark, Salomé is not even referred to by name. Although the motive of Salomé/Herodias's lust for John the Baptist has been present in versions of the myth since the fourth century, nowhere else is Salomé's passion evoked as fully and graphically as in Wilde's drama. Heine's *Atta Troll,* for example, treats Herodias's love satirically, as is evident in the narrator's rhetorical question "Would a woman demand the head of a man she didn't love?" (Caput XIX), and Laforgue's *Salomé* is similarly ironic.

In Wilde's *Salomé,* by contrast, the title heroine's attraction to Jokanaan, as he is called here, is at the center of the play. Her feelings are first conveyed through the use of incantatory, trancelike repetitions in the manner of Maeterlinck, whom Wilde greatly admired: variations on the sentence "I desire to speak with him"[10] after she is drawn to Jokanaan's voice rising up from the cistern where he is being held prisoner, repetitions of "You will do this thing for me" (556ff.) as she attempts to

[9]Quoted in Alan Bird, *The Plays of Oscar Wilde* (London: Vision, 1977), p. 77.
[10]*Salomé,* in *Complete Works of Oscar Wilde* (London: Collier, 1966), p. 556; subsequent page references appear in the text.

persuade the Syrian captain to bring Jokanaan to her, and, most striking, her often reiterated "I will kiss thy mouth" (559ff.) as she is seized with desire for Jokanaan. To be sure, many critics have been put off by this repetitive style, viewing it as a burlesque of Maeterlinck or even as comparable to exercises in language instruction,[11] but seen from the perspective of contemporary drama the technique appears quite modern, anticipating the theater of Pinter, Beckett, and others.

In her obsession with Jokanaan, Salomé becomes oblivious of everything else. When he urges her to seek out the Son of Man, for instance, she asks, "Is he is beautiful as thou art, Jokanaan?" (558). The similes she uses to describe aspects of his person render her lust virtually cannibalistic: she compares his voice to wine, his hair to clusters of grapes, and his mouth to a pomegranate, which she wants to bite "as one bites a ripe fruit" (573). The contrast between the passionate Salomé and the ascetic Jokanaan is underlined by their attitudes toward the act of looking. Whereas she cannot resist the desire to look at him more closely, he refuses to look at her at all and is repeatedly associated with the unseen in his role as precursor of Christ; as the first soldier remarks, "The Jews worship a God that you cannot see" (553).

This emphasis on looking points to the nature of Salomé's obsession with Jokanaan: scopophilia, or a delight in seeing, has been characterized as a central element of fetishism.[12] Writing on the turn of the century, Hans Hofstätter observes:

> Fetishism plays an important role in symbolist art and literature because it replaces the actual fulfillment of a wish by a symbol. This symbol is bound up with the object of longing: it is concretized as a detail of the whole, but a detail in which the whole is both compressed and contained in representative fashion. Such fetishes are the hair, the eyes, the mouth of the beloved, which

---

[11]Beckson, *Oscar Wilde*, p. 133.
[12]Victor N. Smirnoff, "La Transaction fétichique," *Objets du fétichisme*, special issue of *Nouvelle Revue de Psychanalyse*, 2 (1970), 46.

are posited as absolute symbolic signs, all the more so since they
also appear as sexual signs in dream symbolism.[13]

Aspects of Freud's theories on fetishism are illuminating for the
spirit if not the letter of Salomé's devotion to Jokanaan. For
Freud the fetish, a body part or article of clothing which serves
as a substitute for the normal sexual object, represents the maternal penis whose absence the (male) fetishizer perceived as a
child; the fetish, which is usually associated with the last thing
the boy saw before his disturbing discovery of his mother's geni-
talia (feet, shoes, underclothing, etc.), remains a token of triumph over the threat of castration and a protection against it.[14]
Although Salomé's fixation on Jokanaan's body, hair, and
mouth belongs to the more general category of fetishism as an
irrational, obsessive devotion rather than to the perversion
Freud postulates, her passion shares with Freud's definition two
main characteristics, ambivalence and the perception of a lack.
For Freud the fetish stems from the mother's lack of a penis, but
the structure of the fetish is ambivalent since the child both
recognizes this lack and disavows his recognition by creating a
fetish and thus relieving his castration anxiety; his simultaneous
acknowledgment and disavowal lead to both affection and hostility toward the fetish. Similarly, Salomé's fetishization of parts
of Jokanaan's anatomy results from the fact that he is forbidden
to her, or lacking, and his condemnation of her causes her to

[13]Hans H. Hofstätter, *Symbolismus und die Kunst der Jahrhundertwende* (Cologne:
Du Mont Schauberg, 1965), p. 201.

[14]See especially Sigmund Freud, *Three Essays on the Theory of Sexuality* (*Drei
Abhandlungen zur Sexualtheorie,* 1905), *SE,* VII, 153–155; "Fetishism" ("Fetischis-
mus," 1927), *SE,* XXI, 149–157; *An Outline of Psycho-Analysis* (*Abriss der Psycho-
analyse,* 1940), *SE,* XXIII, 202–204; and "Splitting of the Ego in the Process of
Defence" ("Die Ichspaltung im Abwehrvorgang," 1940), *SE,* XXIII, 273–278. In
Freud's definition fetishism is obviously confined to men. Although recent feminist criticism has postulated the existence of female fetishism (e.g., Sarah Kofman, *The Enigma of Woman: Woman in Freud's Writings,* trans. Catherine Porter
[Ithaca: Cornell Univ. Press, 1985], and Naomi Schor, "Female Fetishism: The
Case of George Sand," 1985; rpt. in *The Female Body in Western Culture: Contemporary Perspectives,* ed. Susan R. Suleiman [Cambridge: Harvard Univ. Press, 1986],
pp. 363–372), it is not my intention to do so here, as will become clear.

revile what she has previously praised: "Thy body is hideous. . . .
Thy hair is horrible" (559). Only his mouth escapes her ambivalence, and she literally kills for it.

But what about the source of Salomé's treatment of Jokanaan?
Close analysis of the play as a whole reveals that her behavior is
clearly learned: this daughter's education in a veritable school of
lust, where the principle of immediate gratification reigns, undermines the conventional notion of the femme fatale as a kind
of natural force of virtually mythic proportions. In her fetishization of Jokanaan she is simply following the example of those
around her, who treat her the way she treats him. The opening
lines of the drama, repeated several times, demonstrate the Syrian captain's fascination with her: "How beautiful is the Princess
Salomé to-night!" The page's admonition to him, "You are always looking at her. . . . It is dangerous to look at people in such
fashion" (553ff.), points up another parallel between the captain
and Salomé. And just as her longing to kiss Jokanaan's mouth
compels her to have him decapitated, the captain's unrequited
love for Salomé drives him to suicide.

Salomé's foremost model, however, is surely her uncle and
stepfather, Herod. The first observation made about him in the
play is "He is looking at something," which the second soldier
amends to "He is looking at some one" (553); the "some one" is
of course Salomé, at whom, as his wife Herodias tells him with
irritation, he is "always looking" (561). Herod's lust for his stepdaughter is so overpowering that here, in contrast to other versions of the myth—in, for example, the Bible and Flaubert's
Hérodias, where Salomé's dance precedes Herod's offer—he
coerces her to dance by promising her anything she desires, just
as Salomé uses her power over the Syrian captain to force him to
bring Jokanaan to her. Salomé and Herod are also linked by the
insistent repetition of their monomaniacal desires, her "I will
kiss thy mouth, Jokanaan" and his "Dance for me, Salomé"
(567ff.). Having learned her lesson well, Salomé is simply the
fullest embodiment of the decadence surrounding her, which is
not only exemplified by the contrast between the pagan prac-

tices at Herod's court and the incipient Christianity represented by Jokanaan but also quite obviously reflected in the play's over-wrought style.

The individualized nature of Salomé's sin is further under-mined by her identification with Herodias; although the daugh-ter is not merely her mother's agent, as in other versions of the myth, there are numerous parallels between them. On the most obvious level, attention is called to their shared physical charac-teristics, such as golden eyes and gilded eyelids, which lead Her-odias to think Jokanaan is cursing her when in fact he is con-demning Salomé. Similarly, just as Salomé now shocks Herod's entourage with her carnal interest in the holy man, so had Hero-dias scandalized the populace years before by giving herself to the men of Chaldea, Assyria, and Egypt and by divorcing her husband to marry his half brother. Not surprisingly, Herodias applauds Salomé's demand for the head of Jokanaan. Herod's resigned response to this demand sums up the similarities be-tween the two women: "Of a truth she is her mother's child!" (573). In effect Salomé is for Herod little more than a younger version of Herodias, of whom he has grown tired.

In the end, then, Wilde seems to be less condemning a partic-ular femme fatale than commenting on the decadence of a whole society—perhaps a mask for his own. But there is another mask in the play, one that serves further to demythologize Sa-lomé as a fatal woman: on a disguised, symbolic level she is not a woman at all, but a man. As the one who looks at and admires, as spectator, Salomé assumes vis-à-vis Jokanaan a traditionally male role.[15] This role is borne out by the language she uses in praising him, by her part-by-part celebration of his anatomy. For this kind of anatomical "scattering," introduced by Petrarch, became the standard means by which male poets after him por-

[15]See John Berger, *Ways of Seeing* (Harmondsworth: Penguin, 1972), who observes with regard to painting that "the 'ideal' spectator is always assumed to be male" (64). As we will see in chap. 3, feminist film criticism has paid a good deal of attention to the dichotomy between the female as spectacle and the male as spectator.

trayed female beauty. Nancy Vickers points out that we never see in Petrarch's *Rime sparse* (Scattered rhymes) a complete picture of Laura; she is always presented as a part or parts of a woman. "It would surely seem," Vickers writes, "that to Petrarch Laura's whole body was at times less than some of its parts; and that to his imitators the strategy of describing her through the isolation of those parts presented an attractive basis for imitation, extension, and, ultimately, distortion."[16] By depicting the woman not as a totality but as a series of dissociated parts, the male poet could overcome any threat her femaleness might pose to him. This obsessive insistence on particular body parts in turn produced during the Renaissance the genre of the *blason* or blazon, which praised individual fragments of the female body in a highly ornamental fashion; the new genre even provided an occasion for contests of rhetorical skill in which, for example, one poet pitted his description of a breast against another's celebration of an eyebrow. As Vickers notes, the blazon functioned as a power strategy, since "to describe is, in some senses . . . to control, to possess, and ultimately, to use to one's own ends."[17]

Reexamining Wilde's play in the light of these observations, we find that Salomé's paean to Jokanaan shares much with the traditional male celebration of female anatomy. Her successive tributes to his winelike voice, white body, black hair, and red mouth, a series of mini-blazons reminiscent of the Song of Songs, can be read as an attempt to attain power over him by "taking him apart," as it were. Roland Barthes's comments on the blazon are illuminating in this context:

> *The spitefulness of language:* once reassembled, in order to *utter* itself, the total body must revert to the dust of words, to the listing of details, to a monotonous inventory of parts, to crumbling: language undoes the body, returns it to the fetish. This return is coded under the term *blazon*. . . . [Like the blazon] the sentence

[16]Nancy J. Vickers, "Diana Described: Scattered Woman and Scattered Rhyme," 1981; rpt. in *Writing and Sexual Difference*, ed. Elizabeth Abel (Brighton: Harvester, 1982), p. 97.

[17]Nancy J. Vickers, "'This Heraldry in Lucrece' Face,'" in *Female Body in Western Culture*, p. 219.

can never constitute a *total;* meanings can be listed, not admixed: the total, the sum are for language the promised lands, glimpsed *at the end* of enumeration, but once this enumeration has been completed, no feature can reassemble it—or, if this feature is produced, it too can only be *added* to the others.[18]

The dissociation linked by both Vickers and Barthes with the literary celebration of body parts is heightened in Salomé's address to Jokanaan by her use of incongruous imagery, which is particularly evident in her treatment of his hair. Hair—women's hair—was often fetishized at the turn of the century by male artists and writers.[19] Adopting the male role, Salomé describes Jokanaan's hair in extravagant similes:

> It is of thy hair that I am enamoured, Jokanaan. Thy hair is like clusters of grapes, like the clusters of black grapes that hang from the vine-trees of Edom in the land of the Edomites. Thy hair is like the cedars of Lebanon, like the great cedars of Lebanon that give their shade to the lions and to the robbers who would hide themselves by day. The long black nights, when the moon hides her face, when the stars are afraid, are not so black. The silence that dwells in the forest is not so black. There is nothing in the world so black as thy hair. . . . Let me touch thy hair. [559]

Simple logic tells us that one thing cannot resemble both clusters of grapes— soft and round—and the cedars of Lebanon— straight and tall—at the same time. In the manner of a Renaissance *blasonneur,* Salomé's impulse toward rhetorical display—in this case, decadent rhetorical display—triumphs over her interest in coherence and consistency, and her aesthetic fascination with color supplants her concern with substance. In expressing her desire to touch the admired object, however, Salomé oversteps the bounds of the virtuoso poet and reveals not power but weakness; Jokanaan's rebuke—"Back, daughter of Sodom!

[18]Roland Barthes, *S/Z,* trans. Richard Miller (New York: Hill & Wang, 1974), pp. 113–114.
[19]*Ein Wilder Garten ist Dein Leib: Die Frau um die Jahrhundertwende,* ed. Otto Basil (Vienna: Forum, 1968), pp. 122–123.

Touch me not. Profane not the temple of the Lord God" (559)—
therefore provokes her to reverse the tenor of her blazon: "Thy
hair is horrible. It is covered with mire and dust. It is like a
crown of thorns which they have placed on thy forehead. It is
like a knot of black serpents writhing round thy neck. I love not
thy hair" (559). She then moves on to celebrate the redness of his
mouth, in terms whose implication is revealed only by the original French text: remembering her disguised male status, we find
that the culminating phrase "Laisse-moi baiser ta bouche" ("Let
me kiss thy mouth") takes on added significance when we consider the colloquial meaning of *baiser* ("to have sexual intercourse with").

Salomé's fetishization of Jokanaan is thus doubly forbidden:
on a literal level he is forbidden to her because he is a representative of God, pure and untouchable; on a symbolic level he is
forbidden to her (in her male guise) by the taboo on homosexuality. With his prophecies of Christ, his warnings about the arrival of the angel of death, and his condemnations of Herodias,
Herod, and Salomé, Jokanaan is well suited to evoke the guilt
associated with prohibited objects of desire. Imprisoned in the
same cistern where Salomé's father had been locked up years
before, he is the patriarch par excellence, the quintessential externalization of the paternal superego. Hence Salomé's passion
for him takes on oedipal overtones as well.

Seen in this way, Wilde's *Salomé* emerges less as a misogynistic
denunciation of the femme fatale than as a masked depiction of
one man's prohibited longing for another. Such a strategy
should not seem surprising in a writer who declared, "Man is
least himself when he talks in his own person. Give him a mask,
and he will tell you the truth."[20] This masking structure is similar to one that has been recognized in women's writing. In their
now classic *Madwoman in the Attic*, Sandra Gilbert and Susan

---

[20]"The Critic as Artist," in *Complete Works of Oscar Wilde*, p. 1045. On another
of Wilde's disguised subversions of conventional sexual behavior—*The Picture of
Dorian Gray*—see Ed Cohen, "Writing Gone Wilde: Homoerotic Desire in the
Closet of Representation," *PMLA*, 102 (1987), 801–813.

Gubar use the model of the palimpsest—literally, a parchment reinscribed after an earlier text has been erased—to describe the fiction of nineteenth-century women writers, "works whose surface designs conceal or obscure deeper, less accessible (and less socially acceptable) levels of meaning" and are thus intended "both to express and to camouflage."[21] Gilbert and Gubar demonstrate the ways in which these women writers create subversive, passionate, or melodramatic doubles in their fiction to act out the anger and rebellion that their lives deny them, but dutifully kill these characters off to assuage their guilt at harboring such feelings. Echoing Gilbert and Gubar, Elaine Showalter has suggested that "women's fiction can be read as a double-voiced discourse, containing a 'dominant' and a 'muted' story."[22]

Analogously, Wilde's "double-voiced" treatment of Salomé—as a woman in the "dominant" story, a homosexual man in the "muted" story—reflects his ambivalent attitude: although his is the only literary version of the Salomé myth in which Herod has her killed, Wilde's depiction of her plight at the end of the play contains an undeniable element of sympathy. There is something inherently tragic in the fact that the satisfaction of her desire can be achieved only through the death of the beloved object—a situation that anticipates the famous insight of "The Ballad of Reading Gaol": "Each man kills the thing he loves." Indeed, Salomé's ultimate desire remains frustrated, as her words to Jokanaan's severed head on the charger reveal: "I am athirst for thy beauty; I am hungry for thy body; and neither wine nor fruits can appease my desire" (574). Shortly after the French version of the play was published in 1893, Wilde referred to Salomé in a letter as "that tragic daughter of passion."[23] And yet through her death, symbolically forecast from

[21]Sandra M. Gilbert and Susan Gubar, *The Madwoman in the Attic: The Woman Writer and the Nineteenth-Century Literary Imagination* (New Haven: Yale Univ. Press, 1979), pp. 73, 81.
[22]Elaine Showalter, "Feminist Criticism in the Wilderness," 1981; rpt. in *The New Feminist Criticism: Essays on Women, Literature, and Theory*, ed. Showalter (New York: Pantheon, 1985), p. 266.
[23]Quoted in Hyde, *Oscar Wilde*, p. 150.

the beginning of the play,[24] he expresses his awareness that
neither unbridled female sexuality nor homosexuality could go
unpunished in Victorian society. For a number of reasons it is appropriate both that Wilde used
a female character as a mask for a male homosexual and that a
model derived from women's writing be employed to illuminate
the structure of his play. For it might be said that in his day the
male homosexual possessed "woman's status"—or worse, since
the so-called Labouchère Amendment of the 1885 Criminal Law
Amendment Act had made all male homosexual acts illegal in
Britain.[25] In a traditional, patriarchal society such as this one,
both male homosexuals and women are marginalized. The English feminist, socialist, and homosexual writer Edward Carpenter often drew parallels between the repression of female sexuality and the psychological damage done to homosexuals by his
society in the last decades of the century.

Wilde had feminist sympathies as well. His admiration for
Sarah Bernhardt, one of the least conventional and most self-
consciously masculine of female entertainers and an adamant
advocate of women's rights, is telling. More concretely, his two-
year tenure as editor of *The Woman's World*, which he converted
from a fashion sheet to a magazine that endeavored to be the
"organ of women of intellect,"[26] reflects his special understanding of and respect for women. Infused with a spirit of sexual
equality, the magazine contained articles on women's work and
their position in politics which were far ahead of their time and
with which Wilde was entirely in agreement.[27] On a lighter note,
all of his comedies expose facets of the double standard opera-
tive in his society, posing in various ways the question Jack

[24]See my "Theater of Impotence: The One-Act Tragedy at the Turn of the
Century," *Modern Drama*, 28 (1985), 458–459.
[25]For a detailed description of conditions for homosexuals in Britain at the
time see Jeffrey Weeks, *Coming Out: Homosexual Politics in Britain from the Nineteenth Century to the Present* (London: Quartet Books, 1977).
[26]Quoted in Robert Keith Miller, *Oscar Wilde* (New York: Ungar, 1982), p. 14.
[27]Arthur Fish, "Memories of Oscar Wilde," in vol. I of *Oscar Wilde: Interviews
and Recollections*, ed. E. H. Mikhail (New York: Barnes & Noble, 1979), pp. 152–
153.

Worthing puts to Miss Prism near the end of *The Importance of Being Earnest* when he thinks he has discovered in her his long-lost mother: "Why should there be one law for men, and another for women?" *Lady Windermere's Fan* and *A Woman of No Importance* hinge on the theme of the fallen woman versus the unscathed man, and *An Ideal Husband* demonstrates the unequal balance of power in marriage (all four plays premiered between 1892 and 1895). And for Salomé the consequences of the double standard are fatal: in a precise reversal of the typical femme fatale plot, whereas Herod is allowed his lust, she is killed because of hers. Wilde's stance toward women thus accords with Eve Sedgwick's recent argument against the association of homosexuality with misogyny.[28]

Wilde's sympathy for sexual equality takes on broader significance in the light of recent work on the decadent or dandy and the turn-of-the-century New Woman, which has shown that both character types represented a threat to established culture, especially as far as sex and gender were concerned.[29] Both the dandy and the New Woman opposed the rigid Victorian division between the sexes and moved in the direction of androgyny, or the combination in one person of both masculine and feminine traits,[30] in that the dandy inclined toward male effeminacy and the New Woman toward female mannishness. An 1895 issue of the British humor magazine *Punch* satirized this trend in a poem:

> a new fear my bosom vexes;
> Tomorrow there may be *no* sexes!
> Unless, as end to all pother,
> Each one in fact becomes the other.

[28]Eve Kosofsky Sedgwick, *Between Men: English Literature and Male Homosocial Desire* (New York: Columbia Univ. Press, 1985), pp. 19–20.

[29]See, for example, Linda Dowling, "The Decadent and the New Woman in the 1890's," *Nineteenth-Century Fiction,* 33 (1979), 434–453.

[30]On androgyny see, e.g., Carolyn G. Heilbrun, *Toward a Recognition of Androgyny* (1964; New York: Norton, 1982); June Singer, *Androgyny: Toward a New Theory of Sexuality* (Garden City: Anchor/Doubleday, 1976); and Ellen Piel Cook, *Psychological Androgyny* (New York: Pergamon, 1985).

E'en *then* perhaps they'll start amain
A-trying to change back again!
Woman *was* woman, man *was* man,
When Adam delved and Eve span.
Now he can't dig and she won't spin,
Unless 'tis tales all slang and sin![31]

Once again we may turn to *The Importance of Being Earnest* for a pithy commentary. In her conversation with Cecily in Act III Gwendolen observes, "The home seems to me to be the proper sphere for the man. And certainly once a man begins to neglect his domestic duties he becomes painfully effeminate, does he not? And I don't like that. It makes men so very attractive." While in Salomé the blurring of the sexes is expressed less directly than in this passage, as we have seen it lies just beneath the play's surface, lending a timely, socially specific significance to the "timeless myth" of the femme fatale, and making her as much man as woman.[32]

Aubrey Beardsley's illustrations to *Salomé*, which accompanied the English version published in 1894, reveal his awareness of the ambiguities that Wilde was unwilling to express openly. Few of the drawings actually illustrate scenes from the play; they serve rather as a kind of visual commentary, unmasking disguised themes and associations. Prominent among them is the theme of androgyny implicit in Wilde's double-voiced treatment

[31]Issue of 27 April 1895, p. 203; quoted in Dowling, "The Decadent and the New Woman," pp. 444–445. In "Salomé: The Jewish Princess Was a New Woman," *Bulletin of the New York Public Library*, 78 (1974), 95–113, Jane Marcus argues that both Salomé and Jokanaan are androgynous types of the suffering artist and that Salomé, like the New Woman, is discontented with her stereotypical role as a sex object. Yet Marcus's attempt to present Salomé as spiritualized and saintly overlooks Salomé's objectification of Jokanaan.
[32]In a reading somewhat similar to mine, Kate Millett also views Salomé as the product of Wilde's homosexual desire and guilt, although her interpretation identifies Salomé specifically with Wilde rather than with the male homosexual in general and sees the play as "remarkably contingent in the very midst of the sexual revolution, somehow oblique and aside from the point" (215), rather than as a (disguised) part of this revolution itself; see Millett, *Sexual Politics* (New York: Ballantine, 1969), pp. 214–221.

of Salomé, to which Beardsley adds the element of physical
hermaphroditism, or the possession of both male and female
sexual organs. The original versions of several of the illustrations, which were suppressed as obscene and replaced for the
published edition, contain a number of hermaphrodites, such as
the horned figure with breasts and a penis on the left side of the
suppressed title page (Figure 1) and the serving girl/boy in the
original version of *The Toilette of Salomé* (Figure 2). Similarly, *The
Woman in the Moon* (Figure 3), originally titled *The Man in the
Moon*,[33] has androgynous implications that can be interpreted in
at least two ways. The moon is one of the predominant motifs in
the play, serving as a means by which the characters define
themselves and their obsessions. Yet in nearly every case the
moon is associated with Salomé: in the Syrian captain's comparison of the moon to a "little princess" (552), in the page's
simile likening it to a "dead woman" (552), in Salomé's description of the moon as a "virgin" (555), and in Herod's comparison
of it to a "mad woman" (561). Thus Beardsley's depiction of
Wilde's face in the moon in *The Woman in the Moon*, one of four
caricatures of the author among the illustrations, associates
Wilde with Salomé and, more generally, with femaleness.

From a different perspective, three of the illustrations link
Salomé with maleness—specifically with Jokanaan—by portraying a likeness between their facial features: *John and Salomé*, *The
Dancer's Reward*, and *The Climax* (Figures 4–6). *The Climax*, in
which Beardsley has supplied John's severed head with snaky,
Medusa-like hair (thus recalling Salomé's comparison of his hair
to a "knot of black serpents"), is particularly striking. The
Medusa was a popular theme among romantic and decadent
writers, but she is typically depicted in confrontations with male
characters, since the mythological Medusa had no power over
women. Beardsley's portrayal of Salomé holding up and gazing
longingly at Jokanaan's Medusa-head thus underlines her male-

[33]Haldane Macfall, *Aubrey Beardsley: The Man and His Work* (London: Lane,
1928), p. 52.

Figure 1. Salome: Suppressed Title Page

Figure 2. Salome: Original of The Toilette of Salome

Figure 3. The Woman in the Moon

Figure 4. Salome: John and Salome

74

Figure 5. The Dancer's Reward

Figure 6. The Climax

ness in the play's muted story. On the level of the dominant story, Freud's association of the Medusa's head specifically and decapitation generally with castration is not irrelevant.[34] For Jokanaan's decapitation at the hands of Herod's executioner represents Salomé's disempowerment not only of Jokanaan but of Herod as well: just as Jokanaan is feminized in his status as object, the man whose presumed power was so great that he thought himself able to forbid Messias from raising the dead (565) finds himself subjugated to a woman's will. But Salomé's power over Herod is only temporary, since she is empowered merely as a fetish, as a beautiful female body; once the beautiful woman becomes monstrous, herself imitating the fate of the Medusa, she is destroyed. Neil Hertz's discussion of the emblematization of certain kinds of revolutionary violence in the eighteenth and nineteenth centuries in the Medusa figure—as a "hideous and fierce but not exactly sexless woman"—is illuminating here.[35] For it is precisely Salomé's masculine qualities, in particular her aggressive sexuality, that make her terrifying as a woman and thus intolerable. In Beardsley's drawing Jokanaan's Medusa-head functions as a secret mirror of Salomé's own blurred and monstrous sexuality.

Not surprisingly, Wilde was dissatisfied with Beardsley's drawings and vented his displeasure in the criticism that the illustrations were "Japanese" whereas his play was "Byzantine."[36] Except for those that were obscene, however, he ultimately allowed the drawings to be published with his text, probably because he

---

[34]See Freud, "Medusa's Head" ("Das Medusenhaupt," 1940/1922), *SE*, XVIII, 273–274.

[35]Neil Hertz, "Medusa's Head: Male Hysteria under Political Pressure," in Hertz, *The End of the Line: Essays on Psychoanalysis and the Sublime* (New York: Columbia Univ. Press, 1985), p. 162.

[36]Katharine Worth, *Oscar Wilde* (New York: Grove, 1983), p. 64. The importance of Wilde's displeasure is downplayed by Elliot L. Gilbert, who in arguing against the conventional view that Beardsley's illustrations misrepresent *Salomé* reaches some of the same conclusions I do. Cf. Gilbert, " 'Tumult of Images': Wilde, Beardsley, and *Salome*," *Victorian Studies*, 26 (1983), 133–159.

was aware of the publicity value of Beardsley's notoriety at the
time. Wilde's defense of Salomé in the face of what he saw as a
negative treatment by Beardsley may serve as an apt conclusion
to our discussion of the play. His heroine, he insisted, was a
"mystic," a kind of "St. Theresa" who would have adored the
moon instead of the cross.[37] As so often, he retreats here into
aesthetics to avoid confronting ethics—the ethics of a society
and a religion whose laws were most uncongenial to him.

[37]*Les Muses,* no. 35, 20 May 1970, quoted in Jacqueline Bellas, "L'Équivoque de
Salomé dans la littérature et l'art 'fin de siècle,'" *Poésie et peinture du symbolisme au
surréalisme en France et en Pologne,* special issue of *Cahiers de Varsovie,* 5 (1973), 46.

3 Woman as Spectacle and Commodity: Wedekind's Lulu Plays

Scarcely anyone in the history of German literature has provoked such mixed and violent reactions as Frank Wedekind, self-styled bohemian and passionate nonconformist. In stark contrast to the respectable physician Schnitzler and even to Wilde, who though also an enfant terrible of the literary world never relinquished the trappings of high society, Wedekind punctuated his work in advertising and journalism with stints as an actor and cabaret singer, spent one of the happiest periods of his life in the company of Parisian circus performers, and served a six-month prison term for "libeling the crown" in one of his political poems. Little wonder, then, that Brecht was moved to comment after Wedekind's death in 1918 that "his greatest work was his personality."[1] Looking back with the hindsight that Brecht could not have, we recognize the degree to which his observation obscures the enormous impact Wedekind was to have on Brecht himself and on the many other twentieth-century dramatists whose work would be very different without his example.

None of Wedekind's dramas has been more influential than his so-called Lulu plays, which in their unusual mixture of satir-

---

[1]Quoted in *Der vermummte Herr: Briefe Frank Wedekinds aus den Jahren 1881–1917*, ed. Wolfdietrich Rasch (Munich: Deutscher Taschenbuch, 1967), p. 241.

ic, grotesque, and tragic elements combine some of the most
memorable features of naturalist and symbolist theater and also
anticipate expressionism. Wedekind's initial inspiration for the
subject was twofold: the circus pantomime *Lulu, Une Clownesse
danseuse* by Félicien Champsaur, which he saw at the Nouveau
Cirque in Paris in the early 1890s, and the stories of Jack the
Ripper, whose notorious sex murders in London a few years
before had sent shock waves across half of Europe. The Lulu
material occupied Wedekind longer than any of his other works,
off and on from 1892 to 1913. Because the original drama of
1895 was unwieldy, he expanded it and broke it up into two
plays, *Erdgeist (Earth-Spirit)* and *Die Büchse der Pandora (Pandora's
Box.*[2] Although *Earth-Spirit* was produced in various German
cities from 1898 on, attracting directors of such renown as Max
Reinhardt, *Pandora's Box,* like so many of the plays discussed in
this book, fell victim to the censor's knife, and it was not publicly
performed in Germany until after the abolition of censorship in
1918. Although Wedekind was admired by intellectuals, as
Brecht's above-mentioned tribute to him attests, throughout his
life the general public and popular press tended to regard him
as little more than a pornographer.

The main cause of the scandal surrounding the Lulu plays was
the figure of the heroine herself. Responsible for the deaths not
only of three husbands but of several admirers and possibly of
the wife of her third spouse, Schön, as well, Lulu appears to be a
virtual caricature of the femme fatale. Like Wilde's Salomé, she
is a fin-de-siècle incarnation of an ancient myth; like the biblical
Salomé, the mythological Pandora, created to punish mankind
for Prometheus' theft of fire from the gods, is both beautiful
and a source of evil, reflecting the fundamental and persisting

---

[2]On the differences among the various versions see the standard biography by
Artur Kutscher, *Wedekind: Leben und Werk,* newly edited by Karl Ude (Munich:
List, 1964), pp. 109–136; and David Midgley, "Wedekind's Lulu: From 'Schauer-
tragödie' to Social Comedy," *German Life and Letters,* 38 (1985), 205–232.

ambivalence of men toward the female sex.³ As the titles of both
Lulu dramas suggest and as the animal tamer who introduces
her in the prologue to *Earth-Spirit* expressly states, Lulu is intended to represent "the primal form of woman."⁴ Perhaps it
was the work's evocation of this mythic, primal realm, the source
of so many operas, that inspired Alban Berg in the 1930s to
follow Strauss's example with *Salome* and compose his *Lulu,* a
combined version of the two plays which has become a mainstay
of opera repertory. Whatever the case, whether Lulu is seen as
the manifestation of an "unconditional moral imperative" or as
"consisting of nothing but flesh and vulva,"⁵ she has traditionally
been equated with nature, instinct, animality.

Silvia Bovenschen has shown how this conception of Lulu as
natural phenomenon is a paradigmatic example of male myths
of the feminine.⁶ Yet this perspective does not fully take into
account the extent to which Wedekind depicts the character
Lulu as both a product of her society and a quintessential incorporation of its values. For *Earth-Spirit* and *Pandora's Box* offer

³On the Pandora myth see H. R. Hays, *The Dangerous Sex: The Myth of Feminine
Evil* (New York: Putnam's, 1964), pp. 79–87, and Dora and Erwin Panofsky,
Pandora's Box: The Changing Aspects of a Mythical Symbol, 2d ed. (New York:
Pantheon, 1962). Expressing his disappointment with Reinhardt's 1902 production of *Earth-Spirit* in Berlin, Wedekind criticized Gertrud Eysoldt's performance
as "Salomé-like" and therefore misrepresentative of his heroine's childlike,
unself-conscious nature; Frank Wedekind, "Was ich mir dabei dachte," vol. IX of
Gesammelte Werke (Munich: Müller, 1924), p. 440. As we shall see, however, there
are in fact numerous parallels between Salomé and Lulu.
⁴Wedekind, *The Lulu Plays and Other Sex Tragedies,* trans. Stephen Spender
(London: Calder, 1977), p. 11. Subsequent parenthetical references to this edition of *Earth-Spirit,* abbreviated as *ES,* include act, scene, and page number;
references to *Pandora's Box (PB)* consist of act and page number only, as each act
is confined to one setting.
⁵The first characterization is Wilhelm Emrich's, "Frank Wedekind: Die Lulu-
Tragödie," in his *Protest und Verheißung: Studien zur klassischen und modernen
Dichtung* (Frankfurt: Athenäum, 1960), p. 206, the second is Peter Michelsen's,
"Frank Wedekind," in *Deutsche Dichter der Moderne: Ihr Leben und Werk,* ed. Benno
von Wiese, 2d ed. (Berlin: Schmidt, 1969), p. 55.
⁶Silvia Bovenschen, *Die imaginierte Weiblichkeit: Exemplarische Untersuchungen zu
kulturgeschichtlichen und literarischen Präsentationsformen des Weiblichen* (Frankfurt:
Suhrkamp, 1979), pp. 43–59.

one of the fullest portrayals in dramatic literature of the cultural construction of a woman into spectacle and commodity, two roles conventionally played by women in consumer economies. Far from being removed from the workings of her society— Wilhelmine Germany undergoing a belated industrial revolution—Lulu reveals the ways in which its dominant ideologies of patriarchy and capitalism reinforce each other as mechanisms of objectification. Just as Salomé's wanton behavior toward Jokanaan is conditioned by her stepfather's lustful treatment of her, Lulu is not simply born but made, shaped by her particular upbringing and education.

For writers in the German literary tradition from Goethe to Thomas Mann, perhaps no theme has been more central than the importance of education—*Bildung*—in human development. Wedekind is no exception. The prelude to one of his first plays, *Die junge Welt* (The young world; originally published as *Kinder und Narren* [1891] [Children and fools]), satirically depicts the restrictive education received by girls at the turn of the century; the farce *Fritz Schwigerling* (later retitled *Der Liebestrank* [1899] [The love potion]) and the novel fragment *Mine-Haha oder Über die körperliche Erziehung der jungen Mädchen* (1901) (Mine-Haha, or on the physical education of young girls) present detailed pedagogical programs, emphasizing especially the importance of physical fitness in the upbringing of children. But the most enduring treatment of education in Wedekind's oeuvre is the early drama *Frühlings Erwachen* (1891) *(Spring Awakening)*. Anticipating Freud's "Sexual Enlightenment of Children" (1907), Wedekind's play graphically demonstrates the detrimental results of the failure to provide children with what would today be called "sex education": one girl dies from the effects of a botched abortion, having become pregnant after her embarrassed mother was unable to explain to her the mechanics of reproduction, and her pubescent lover is sent to a reformatory because the illustrated description of sexual intercourse with which he enlightened a schoolmate is blamed for the schoolmate's breakdown and suicide (in fact brought on by his failure to be promoted to the next grade).

  Despite Wedekind's repeated stabs at the naturalist movement
in general and Gerhart Hauptmann in particular, in the Lulu
plays as well as in his other works he calls attention to the influence of early environment and training on the subsequent life of
the adult. The question posed to the judge at Lulu's murder trial
by her teenage admirer, Hugenberg (aside from Countess
Geschwitz, he is the only character in the two dramas with what
might be called a soul), should not be overlooked: "How can you
tell what would have become of you if as a ten-year-old child
you'd had to knock about barefoot at night in cafés?" (PB I, 122).
For the period of Lulu's life to which Hugenberg refers is that
spent with her first major shaping figure, or at least the first we
learn about, the mysterious tramp Schigolch, who knew her
"when all there was to see of [her] was [her] two big eyes" (ES II,
ii, 44). Many critics have stressed Lulu's mythical qualities and
blurred origins—Schigolch's dry observation that she "never
had" a father (ES IV, vi, 88), Schön's claim that she did not know
her mother and that her mother "has no grave" (ES II, iv, 55).
Less crucial for Lulu's development than the absence of her
biological parents, however, are the presence and influence of
her two incestuous foster fathers, Schigolch and Schön.

  Having first encountered Lulu as a ragged twelve-year-old
making her way by petty thievery and by selling flowers on the
street, Schön has always assumed that Schigolch is her father,
although the text never confirms this assumption. Whereas the
education provided her by the bum, pimp, and murderer
Schigolch is anything but middle-class, he is far from the primeval, asocial creature that some critics have seen him to be, for
example, associating his name with Molch, the German word for
"salamander."[7] Considering his character, we can derive a more

[7]Friedrich Rothe, Frank Wedekinds Dramen: Jugendstil und Lebensphilosophie
(Stuttgart: Metzler, 1968), p. 35n.

appropriate reading of his name from the nearly exact equivalence of its inverse with *logisch,* the German for "logical." For Schigolch is nothing if not a shrewd thinker, managing to survive without a job by living outside the law and teaching Lulu to do the same, as her attempt to steal Schön's watch as a child demonstrates. As important to Schigolch as money is sex. Even in his old age he comes begging to Lulu for funds to support his mistresses, and in the midst of his and Lulu's desperately impoverished circumstances in London at the end of *Pandora's Box* he is preoccupied with trying to seduce the keeper of a nearby pub. A number of remarks Schigolch lets fall, such as his admission that he, like so many others, originally wanted to marry Lulu (*ES* IV, vi, 88), suggest that the erotic relationship between them began when she was a child. And his powerful sexuality doubtless influenced her by its example, just as Herod's does his stepdaughter Salomé in Wilde's play.

In their attention to the eroticism in the relationships of Salomé and Lulu with their father figures, Wilde and Wedekind dare to explore terrain from which Freud shied away. Freud initially postulated that the hysteria of many of his female patients was the result of sexual advances made by their fathers, but he later rejected this "seduction theory" in favor of the view that his patients' revelations were simply sexual fantasies. In recent years much debate has centered on the question of whether Freud abandoned the seduction theory because of contrary evidence or simply because he was reluctant to expose such shocking facts to the world and feared the professional opposition that his disclosure would arouse.[8] Whichever the case, his thoughts on the subject were later incorporated into his writings on infantile sexuality and the Oedipus complex, and he never gave up his belief that "the number of women who remain till a

---

[8]The latter position is taken by Jeffrey M. Masson, *The Assault on Truth: Freud's Suppression of the Seduction Theory* (New York: Farrar, Straus & Giroux, 1984), the former by Janet Malcolm, *In the Freud Archives* (New York: Knopf, 1984). On this question see also William J. McGrath, *Freud's Discovery of Psychoanalysis: The Politics of Hysteria* (Ithaca: Cornell Univ. Press, 1986), pp. 197–229.

late age tenderly dependent on a paternal object, or indeed on their real father, is very great."[9] Wilde's and Wedekind's metaphorical treatment of father–daughter attraction (involving not biological fathers but rather step- or foster fathers) shows the degree to which such ideas were in the air at the time. That they were not only in the air but also realized is very likely, especially in light of recent work on incest. Seeking to explain the overwhelming predominance of father–daughter incest in Western societies, Judith Herman and Lisa Hirschman observe:

> Although custom will eventually oblige [the little boy] to give away his daughter in marriage to another man (note that mothers do not give away either daughters or sons), the taboo against sexual contact with his daughter will never carry the same force, either psychologically or socially, as the taboo which prohibited incest with his mother. *There is no punishing father to avenge father–daughter incest.* . . . A patriarchal society, then, most abhors the idea of incest between mother and son, because this is an affront to the father's prerogatives. Though incest between father and daughter is also forbidden, the prohibition carries considerably less weight and is, therefore, more frequently violated.[10]

This observation sheds retrospective light on the prevalence of the theme of father–daughter incest in the works of Wedekind and his contemporaries.

In contrast to the children in *Spring Awakening*, the young Lulu suffers not from a lack but from an excess of sexual knowledge. Her most significant lesson at the hands of her sexual educator Schigolch is her entrance into the world of prostitution, an initiation he reveals to us with his comment, in the last act of *Pandora's Box*, that it was as difficult for her to take to the streets twenty years before as it is now. (The corruption of Lulu is satirically echoed in the second act of *Pandora's Box* in the fate

[9]Freud, "Femininity" ("Die Weiblichkeit," 1933), *SE*, XXII, 119.

[10]Judith Herman and Lisa Hirshman, "Father–Daughter Incest," in *The Signs Reader: Women, Gender, and Scholarship*, ed. Elizabeth and Emily K. Abel (Chicago: Univ. of Chicago Press, 1983), pp. 262–263; italics in the original. See also Herman with Hirschman, *Father–Daughter Incest* (Cambridge: Harvard Univ. Press, 1981).

of the twelve-year-old Kadidja, whose mother introduces her to
wealthy older gentlemen who lust for her and, after the
Jungfrau ["virgin"] shares that support them have become
worthless, decides to take her out of school and let her try out
for the variety theater. In introducing Lulu to prostitution,
Schigolch lays the foundation in her youth for the role that she is
increasingly to play in her adult life—the role of commodity, or
object of exchange.[11]
     This, then, is the product "snatched . . . from the clutches of
the police" (*ES* IV, viii, 95) by Schön, Lulu's second father figure: a girl familiar at the age of twelve with street theft, child
molestation, and prostitution. Numerous statements call attention to his function as shaping figure for Lulu, such as his own
repeated reminders to her of the sacrifices he has made for her
education; other characters also credit him with the responsibility for her development. The effects of this phase of her education are evident, for instance, in the repulsion she feels for her
lesbian admirer Geschwitz, insofar as heterosexuality is the
result of instinct conditioning.[12] The period she spent with
Schigolch, by contrast, had been for her one of undifferentiated
sexuality, reflected in the name Lulu, used solely by him. Lulu
not only is a name given to both sexes in Germany but also
is akin to the bisyllabic consonant-vowel words first learned
by children and associated with their earliest needs: "mama,"
"papa," "kaka," "pipi."[13] When Schigolch visits Lulu at the home

[11]In connection with Schigolch's influence on Lulu see Hauke Stroszek, "'Ein
Bild, vor dem die Kunst verzweifeln muß': Zur Gestaltung der Allegorie in
Frank Wedekinds Lulu-Tragödie," in *Literatur und Theater im Wilhelminischen
Zeitalter*, ed. Hans-Peter Bayerdörfer et al. (Tübingen: Niemeyer, 1978), pp.
230–232; Stroszek draws parallels between Schigolch and Hephaestus (Vulcan),
the mythological creator of Pandora.
     [12]Cf. Horst Albert Glaser, "Arthur Schnitzler und Frank Wedekind: Der dop-
pelköpfige Sexus," in *Wollüstige Phantasie: Sexualästhetik der Literatur*, ed. Glaser
(Munich: Hanser, 1974), p. 178.
     [13]This observation is made by Thomas Medicus, *"Die große Liebe": Ökonomie und
Konstruktion der Körper im Werk von Frank Wedekind* (Marburg: Guttandin &
Hoppe, 1982), pp. 102–103, with reference to Roman Jakobson, "Warum
'Mama' und 'Papa'?" in Jakobson, *Aufsätze zur Linguistik und Poetik* (Frankfurt:
Ullstein, 1979). In the dialect of Viennese children, "lulu" is the equivalent of the
American "pee-pee" or "wee-wee."

of her second husband, Schwarz, after not seeing her for several years, she tells him that no one has called her Lulu for ages and that the name now sounds to her "completely out of date" (*ES* II, ii, 42), a characterization that indicates the progress she has made under the tutelage of Schön. For the most part, however, Schön's education of Lulu affects her only superficially. As a newspaperman, a controller of public opinion, an advertiser and marketer whose very name (meaning "beautiful") announces his aesthetic sense, he is well qualified to mold her into a beautiful object of desire. That there is indeed little substance beneath this attractive surface is perhaps most evident in the parodied cathechism put to her by Schwarz:

Schwarz: Can you speak the truth?
Lulu: I don't know.
Schwarz: Do you believe in a creator?
Lulu: I don't know.
Schwarz: Is there anything you can swear by?
Lulu: I don't know. Leave me alone! You're mad.
Schwarz: What do you believe in, then?
Lulu: I don't know.
Schwarz: Have you no soul, then?
Lulu: I don't know.
Schwarz: Have you ever been in love?
Lulu: I don't know.
Schwarz: (*rises, walks over to the left. To himself*) She doesn't know!
Lulu: (*without moving*) I don't know. [*ES* I, vii, 34–35][14]

In his depiction of Lulu as a virtual nonentity, devoid of beliefs and opinions, Wedekind takes part in the time-honored tradition that defines the feminine in terms of an absence or lack of the masculine norm. This tradition, which as we have seen finds a foremost exponent in Freud, has received one of its fullest

[14]This frequently cited passage is the clearest example of the repetitiveness of much of the dialogue in the two plays, a feature typical of the deliberately unnatural, stylized, at times even absurd quality of the language. See Anna Kuhn, *Der Dialog bei Frank Wedekind: Untersuchungen zum Szenengespräch der Dramen bis 1900* (Heidelberg: Winter, 1981), pp. 82–161.

critiques in the writings of the French psychoanalyst Luce
Irigaray. A good deal of her work responds either implicitly or
explicitly to the neo-Freudian school of which she was originally
a member, in particular to those papers of Lacan in which he
expounds his theory that woman has been excluded from participation as a subject in the order of language, that she is in
effect linguistically castrated.[15] Much of Irigaray's *Speculum de
l'autre femme* (1974) *(Speculum of the Other Woman)*, as well as
several of the essays in *Ce Sexe qui n'en est pas un* (1977) *(This Sex
Which Is Not One)*, criticizes the Freudian model that denies sub-
jectivity to woman and instead views her as man's specularized
other or negative reflection. Irigaray describes the basis of
Freud's model as

> an economy of representation . . . whose meaning is regulated by
> paradigms and units of value that are in turn determined by male
> subjects. Therefore, the feminine must be deciphered as inter-
> dict: within the signs or between them, between the realized
> meanings, between the lines . . . and as a function of the (re)pro-
> ductive necessities of an intentionally phallic currency, which, for
> lack of the collaboration of a (potentially female) other, can im-
> mediately be assumed to need *its* other, a sort of inverted or
> negative alter ego—"black" too, like a photographic negative.[16]

Irigaray goes on to elaborate on woman's function in sustaining
the male ego: "Now, if this ego is to be valuable, some 'mirror' is
needed to reassure it and re-insure it of its value. Woman will be
the foundation for this specular duplication, giving man back
'his' image and repeating it as the 'same'" (54).
    Lulu serves precisely this kind of mirroring function for her

----

[15]For Lacan's writings on femininity see *Feminine Sexuality: Jacques Lacan and
the "école freudienne,"* trans. Jacqueline Rose, ed. Rose and Juliet Mitchell (1982;
New York: Norton, 1985). On these writings see, e.g., Jane Gallop, *The Daughter's
Seduction: Feminism and Psychoanalysis* (Ithaca: Cornell Univ. Press, 1982); the
introductions by Mitchell and Rose to *Feminine Sexuality;* and Alice Jardine,
Gynesis: Configurations of Woman and Modernity (Ithaca: Cornell Univ. Press,
1985), pp. 159–169.
    [16]Luce Irigaray, *Speculum of the Other Woman*, trans. Gillian C. Gill (Ithaca:
Cornell Univ. Press, 1985), p. 22. Subsequent page references to this edition
appear in the text.

male admirers: as a veritable tabula rasa, she is perfectly suited
to reflect back to them their particular perceptions of and pro-
jections onto her. Her function as mirror is underlined by the
series of names they give her: ignorant of her "primal name,"
Lulu, Schön romanticizes her origins by calling her Mignon, the
name of the mysterious girl in Goethe's *Wilhelm Meister* whose
elderly companion, the harper, is considerably more appealing
than Schigolch; the first man to whom Schön marries Lulu
off, the wealthy but senile Dr. Goll, calls her Nelli, perhaps a
patronizing recollection of Dickens's Little Nell; the painter
Schwarz, to whom Lulu is, in her own words, "his wife, his wife,
and nothing but his wife" (*ES* II, iii, 47), renames her Eve. Like
all the others, her next suitor, the colonial explorer Prince Escerny, projects onto her his own fantasies of what he would like her
to be: "Yours is a generous nature, unselfish. You cannot bear to
see anyone suffer. You are the embodiment of mortal happiness. As a wife you would make a man supremely happy. . . .
Your being is all candour . . . you would make a poor actress"
(*ES* III, iv, 71–72; Wedekind's ellipses). As Lulu has by this
point already brought on Goll's fatal heart attack (through her
flirtations with Schwarz) and then driven Schwarz to suicide
(through Schön's revelation to him of her true background), the
dramatic irony of this passage requires little comment. Contrary
to Escerny's image of her, Lulu is in fact a consummate actress,
consisting by her own admission of a series of roles; the statement she makes to Schön just before shooting him in self-de-
fense—"I've never in the world wanted to be anything but what
I've been taken for, and no one has ever taken me for anything
but what I am" (*ES* IV, viii, 97)—should be viewed in light of her
earlier rhetorical question to his son Alwa: "If I hadn't known
more about acting than they do in the theatre I wonder what
would have become of me" (*ES* III, i, 67).

Lulu's chameleon-like character—a beautiful surface without
substance—is highlighted by her love of costumes. The ability to
change clothes quickly, which Alwa says she learned as a child, is
in Goll's words her "own sphere" (*ES* I, ii, 19). Her first response

after a disaster is to change her clothes, as if thereby to rid
herself of any unpleasant effects, and her various outfits allow
her to slip with ease from one role to another: from middle-class
wife to pierrot to flower girl to cancan dancer to ballerina to
Queen of the Night to Ariel to East Indian sailor to jockey. It is
surely no accident that the stage directions of both plays devote
considerably more attention to descriptions of clothing, in particular Lulu's clothing, than to details of physiognomy. In her
talent as a role-player Lulu is perhaps intended—in anticipation
of Mann's Felix Krull—to represent a type of the artist, her
theatrical skills constituting a creative power otherwise denied to
the sterile femme fatale. In any case, it is clear that she is to be
seen not as the incorporation of a natural principle, as has so
often been claimed, but as the embodiment of artifice, carefully
oiling, powdering, and dressing herself in an almost dandified
manner (in an early version of the play she is even suspected of
dyeing and artificially curling the hair in her armpits).[17] The
extent to which she has learned the social graces is grotesquely
caricatured at the end of *Earth-Spirit* in the non sequiturs with
which she interrupts Schön's jealous raging as he is on the verge
of shooting her: "How do you like my new dress?" and "Please
order the carriage. We'll drive to the opera" (*ES* IV, viii, 95, 96).
The irony, of course, is that he has helped create this "whore," as
he calls her here, having shaped her into a creature to be desired
by other men in order to free himself to marry someone more
appropriate to his respectable middle-class status. The effectiveness of his training is evident on numerous occasions, as when
Alwa and Escerny spend an entire scene discussing which ballerina costume suits Lulu better, the pink or the white (*ES* III, vi,
73).

Lulu's exhibitionist fascination with dress and style is crucial to
her feminine function as an image of visual perfection, inviting
the male gaze. Because her role as beautiful spectacle is so pronounced, it can be usefully illuminated by recent work on narra-

[17]Midgley, "Wedekind's Lulu," p. 212.

tive cinema, the genre in which, as Teresa de Lauretis writes, "the representation of woman as spectacle—body to be looked at, place of sexuality, and object of desire—so pervasive in our culture, finds . . . its most complex expression and widest circulation."[18] In her highly influential article "Visual Pleasure and Narrative Cinema," Laura Mulvey uses psychoanalysis to explore the ways in which the fascination of film is reinforced by social patterns that have molded directors and viewers alike. Because of the sexual imbalance characteristic of these patterns, she writes, the pleasure in looking afforded by cinema has conventionally been split between the male as active bearer of the look and the female as passive receptor of it:

> The determining male gaze projects its fantasy on to the female figure, which is styled accordingly. In their traditional exhibitionist role women are simultaneously look at and displayed, with their appearance coded for strong visual and erotic impact so that they can be said to connote *to-be-looked-at-ness*. Woman displayed as sexual object is the leitmotif of erotic spectacle: from pinups to strip-tease, from Ziegfeld to Busby Berkeley, she holds the look, plays to and signifies male desire. Mainstream film neatly combined spectacle and narrative.[19]

Thus narrative cinema exploits in paradigmatic fashion the dichotomy between man as spectator and woman as spectacle which has informed the history of painting and which we saw Salomé reverse vis-à-vis Jokanaan in her role as disguised male. As Mulvey goes on to observe, however, in psychoanalytic terms the female figure also connotes to the male viewer the lack of a penis, implying a threat of castration and hence unpleasure. For the male unconscious there are two solutions to this problem: either to show that the woman's castration is the result of guilty

[18]Teresa de Lauretis, *Alice Doesn't: Feminism, Semiotics, Cinema* (Bloomington: Indiana Univ. Press, 1984), p. 4.
[19]Laura Mulvey, "Visual Pleasure and Narrative Cinema," 1975; rpt. in *Narrative, Apparatus, Ideology: A Film Theory Reader,* ed. Philip Rosen (New York: Columbia Univ. Press, 1986), p. 203. See also E. Ann Kaplan, *Woman and Film: Both Sides of the Camera* (New York: Methuen, 1983).

conduct or to disavow her castrated state by turning her into a
fetish—in other words, either devaluation or overvaluation. The
first alternative produces the female criminal as cinematic character, the second the female star. Both strategies for neutralizing
the male viewer's anxiety can be found in the same film, as Kaja
Silverman demonstrates with reference to Ophüls's *Lola Montès*
(1955); documenting the rise and descent of an actual nineteenth-century courtesan, the movie both establishes Lola as fall-
en woman and circles around her as spectacle.[20]

It is not insignificant that both Lola Montès and Lulu are first
glimpsed on display, immobile, in a circus. For like Ophüls's
film, Wedekind's Lulu plays combine the strategies of overvaluation and devaluation of the female in portraying the rise and fall
of a femme fatale, and Lulu's rise, like Lola's, is marked by her
function as fetishized spectacle. This function is most apparent
in three scenes in *Earth-Spirit* which might be called embedded
spectacles (within the overall spectacle of the drama itself): the
prologue in front of the circus tent, Lulu's appearance first in
and then posing for her portrait, and her performance as a
dancer. All three of these scenes, focusing on her as a sensually
alluring figure, are analogous to those scenes in narrative
cinema which, in Mulvey's words, "freeze the flow of action in
moments of erotic contemplation [of a beautiful female star]"
(203).

It is difficult to imagine more of a spectacle atmosphere than
the circus setting in which the prologue to *Earth-Spirit* takes
place. As instructed by the animal tamer, who first previews
Lulu as "the wild and lovely animal, the true" (*ES*, 10), a worker
carries her in and sets her down in front of the big top, where
she sits silently while the animal tamer fondles her and tells her
how to behave. His significance is clear from an observation
made by Louise Brooks, whose portrayal of Lulu in Pabst's 1928
silent film *Pandora's Box* brought her overnight fame. In her

---

[20]Kaja Silverman, *The Subject of Semiotics* (New York: Oxford Univ. Press,
1983), pp. 226–230.

autobiography Brooks comments, "The finest job of casting that
G. W. Pabst ever did was casting himself as the director, the
Animal Tamer, of his film adaptation of Wedekind's 'tragedy of
monsters.'"[21] Both Lulu's treatment as an animal and the costume she wears—that of a pierrot, a stock character of com-
media dell'arte (as Pedrolino) and old French pantomime—emphasize her silence. Hardly any other work of literature provides
better evidence than *Earth-Spirit* for what Mary Jacobus says
might be "the hidden message which a feminist critique un-
covers": "'Shut up already.'"[22]

Our next glimpse of Lulu is not of the living character but of
her portrait as pierrot, which Goll has commissioned Schwarz to
paint. Gazing at this spectacle alongside the picture of his fiancée on which Schwarz is also working, Schön gives us an early
indication of Lulu's role as attractive surface without core, commenting that she is "a diabolic beauty," whereas his fiancée's
portrait shows "more substance" (*ES* I, i, 15). But perhaps the
most striking instance in the entire drama of Lulu's role as silent
spectacle occurs in the next scene, in which she stands on a
raised platform posing for Schwarz in her pierrot costume while
Goll and Schön sit watching. Since this is the only one of the
three embedded spectacles in the play which allows us to observe
Lulu's spectators observing her, the voyeuristic pleasure that
underlies the fascination of drama is particularly great here,
insofar as the theatergoer identifies with Goll and Schön in a
kind of doubling effect. An illuminating analogy is again provided by narrative cinema, much of whose appeal is also based
on voyeurism: the visual dynamics of this scene in *Earth-Spirit*
are similar to those of Alfred Hitchcock's film *Marnie* (1964).

[21]Louise Brooks, *Lulu in Hollywood* (New York: Knopf, 1974), p. 94. One could
obviously study the role of woman as spectacle in Pabst's film as well, but to do so
would require a different methodology, and my focus in this book is on dramatic
characters. On the film see, e.g., Thomas Elsaesser, "Lulu and the Meter Man:
Pabst's *Pandora's Box*," in *German Film and Literature: Adaptations and Transformations*, ed. Eric Rentschler (New York: Methuen, 1986), pp. 40–59.

[22]Mary Jacobus, "The Difference of View," in *Women Writing and Writing about
Women*, ed. Jacobus (London: Croom Helm, 1979), p. 14.

Raymond Bellour, noting that in American English "one says, when describing a woman: 'her looks'; as though her 'looks' were nothing but that image constituted through the looks given her by men,"[23] points out that Hitchcock has inserted himself into the chain of male looks that constitute Marnie: after a segment in which Marnie's employer and a client of his elaborate on her "looks" to the police following her theft and disappearance, Hitchcock himself appears in the hall of the hotel where she has gone, first watching her walk down the hall and then turning toward the spectator, "staring at the camera which he is, whose inscription he duplicates. The spectator in turn (re)duplicates this inscription through his identification with both Hitchcock and the camera" (73). The "looks" given to Lulu in this scene of Wedekind's play render her artlike: Schön tells her she is a "picture before which Art must despair" and instructs Schwarz to "treat her as a still-life" (*ES* I, ii, 19, 21). Schön's fantasy is clear: if this woman he helped create would only behave like a work of art—silent, framed, and immobile—all his troubles would be over.

If this fantasy is not realized, the actual work of art Schwarz produces—the painting of Lulu in her pierrot costume—does remain. Displaying her at the peak of her beauty, the painting continues throughout both plays to be crucial to her identity as a desirable female, to what might be called her ego ideal. For her status as an attractive woman, as a pretty package, is more than merely pleasurable for Lulu; she regards it as her salvation. This is especially evident at the end of *Earth-Spirit*, where she attempts to use her appearance to persuade Alwa not to turn her over to the police for murdering his father: "Don't let me fall into the hands of the law. It would be such a pity! I'm still so young. I'll be true to you all my life. *Look at me, Alwa, look at me, man! Look at me!*" (*ES* IV, viii, 99; emphasis mine). Lulu's need to see her portrait as soon as she gets out of prison is evidence of

[23]Raymond Bellour, "Hitchcock, The Enunciator," *camera obscura*, 2 (Fall 1977), 70–71; subsequent page references appear in the text. See also Sandy Flitterman, "Woman, Desire, and the Look: Feminism and the Enunciative Apparatus in Cinema," *Ciné-Tracts*, 2, no. 1 (Fall 1978), 63–68.

the same phenomenon, as is the fact that, when she is later so
down-and-out that her looks have faded, she cannot bear to see
the beautiful portrait with which she can no longer identify.
Lulu's reliance on her portrait as mirror reflection is bound
up with her narcissism, a condition not incongruous with her
education into beautiful surface without substance. Like Schnitzler's actress, she is constantly parading her awareness of her
attractiveness, claiming to Goll while posing for Schwarz that she
looks "equally well from all sides" (*ES* I, ii, 21) and to Alwa that
when she saw herself in the mirror in her Parisian evening
gown, she "wished [she] were a man . . [her] own husband" (*ES*
IV, vii, 90). Escerny observes that "when she dances her solo she
is intoxicated with her own beauty—seems to be idolatrously in
love with it" (*ES* III, ii, 69). And, as Freud was to do a few years
later, Wedekind presents the narcissistic woman as all the more
fascinating for her self-contentment. Again and again Lulu is
placed before mirroring surfaces. The mirrors in her dressing
room give way to a gleaming dustpan when she is in prison, and
in the opinion of the white-slave dealer Casti-Piani, the picture
of her as Eve before the looking-glass is her grandest (*PB* II,
135). Her self-involvement is epitomized in the early scene
where she is left alone with Schwarz; when he commands her to
look him in the eyes, she responds, "I can see myself as a pierrot
in them" (*ES* I, vii, 34). The melancholy introspection conventionally associated with the pierrot figure in nineteenth-century
literature and painting is replaced here by narcissistic self-ab-
sorption.[24] But Lulu's narcissism is essential to her sociocultural
construction as a paradigmatic female. In the words of Judith
Kegan Gardiner, "In film, as in literature and life, women are
accustomed to seeing themselves being seen, to valuing themselves according to others' evaluations of their appearance."[25]

[24]Jeannine Schuler-Will, "Wedekind's Lulu: Pandora and Pierrot, the Visual
Experience of Myth," *German Studies Review*, 7 (1984), 36. On the pierrot figure
see also Robert F. Storey, *Pierrot: A Critical History of a Mask* (Princeton: Princeton
Univ. Press, 1978).
[25]Judith Kegan Gardiner, "Mind Mother: Psychoanalysis and Feminism," in
Making a Difference: Feminist Literary Criticism, ed. Gayle Greene and Coppélia
Kahn (London: Methuen, 1985), p. 128.

As the one largely responsible for Lulu's identity as spectacle, Schön has affinities with a number of artist figures. Enamored of his creation, he is both a Pygmalion and a Henry Higgins, having rescued Lulu from her existence as an indigent flower girl.[26] Unable to separate himself from his work of art, with whom he says he has so grown together that, were he to divorce her, half of himself would go with her (*ES* IV, viii, 97), he is also a René Cardillac, E. T. A. Hoffmann's prototype of the romantic artist in "Das Fräulein von Scuderi," who is irresistibly compelled to repossess the jewelry he fashions. And he is of course a Frankenstein as well, ultimately destroyed by the monster he has created. Lulu is anything but art for art's sake, however. She has for Schön, as for her first foster father, Schigolch, concrete monetary value, and she is exchanged accordingly: having passed her to Schwarz after Goll's death, Schön seeks to comfort Schwarz in his despair at learning of her infidelities with his repeated exclamation "You married half a million!" (*ES* II, iv, 50ff.)[27] Following Schwarz's suicide Schön puts her up for sale again, making her into a dancer "so that someone should come and take me away," as she puts it (*ES* III, ix, 76). In this third embedded spectacle in the play Schön is intent on keeping his beautiful product well exposed, telling her to remain more downstage, urging Alwa to make her costumes more revealing, and forcing her to dance even though she does not want to appear before his fiancée (*ES* III, i, viii).

In his extensive discussion of the commodity in the first part of *Capital*, Marx describes the commodity–guardian relationship in the following statement and footnote:

> Commodities cannot themselves go to market and perform exchanges in their own right. We must, therefore, have recourse to

[26]For an analysis of *Earth-Spirit* in terms of the Pygmalion myth, see Edward P. Harris, "The Liberation of Flesh from Stone: Pygmalion in Frank Wedekind's *Erdgeist*," *Germanic Review*, 52 (1977), 44–56.
[27]For an insightful discussion of the Lulu plays in the context of the commercialization of the arts in Wedekind's era, see Peter Jelavich, *Munich and Theatrical Modernism: Politics, Playwriting, and Performance, 1890–1914* (Cambridge: Harvard Univ. Press, 1985), pp. 101–115.

their guardians, who are the possessors of commodities. Commodities are things, and therefore lack the power to resist man. If they are unwilling, he can use force; in other words, he can take possession of them.*

*In the twelfth century, so renowned for its piety, very delicate things often appear among these commodities. Thus a French poet of the period enumerates among the commodities to be found in the fair of Lendit, alongside clothing, shoes, leather, implements of cultivation, skins, etc., also *"femmes folles de leur corps."***

**"Wanton women."[28]

The relevance of this description to Lulu and her father figures is obvious. Lulu's function as commodity can be seen to fit into a larger framework defined by Irigaray. Echoing Claude Lévi-Strauss, Irigaray goes so far as to claim that Western culture is based on the exchange of women. Taking Marx's analysis of commodities as her point of departure, she writes that women, like commodities, are used and passed from one man or group of men to another; like commodities women are products of men's labor and hence serve as signs of male power.[29]

The commodity–guardian parallel holds true for Lulu's relationships not only with her father figures but with other men as well. Moreover, the consumer society within which she functions as a commodity, first as a child with Schigolch and then as an adult, leaves its mark on the language of both plays. Married to Schwarz, Lulu complains that he is "wasting" her (*ES* II, i, 40) ("Du vergeudest mich"), and Alwa later uses the same word in warning her as a dancer not to "waste" ("vergeuden") her

[28]Karl Marx, *Capital*, trans. Ben Fowkes (Harmondsworth: Penguin, 1976), I, 178.

[29]Irigaray, *This Sex Which Is Not One*, trans. Catherine Porter with Carolyn Burke (Ithaca: Cornell Univ. Press, 1985), pp. 170–197. Cf. also Rachel Bowlby, who writes in *Just Looking: Consumer Culture in Dreiser, Gissing, and Zola* (New York: Methuen, 1985) that the passage from Marx which I quoted above suggests "that a productive channel of investigation might be opened up by considering what woman as ideological sign, and women as subjects caught or participating in various levels of social relations, have in common with commodities—with the things which a buyer consumes" (27).

strength before her final appearance (*ES* III, i, 65). More graphically, lamenting the literary trends that have led to a decline in
the popularity of the circus, the animal tamer tells his audience
at the beginning of the prologue to *Earth-Spirit*, "My pensioners
are short of fodder / So at the moment they devour each other"
("sich verzehren"); within the same realm of imagery, Alwa compares the atmosphere in the theater where Lulu is dancing to the
frenzy of a menagerie at feeding time (*ES* III, ii, 68). The degree
to which Lulu has internalized her role as object of consumption
is evident in the reason she gives Schigolch for oiling and powdering herself so carefully each day: "I want to be good enough
to eat" ("zum Anbeißen"; *ES* II, ii, 44). The process of consumption is not one-sided, however, as Casti-Piani's comment about
Lulu's "heavy consumption" of men ("starken Verbrauch"; *PB*
II, 135) makes clear.
     The commodification of Lulu is most apparent in *Pandora's
Box*. Whereas her function as fetishized spectacle predominates
during her rise as a femme fatale, her role as commodity pre-
vails during her fall, which begins with her murder of Schön at
the end of *Earth-Spirit;* in the terms that Mulvey sets out and
Silverman takes up in discussing the fortunes of Lola Montès, it
is at this point that overvaluation gives way to devaluation, that
star becomes criminal. *Pandora's Box* presents us with one male
character after another trying to "cash in on" Lulu: the variety
acrobat Rodrigo, guided by his conviction that "it's not half as
much of an effort for a woman to support her husband as the
other way about" (*PB* I, 122), plans to train her as a trapeze artist
after their marriage and then live on her income; Casti-Piani
intends to make a large sum by selling her into prostitution in
Egypt; and after her escape from prison both threaten to turn
her back over to the police if she refuses to comply with their
wishes. Even Alwa has profited from her, by taking her life as
the subject of his play. In the tradition of her mythological an-
cestor *Pan-dora*, Lulu not only is "all-gifted" but becomes a "gift
for all."
     Schigolch's sending Lulu down into actual street prostitution

in London in the final act of *Pandora's Box*, thereby completing the circle he had begun in her childhood, is thus simply the most literal manifestat:)n of a process that has been going on throughout both dramas. Appropriately, her customers can be read as grotesque versions of her husbands and suitors: the deaf-mute Hunidei, who keeps putting his hand over her mouth, parallels Goll, who commissioned Schwarz to "silence" Lulu into a portrait; the brutal African prince Kungu Poti is reminiscent of Prince Escerny, who is in his own words "forced to exercise a quite inhuman despotism" on his voyages of exploration (*ES* III, iv, 70–71); the Swiss professor Hilti, who responds to Lulu's question about whether his fiancée is pretty by answering "Yes, she has two million" (*PB* III, 170), echoes Schön, who equates Lulu with half a million; and Jack the Ripper, after murdering Lulu, utters the same phrase that Schön had used after enlightening Schwarz about her true character (and thus occasioning his suicide): "That was a good piece of work!" (*PB* III, 174–175).[30] But the crassest example of Lulu's commodification was eliminated from the final edition of the play. In the early manuscript version, Jack, the quintessential embodiment of male sexuality perverted, tucks a newspaper package into his breast pocket after murdering and dissecting Lulu and speculates about how much money the London Medical Club will pay for this "prodigy"—the part of Lulu denoted, in vulgar parlance, by the "box" of the play's title.[31]

But what about Wedekind's attitude toward Lulu's grisly fate? Are we to view it as a wish-fulfillment fantasy of male revenge for the snares of female sexuality or as a condemnation of woman's utmost victimization? The drama has been read both ways, and indeed, the Lulu plays offer one of the most profound

[30]For a somewhat different set of equivalences see Hans-Jochen Irmer, *Der Theaterdichter Frank Wedekind: Werk und Wirkung* (Berlin: Henschelverlag, 1975), p. 144. It is interesting to note that Schön and Jack were played on various occasions by Wedekind himself.

[31]Midgley, "Wedekind's Lulu," p. 223. The German *Büchse* has the same anatomical connotation as the English "box," as Freud points out in *The Interpretation of Dreams* (*Die Traumdeutung*, 1900), *SE*, IV, 154.

examples in turn-of-the-century literature of the ambiguity characteristic of male portrayals of women. On the one hand the character Lulu is, as we have seen, clearly a product of her socialization; her roles as spectacle and commodity grow out of a patriarchal capitalist system in which men control both women and money. The implication of this view—that women are not inherently inferior or evil and that the only way to improve their lot is to abolish capitalism—places Wedekind on the side of socialist thinkers such as Engels and Bebel, who supported the feminist struggle for equal rights while doubting its effectiveness as long as the current economic structure remained intact.[32] Certainly Wedekind's drama *Der Marquis von Keith* (1900), a harsh portrayal of the emotional and spiritual bankruptcy of human beings in a capitalist society, would support this kind of categorization.

On the other hand, to identify Wedekind with the feminist cause is misleading, since in the Lulu plays as well as in other works he seems to take pleasure in making fun of the turn-of-the-century women's movement. At the end of *Pandora's Box* Geschwitz, following her ludicrous failed attempt to hang herself in despair at Lulu's indifference to her, resolves to return to Germany to study law and fight for women's rights. Similarly, in the prelude to *Die junge Welt*, mentioned earlier in the context of Wedekind's concern with education, several girls form a women's rights group and vow not to marry until the sexual inequalities characterizing the education of women have been completely removed, yet in the course of the play one after the other forgets her pledge and enters a traditional marriage. And in *Tod und Teufel* (1905) *(Death and Devil)* Casti-Piani reappears to convince a prudish member of the International Society for the Suppression of White Slave Traffic that the ability to sell their bodies is women's only advantage over men and that sen-

---

[32]For precisely such an interpretation see D. C. G. Lorenz, "Wedekind und die emanzipierte Frau: Eine Studie über Frau und Sozialismus im Werke Frank Wedekinds," *Seminar*, 12 (1976), 38–56.

sual pleasure is the one joy in a world deadened by the hypocrisy of bourgeois society. But his belief that prostitution is the result of female sexual desire is unmasked as an illusion through the confession of one of the girls in his bordello, who reveals that her work there has failed to satisfy her raging masochistic lust. Her stance echoes Lulu's description to Alwa of her recurrent (and prophetic) dream of being attacked by a sex murderer (*PB* I, 126), which she immediately follows with a request for a kiss. Wedekind's attribution of masochism to women, paralleling Freud's views, as well as other evidence of his belief in the existence of polar differences between the sexes, places him on the side of notorious "hysterizers" such as Schopenhauer, Nietzsche, and even Weininger.[33]

Evidently Wedekind is not to be pinned down. In their open-endedness the Lulu plays encourage critics, directors, and even audiences to project their own preconceived notions of femininity onto Lulu, thus imitating the male characters in the dramas themselves. Created by a man to represent "woman"—in her "primal form"—Lulu is of necessity marked by ambivalence. For ambivalence has typified depictions of the female ever since Hesiod told the story of Pandora, who is remembered for bringing into the world not only evil but also hope.

[33]For comparisons between Wedekind and such thinkers see, e.g., Audrone B. Willeke, "Frank Wedekind and the 'Frauenfrage,'" *Monatshefte*, 72 (1980), 26–38, and J. L. Hibberd, "The Spirit of the Flesh: Wedekind's Lulu," *Modern Language Review*, 79 (1984), 336–355.

PART III

The Law of the Father

Leaving the world of the femme fatale, or sterile daughter, in her decadently opulent Middle Eastern milieu on the one hand and her lurid urban environment on the other, we now turn our attention to a very different type of daughter, the simple peasant girl. Set in rural locales—county Mayo, Ireland, and Silesia, Germany, respectively—that are relatively conservative in matters of family and religion, John Synge's *Playboy of the Western World* and Gerhart Hauptmann's *Rose Bernd* offer model illustrations of the father's power over his daughter, exercised in both dramas through his choice of her (unloved) marriage partner. The two works can thus be read as paradigmatic depictions of woman's "daughterly" place in patriarchal societies, for as Juliet Mitchell has written, "It is quite specifically the importance of the *father* [rather than of men in general] that *patriarchy* signifies."[1] At the same time, however, both plays call into question the rigid sex-typed distinctions that prevailed at the turn of the century.

[1] Juliet Mitchell, "On Freud and the Distinction between the Sexes," 1974; rpt. in Mitchell, *Women: The Longest Revolution* (New York: Pantheon, 1984), p. 232.

4 "I've Lost Him Surely": Synge's *Playboy of the Western World*

At first glance a play as firmly rooted in Irish culture as *The Playboy of the Western World* (1907) may seem out of place in a study of European drama. As Synge pointed out in response to critics who attacked his play as improbable, the central motif of Christy Mahon's (purported) murder of his father and the reaction in Mayo was based on two actual events, the case of a man who had assaulted a woman on Achill Island and managed with the aid of peasant women to hide and eventually escape to America, and the story of an old man of Aran who claimed to have concealed for six months a man who had killed his father.

Although *The Playboy* is rich in local color, its focus on the archetypal theme of patricide links it to ancient Western drama and gives it a universality that has helped carry it well beyond its national boundaries. Unlike his compatriots Wilde and Shaw, Synge did not leave Ireland permanently, and on the surface his oeuvre seems less touched by continental influences than theirs, but he in fact spent the better part of the years from 1895 through 1902 in Paris, and he was thoroughly familiar not only with modern French literature but with the work of his contemporaries in other countries. Ann Saddlemyer provides a good description of Synge's cosmopolitanism:

As occasional critic to literary magazines in Paris and in London (for which he reviewed works in both French and English), he constantly re-examined the so-called Irish Renaissance in terms of the history of literary movements in Europe, based on his own travels and extensive reading. This familiarity can be seen in his prefaces and notebooks: the history of the drama is cited in Spain, England and France; Ibsen and the Germans are paralleled with Ben Jonson and Molière; Zola and Ibsen again set beside Mallarmé and Huysmans; Villon, de Musset, Vogelweide and Leopardi are translated into Anglo–Irish; even the clergy of the west are placed against the characterization of the Cloth in other countries. His first play was attempted in German, his first poetic cycle set in Paris. Constantly in all his writings Ireland is set against the background of Europe, the Irish theatre movement viewed in terms of the history of world drama.[1]

Moreover, friendships with such people as Thérèse Beydon in Paris, an art teacher and feminist, and Hope Rea in Italy, an American art historian "whose life-styles and attitudes were liberal and who treated him as an equal,"[2] helped keep Synge abreast of European trends of the day such as feminism, traces of which are discernible in *The Playboy.*

Perhaps not surprisingly, most interpretations of the play have centered on Christy Mahon. Yet there is much more to this drama than its treatment of the father–son conflict; Synge himself wrote, "There are, it may be hinted, several sides to 'The Playboy.'"[3] As significant as Christy is the character with whom the play begins and ends, Margaret (Pegeen Mike) Flaherty. Indeed, the drama can be seen to revolve in part around the tension between her ties to her father and her rebellion against him, a tension that epitomizes the theme at the center of this book: the clash at the turn of the century between women's sense of duty to the patriarchal establishment and their desire for autonomy and equality. As we shall see, this tension explains

[1] Ann Saddlemyer, *J. M. Synge and Modern Comedy* (Dublin: Dolmen, 1968), pp. 10–11.

[2] Andrew Carpenter, "Synge and Women," *Etudes Irlandaises*, 4 (1979), 97.

[3] John M. Synge to Editor, *Irish Times*, 30 January 1907, in *The Collected Letters of John Millington Synge*, ed. Ann Saddlemyer (Oxford: Clarendon, 1983), I, 286.

both Pegeen's attraction to Christy, who as a (purported) father-killer embodies the ideal that she would like to achieve meta-phorically, and her ultimate rejection of him.

The contradiction between Pegeen Mike's closeness to her fa-ther and her wish to free herself from him arises from the fact that she has been, as she tells Christy, "my whole life with my father only."[4] On the one hand, in a situation common in nine-teenth-century fiction, Pegeen, lacking a mother (typically the primary identity figure for a girl) has developed into a woman of unusual independence and strength of will.[5] On the other hand, in assuming joint responsibility for the pub, she has slipped into the role vis-à-vis her father which her mother would have played, thus realizing the girl's oedipal fantasy as Freud con-ceives it: "an affectionate attachment to her father, a need to get rid of her mother as superfluous and to take her place."[6] More-over, it is only to be expected that Michael Flaherty, in the ab-sence of his wife, would feel an unusually great tenderness to-ward his daughter.

This dichotomy in Pegeen is reflected even in her name, "Pegeen" being of course a nickname for "Margaret," which is a variant of "Mary," sign of the Mother par excellence, and "Mike" a man's name and the name of her father. At the outset of the play her submissive side predominates: in her first lines she lists the articles necessary to make the outfit in which she intends to marry the timid but well-to-do Shawn Keogh, her cousin and her father's choice. Having "no father to kill"— that is, doomed to remain eternally immature—this cowardly "stereotype of the

[4]Synge, *Plays*, bk. 2, vol. IV, of *Collected Works*, ed. Ann Saddlemyer (1968; Gerrards Cross: Colin Smythe, 1982), Act II, p. 111; subsequent parenthetical references to this edition include act and page number.

[5]Cf. Marianne Hirsch's observation in "Mothers and Daughters," *Signs*, 7 (1981): "the powerful and celebrated nineteenth-century mother is so inhibiting a force for her daughter's development that she needs to be removed from the fiction" (216). See also Susan P. MacDonald, "Jane Austen and the Tradition of the Absent Mother," in *The Lost Tradition: Mothers and Daughters in Literature*, ed. Cathy N. Davidson and E. M. Broner (New York: Ungar, 1980), pp. 58–69.

[6]Sigmund Freud, "The Development of the Libido and the Sexual Organiza-tions" ("Libidoentwicklung und Sexualorganisation," 1917), *SE*, XVI, 333.

unmasculine"[7] bows to the paternal authority of Father Reilly, whose precepts he constantly invokes. In being engaged to Shawn, then, Pegeen Mike is actually under the sway of four fathers: her own; his delegate, Shawn; Father Reilly; and the Holy Father, whose deputy he is. But the true nature of her feelings for Shawn is indicated by the stage directions designating the tone of her lines to him: "with rather scornful good humour"; "with scorn"; "impatiently" (I, 59).

Insofar as a father who forces his daughter to marry a man she does not love tightens his own hold on her, since it ensures that she will always love *him* and never really leave him,[8] Michael Flaherty's intentions as the play begins are evident. It is also evident, however, that a young woman like Pegeen, characterized by Michael's crony Jimmy Farrell as a "fine, hardy girl would knock the head of any two men in the place" (I, 63), cannot subordinate herself to her father's will for long. Her early rhetorical question to Shawn, showing that she is dissatisfied not only with him and her father but with her entire environment, suggests that she is on the verge of rebellion: "Where now will you meet the like of Daneen Sullivan knocked the eye from a peeler, or Marcus Quin, God rest him, got six months for maiming ewes, and he a great warrant to tell stories of holy Ireland till he'd have the old women shedding down tears about their feet. Where will you find the like of them, I'm saying?" (I, 59). As if in response to her question, just such a person (or one she imagines to be) arrives. That what Christy represents opposes the world of her father is symbolized by the fact that his courtship of Pegeen is allowed to develop because Michael is absent. The connection between Michael's neglect of Pegeen and Christy's success in winning her admiration is stressed by her repeated complaints about her father's irresponsibility in leaving her alone overnight to attend a wake. "If I am a queer

[7]Horst Breuer, "Männlichkeit in J. M. Synge's 'Playboy of the Western World,'" *Germanisch-Romanische Monatsschrift*, 32 (1982), 306.

[8]Cf. Shirley Nelson Garner, "*A Midsummer Night's Dream*: 'Jack shall have Jill; / Nought shall go ill,'" *Women's Studies*, 9 (1981), 55.

daughter," she says, "it's a queer father'd be leaving me lonesome these twelve hours of dark, and I piling the turf with the dogs barking, and the calves mooing, and my own teeth rattling with the fear" (I, 63).

With Christy's arrival at the pub and her father's departure, Pegeen's independent side comes increasingly to the fore. To understand the changes in her we must look closely at her contributions to Christy's identity as a parricide and playboy. Significantly, it is she who first evokes his admission that he murdered his father: when he accuses her of not speaking the truth about him, she responds, "Not speaking the truth, is it? Would you have me knock the head of you with the butt of the broom?" whereupon he replies, Don't strike me. . . . I killed my poor father, Tuesday was a week, for doing the like of that" (I, 73). Because of this single statement, she proceeds to build Christy up into a grand figure of heroic proportions. She makes of him, first, her protector, as pot-boy: "If I'd that lad in the house, I wouldn't be fearing the loosèd khaki cut-throats, or the walking dead" (I, 75); she then projects royal blood into his veins: "You should have had great people in your family, I'm thinking, with the little small feet you have, and you with a kind of quality name, the like of what you'd find on the great powers and potentates of France and Spain" (I, 79); next she casts him as a ladies' man, replying in response to a compliment of his, "You've said the like of that, maybe, in every cot and cabin where you've met a young girl on your way" (I, 81); and finally she envisions him as a poet—"I've heard all times it's the poets are your like, fine, fiery fellows with great rages when their temper's roused" (I, 81)—a comparison she reiterates during their love scene in the third act.

It is largely through Pegeen's imputation of these identities to Christy that he assumes them; at her suggestion and through her encouragement he really does become courageous, charming, lyrically adept, in short, a true playboy in all senses of the word at the time—consummate role-player, skillful athlete or game-player, and general "star." For as we learn in the course of the drama, there is little basis for attributing any of these roles to the son old Mahon characterizes as a "dirty, stuttering lout," a "lier on walls, a talker of folly, a man you'd see stretched the half of the day in the brown ferns with his belly to the sun" (II, 121), and "the laughing joke of every female woman where four baronies meet" (II, 123). Christy is as inherently inferior to his peers as Pegeen is inherently superior to hers. What, then, motivates her to form such an exalted image of him?

As Patricia Meyer Spacks has written, Christy's murder of his father represents a "metaphor of achievement," demonstrating his attainment of the self-confidence and maturity that come with release from parental domination.[9] It is little wonder that this kind of achievement should seem highly desirable to a passionate, strong-willed, imaginative woman like Pegeen, who as a girl "was tempted often to go sailing the seas" (III, 151). Given the conventions of her narrowly provincial society, however, as a woman she can realize such an achievement only vicariously. She therefore projects onto Christy, who in killing his father has accomplished what she wants metaphorically to do, characteristics that she would like to have herself. Having endowed him with these characteristics, she then takes back or imitates certain of them, such as the ability to speak like a poet, and no one is more astonished at her transformation than she is: "And to think it's me is talking sweetly, Christy Mahon, and I the fright of seven townlands for my biting tongue" (III, 151).

Christy's function as ideal alter ego for Pegeen is reinforced by parallels between their fathers and between their relationships with the two men. Although old Mahon is cantankerous and Michael Flaherty jovial, for example, both are part of the long-standing tradition in Irish literature (and life?) of the alcoholic patriarch. Flaherty gets so drunk at the wake that he has to be brought home in an ass cart, and he chides Christy for not

[9]Patricia Meyer Spacks, "The Making of the Playboy," in *Twentieth-Century Interpretations of "The Playboy of the Western World,"* ed. Thomas R. Whitaker (Englewood Cliffs, N.J.: Prentice-Hall, 1969), p. 84.

giving his father a wake so that they could have drunk "a smart drop to the glory of his soul" (III, 153); his main objection to Christy's murdering Shawn in the pub is that it is filled with whiskey for the men's drinks that evening. As for Mahon, his past ravings sound very much like delirium tremens: "There was one time I seen ten scarlet divils letting on they'd cork my spirit in a gallon can; and one time I seen rats as big as badgers sucking the life blood from the butt of my lug . . . and I a terrible and fearful case, the way that there I was one time screeching in a straitened waistcoat with seven doctors writing out my sayings in a printed book" (III, 143–145).

And yet Mahon has managed to raise Christy on his own, the boy's mother having died bearing him, just as Flaherty has had sole care of Pegeen. Similarly, just as Pegeen works for her father in the pub, Christy's life with Mahon has consisted of "toiling, moiling, digging, dodging from the dawn till dusk with never a sight of joy or sport saving only when I'd be abroad in the dark night poaching rabbits on hills" (I, 83). Finally, as Flaherty has done with Pegeen, Mahon has attempted to coerce his son into marrying an unloved partner simply for money. In Christy's words, his intended wife is "a walking terror from beyond the hills, and she two score and five years, and two hundredweights and five pounds in the weighing scales, with a limping leg on her, and a blinded eye, and she a woman of noted misbehaviour with the old and young" (II, 101). To Christy the worst of it is that "she did suckle me for six weeks when I came into the world" (II, 103), and it is of course this planned match, constituting what has been called "a kind of inversion of the Oedipal situation,"[10] that incites Christy to "kill" his father. It is at this point that the parallels between the two father–child relationships end; as Pegeen tells Christy, "I never killed my father. I'd be afeard to do that, except I was the like of yourself with blind rages tearing me within" (I, 81). But through her glorifica-

[10]Dierdre Laigle, "The Liberation of Christy Mahon," *Cahiers du Centre d'Études Irlandaises*, 2 (1977), 55.

tion of and love for a parricide Pegeen demonstrates her unconscious desire to do what repels her conscious mind: to rid herself
of the father who has consigned her to a loveless marriage in an
environment that is sure to stifle her.

Pegeen's identification with Christy is so strong that she occasionally exhibits conventionally masculine characteristics, while
at the same time he often displays traditionally feminine traits.
Such reversals are typical in comedy, where humorous effects
are frequently achieved by the inversion of conventional values
and norms of behavior. But in a drama where role-playing is as
important as in *The Playboy,* the reversal of gender roles deserves
especially close attention. Carolyn Heilbrun provides a concise
summary of gender distinctions: "According to the conventional
view, 'masculine' equals forceful, competent, competitive, con-
trolling, vigorous, unsentimental, and occasionally violent; 'feminine' equals tender, genteel, intuitive rather than rational, passive, unaggressive, readily given to submission. The 'masculine'
individual is popularly seen as a maker, the 'feminine' as a nour-
isher."[11]

Applying such categorizations to *The Playboy,* we find that
much about Christy is "feminine," particularly in the early parts
of the play. Before he appears on stage, Shawn says that he has
heard him "groaning out and breaking his heart" (I, 61) in a
ditch near the pub; Synge's first description characterizes him as
a "slight young man . . . very tired and frightened and dirty,"
who speaks "in a small voice" (I, 67), and he initially strikes
Pegeen as a "soft lad" (I, 71). Furthermore, with his fondness for
looking at himself in mirrors and his peacock pride at his appearance in the new clothes Shawn gives him, he displays a kind
of vanity stereotypically associated with women. And yet because
of his patricide, Pegeen is able to overlook all these features,
thus demonstrating her adherence to the conventional notion

[11]Carolyn Heilbrun, *Toward a Recognition of Androgyny* (1964; New York: Norton, 1982), p. xiv.

that the masculine principle is "predicated on the ability to kill."[12]

Pegeen in fact often exhibits a hardiness and boldness that render her more of a "playboy" than Christy. When he seeks to justify his "oddness" to her by explaining that he has lived "lonesome in the world" (II, 111), she replies that she is not odd, even though she has lived her whole life with her father alone. Similarly, she does not shrink from details of physical suffering, as other girls probably would do, but tells Christy how "Jimmy Farrell hanged his dog from the license and had it screeching and wriggling three hours at the butt of a string" (I, 73). Possessing in Shawn's words "the divil's own temper" (II, 115), she breaks out "into wild rage" (I, 89) when the Widow Quin accuses her of indiscriminate man-chasing, and in menacing Christy with the broom in Act I she is the first character in the play to threaten violence. After she returns the next morning from milking to find Christy surrounded by admiring village girls, she treats him with an imperiousness that reduces him to apologetic meekness. Most notably, after Christy's (second) attempted murder of old Mahon, Pegeen is the only one who is "man" enough to go up to him and slip the noose over his head and, when he twists his legs around the table, to burn him so that he will let go.

One of the central questions posed by *The Playboy* is of course why Pegeen and the other villagers are so horrified at witnessing precisely what had enthralled them as a tale, Christy's attempted patricide. One can find a partial explanation in the claim that, while no one loves a good yard more than the Irish, for them reality is another matter. But I am also persuaded by Gérard Leblanc's suggestion:

> One may . . . be tempted to see in the *Playboy* another dramatization of a universal model complicated by specific socio-historical

[12]Marilyn French, *Shakespeare's Division of Experience* (New York: Summit, 1981), p. 21.

circumstances in Ireland, where the son's emancipation was—and
is still—delayed much later than in other European countries.
Ireland is a fathers' country and the violent liberation of Christy
Mahon may pass for the vicarious fulfilment of a deepfelt unsocial wish shared by the villagers of Mayo and perhaps too, by the
Dublin spectators of January 1907 who more or less consciously
sensed that the symbolic undertones of parricide might threaten
the whole moral and social fabric of their world.[13]

Pegeen's radical turnabout after she learns that Christy's father
is alive, manifested in her characterization of Christy as "nothing
at all" (III, 161) and in her physical cruelty to him, represents a
special variation on this model. As we have seen, her glorification of him as a heroic playboy is inspired solely by her belief
that he has killed his father; it is this belief alone that blinds her
to his weaknesses and leads her to project a series of idealized
identities onto him. Once his claim is unmasked as a falsehood,
he truly becomes "nothing" in her eyes. In her case the "deepfelt
unsocial wish" vicariously fulfilled by Christy is less the overthrow of Ireland's English oppressors than the rebellion against
her own personal oppressor, her father. It is likely that in actually witnessing Christy's attempt as patricide (rather than simply
hearing about it) she becomes conscious of this wish, whereupon
her loyalty to Flaherty and to social convention—evident, for
example, in her earlier willingness to marry a man she did not
love because her father chose him—again takes over.

   Whatever the case, it seems certain that the blurring of gender
distinctions culminating in Pegeen's show of violence was as responsible as Christy's notorious mention of "a drift of chosen
females, standing in their shifts" (III, 167) for the bewilderment
of the play's audiences and the riots occasioned by its first performances in Dublin and the United States. As Synge realized
even at the time, the opening of *The Playboy* in Dublin's Abbey
Theatre was truly "an event in the history of the Irish stage."[14]

---

[13]Gérard Leblanc, "The Three Deaths of the Father in *The Playboy of the
Western World*," *Cahiers du Centre d'Études Irlandaises*, 2 (1977), 33–34.
[14]Synge to Molly Allgood, 27 January 1907, in *Collected Letters*, I, 285.

Indeed, few works in the history of *world* drama have caused comparable upheavals. The first performance was greeted by hissing, the second by shouting, hooting, and trumpet-blowing so loud the actors could not be heard, and similar responses continued for several nights thereafter; fights broke out and police were brought in to stand guard. The furor moved Yeats to hold a public debate on the freedom of the theater about a week after the premiere.[15] The play provoked even Joseph Holloway, the architect whose attendance at Abbey productions was so regular that he was regarded as virtually a member of the company and became its diarist, to call Synge "the evil genius of the Abbey" and "the dramatist of the dungheap."[16] Critics railed from all sides against the bawdy language of the play and its apparent celebration of patricide, but a newspaper review of the first performance reveals that what most scandalized audiences was Synge's depiction of women: the review refers to *The Playboy* as "this unmitigated, protracted libel upon Irish peasant men and, worse still, upon Irish peasant girlhood."[17] Similarly, William and Frank Fay, two of the cofounders of the Abbey Theatre, begged Synge to make Pegeen "a decent likable country girl," and in a letter to Synge the Abbey playwright Padraic Colum called her "a creation distinctly and acted splendidly. Still I think she would have stood by her man when he was attacked by a crowd. The play does not satisfy me."[18] Such reactions bear

[15]The fullest account of the riots is that of James Kilroy, *The "Playboy" Riots* (Dublin: Dolmen, 1971). See also the standard biography by David H. Greene and Edward M. Stephens, *J. M. Synge: 1871–1909* (New York: Macmillan, 1959), pp. 234–271, and Richard M. Kain, "The *Playboy* Riots," in *A Centenary Tribute to John Millington Synge, 1871–1909: Sunshine and the Moon's Delight*, ed. S. B. Bushrui (New York: Barnes & Noble, 1972), pp. 173–188.

[16]*Joseph Holloway's Abbey Theatre: A Selection from His Unpublished Journal*, ed. Robert Hogan and Michael J. O'Neill (Carbondale: Southern Illinois Univ. Press, 1967), pp. 81, 85.

[17]"The Abbey Theatre, 'The Playboy of the Western World,'" *Freeman's Journal*, 28 January 1907, p. 10, as quoted in Kilroy, *"Playboy" Riots*, p. 7.

[18]The Fay quotation is found in *My Uncle John: Edward Stephens's Life of J. M. Synge*, ed. Andrew Carpenter (London: Oxford Univ. Press, 1974), p. 188. The Colum passage is in Greene and Stephens, *J. M. Synge*, p. 248.

out T. R. Henn's claim that by Synge's day the chastity and purity of Irish womanhood had become a national myth.[19]

Synge's flaunting of this myth is evident in other works as well. His first completed play, *The Shadow of the Glen* (1904), in which Nora Burke goes in search of other men after she mistakenly thinks her husband has died, was denounced as libelous of Irish women because of its portrayal of her mercenary and "adulterous" inclinations. In fact the drama shows, through Nora's descriptions of her life with her husband, considerable insight into the frustration and loneliness of a woman who had married a much older man for his money and who lived with him in an isolated, out-of-the-way place. A similar juxtaposition of sexual realism with an attention to existential questions appears in *The Tinker's Wedding* (1907): the tinker Sarah Casey thinks that marriage to Michael Byrne will ease the pains of aging but is disabused of this notion by Michael's lusty, hard-drinking mother, Mary. In their strength and tenacity Nora, Sarah, and Mary are comic sisters of the tragic Maurya in *Riders to the Sea* (1903), who bears the successive drownings of her husband, father-in-law, and six sons with monumental stoicism, and of the title character in *Deirdre of the Sorrows* (1910), who is single-minded in her rejection of the much older Conchubor in favor of the young and attractive Naisi, even though she knows it will mean death for herself and Naisi. These powerful female figures dominate our memory of the dramas. As Ann Saddlemyer writes, "In nearly all of Synge's plays the women are not only more clearly defined than most of the men but also treated with a sympathetic complexity which frequently determines plot, mood and theme."[20] The extent to which Synge's women characters cross the conventional gender boundaries of the day suggests that his encounter

---

[19]*The Plays and Poems of J. M. Synge*, ed. T. R. Henn (London: Methuen, 1963), p. 61.

[20]Ann Saddlemyer, "Synge and the Nature of Woman," in *Woman in Irish Legend, Life, and Literature*, ed. S. F. Gallagher (Gerrards Cross: Colin Smythe, 1983), p. 58.

with feminism through his friendships with Rea, Beydon, and others left more than a merely superficial impression.

But nowhere is the blurring of gender roles more evident than in Synge's most well-known female character, Pegeen Mike. Her complex relationship with Christy, alternating as it does between identification and rejection, is further illuminated by contrast with another of Synge's masterful women and one of his favorite characters,[21] the Widow Quin. Unlike Pegeen, the Widow Quin is not restricted by a father and can thus act freely and uninhibitedly. Indeed, she stands apart from her entire community both geographically and morally. In her "little houseen, a perch off on the rising hill" (I, 89), she lives at a lofty remove from the other villagers. Her description of her daily routine is one of the most evocative of the many portrayals of loneliness in Synge's works: "I'm above many's the day, odd times in great spirits, abroad in the sunshine, darning a stocking or stitching a shift, and odd times again looking out on the schooners, hookers, trawlers is sailing the sea, and I thinking on the gallant hairy fellows are drifting beyond, and myself long years living alone" (II, 127).

The Widow Quin's genuine isolation is of an entirely different magnitude from the "lonesomeness" Pegeen feels on being deserted by her father for a night and accentuates the fact that it is the Widow Quin, rather than Pegeen, who belongs to the world outside the tight social order of the Mayo village, as Christy soon realizes; in response to her description of her loneliness (II, 127), he remarks, "You're like me, so." Moreover, the moral isolation the Widow experiences because of her accidental murder of her husband prefigures the rejection of Christy at the end of the play because of his attempted murder of his father. Michael Flaherty provides an early indication of the village attitude toward the Widow Quin with his rhetorical question to Christy:

[21]Nicholas Grene, *Synge: A Critical Study of the Plays* (London: Macmillan, 1975), p. 140.

"What would the polis want spying on me, and not a decent house within four miles, the way every living Christian is a bona fide saving one widow alone?" (I, 67). One of the village girls tells Christy that "all dread [the Widow] here" (II, 105), and Pegeen goes so far as to accuse her of rearing a black ram "at [her] own breast" (I, 89).

In fact the Widow Quin is no witch but rather the most down-to-earth character in the play. As a woman with a good deal of experience behind her, one who has "buried her children and destroyed her man" (I, 89), she is a hard-bitten, clear-sighted realist. In contrast to the romantic Pegeen Mike, she does not seek to escape the world in her imagination, having transcended it in actuality. Unlike Pegeen, she does not project onto Christy the roles of heroic parricide, aristocrat, ladykiller, or poet but sees him as he is: "It'd soften my heart to see you sitting so simple with your cup and cake, and you fitter to be saying your catechism than slaying your da" (I, 87). It is in keeping with her isolated position that the Widow Quin is shocked neither by the revelation that Christy did not succeed in killing his father nor by his second attempt to do so. In supporting the father-killer throughout and even helping him escape on several occasions, she distinguishes herself from all the other villagers. And whereas Pegeen loves Christy only conditionally, ultimately rejecting him and returning to the fold of her father's community, the Widow remains attached to him despite the changes in his fortunes, her fidelity recalling, as Michael Collins has observed, the norm in Shakespeare's Sonnet 116: "Love is not love / Which alters when it alteration finds."[22]

In the final version of *The Playboy* the Widow Quin does not win Christy, as she does in earlier versions. Yet the drama's closing spotlight is of course not on her loss—she is, after all, "formed . . . to be living lone" (I, 89)—but rather on Pegeen Mike's. Although both Christy and Pegeen are reunited with

[22]Michael J. Collins, "Christy's Binary Vision in *The Playboy of the Western World*," *Canadian Journal of Irish Studies,* 7, no. 2 (1981), 79.

their respective fathers in the end, the resolution of the play has very different implications for each. Christy, as we have seen, undergoes a profound development in the course of the drama, growing into the roles projected onto him by the villagers and above all by Pegeen; his imperious claim to his father near the play's end that he is "master of all fights from now" (this and all subsequent quotations from the play are from III, 173) shows that through his attempts at patricide he has won old Mahon's respect and has in effect switched places with him. Pegeen, by contrast, remains under the sway of her father and thus unchanged. While old Mahon reacts "with a broad smile" to Christy's new-found self-confidence as the two leave behind them these "fools," Flaherty's last words underline his power over his daughter and the compliance and conventionality to which it restricts her: "By the will of God, we'll have peace now for our drinks. Will you draw the porter, Pegeen?" The crossing of gender boundaries represented by Pegeen's vicarious overthrow of her father through her identification with Christy proves to be temporary.

Nowhere is the difference between Christy's development and Pegeen's static nature more evident than in their respective last lines. Christy's departing words are triumphant, announcing his imminent liberation from the narrow-mindedness of communities such as this Mayo village: "Ten thousand blessings upon all that's here, for you've turned me a likely gaffer in the end of all, the way I'll go romancing through a romping lifetime from this hour to the dawning of the judgment day." The tone of the famous lines with which Pegeen, putting her shawl over her head, closes the play is altogether different: "Oh my grief, I've lost him surely. I've lost the only playboy of the western world." Her words do more than reveal her awareness that Christy, having grown to be what she had imagined he was, is worth having after all; symbolically her lamentation points to her loss of that part of herself which might have set her free from her father and from the loveless marriage he has arranged for her. Indeed, Pegeen is worse off at the play's end than at its begin-

ning, for she has known Christy, felt true passion, experienced
the liberation brought by identification with the father-killer—
and then lost it all.

Thus Synge's great comedy ends in the same dark key as his
two tragedies, *Riders to the Sea* and *Deirdre of the Sorrows*. The
Playboy's conclusion is one of the best examples of what Arthur
Ganz has called "the essential sadness lying beneath even the
brightest of Synge's plays."[23] But because a comedy whose title
character is a man ends with the words of a grieving woman, we
are inevitably moved to think about the relationship between
comedy and woman's place. Among the first critics to do so was
George Meredith, whose essay on comedy (1877) goes so far as
to claim that there can be no comedy without sexual equality:
"Where women are on the road to an equal footing with men, in
attainments and in liberty—in what they have won for themselves, and what has been granted them by a fair civilization—
there, and only waiting to be transplanted from life to the stage,
or the novel, or the poem, pure comedy flourishes, and is, as it
would help them to be, the sweetest of diversions, the wisest of
delightful companions."[24]

As its tone might suggest, however Meredith's analysis fails to
take into account the status of female characters at the *end* of the
play, novel, or story, and his definition has been modified by
recent feminist criticism, notably in commentaries on Shakespeare. Linda Bamber, for example, writes that the disruption
of the social order commonly found in comedy often consists in
Shakespeare's plays of the reversal of traditional sexual hier-
archies: "The natural order, the status quo, is for men to rule
women. When they fail to do so, we have the exceptional situation, the festive, disruptive, disorderly moment of comedy." And
yet, she continues, "whenever Shakespeare's comedies challenge

[23]Arthur Ganz, *Realms of the Self: Variations on a Theme in Modern Drama* (New
York: New York Univ. Press, 1980), p. 28.
[24]George Meredith, "An Essay on Comedy," in *Comedy*, ed. Wylie Sypher
(1956; Baltimore: Johns Hopkins Univ. Press, 1980), p. 32.

the limits to sexual equality, they end by strenuously reaffirming those limits."[25] Insofar as the restoration of the social order toward which comedy moves typically includes a traditional, male-dominated marriage, comedy and sexual equality are in fact usually at odds with each other, Meredith notwithstanding.

The situation is rather different in *The Playboy*. Although the drama conforms superficially to the comic pattern, in that the status quo of the Mayo community triumphs and a traditional marriage is in the offing, obviously boy does not get girl, and girl gets the wrong boy; the final focus is not on union but on isolation. One is reminded of Synge's own comment that "'The Playboy of the Western World' is not a play with 'a purpose' in the modern sense of the word, but although parts of it are, or are meant to be, extravagant comedy, still a great deal that is in it, and a great deal more that is behind it, is perfectly serious, when looked at in a certain light."[26] One "serious" aspect is surely Pegeen's fate, which verges on tragedy—not death, as in the cases of Wilde's Salomé and Wedekind's Lulu, but the failure of self-realization, symbolized by a union with Christy. In contrast to the comedies of Shakespeare and others, then, in Synge's play comic tone and egalitarian impulse do not oppose but rather support each other, since Pegeen's liberating identification with Christy is directed, in terms of her development, toward a comic

[25]Linda Bamber, *Comic Women, Tragic Men: A Study of Gender and Genre in Shakespeare* (Stanford: Stanford Univ. Press, 1982), pp. 29, 32. On women and comedy see also, e.g., Judith Wilt, "The Laughter of Maidens, the Cackle of Matriarchs: Notes on the Collision between Comedy and Feminism," *Women and Literature*, 1 (1980), 173–196; several essays in *The Woman's Part: Feminist Criticism of Shakespeare*, ed. Carolyn R. S. Lenz, Gayle Greene, and Carol T. Neely (Urbana: Univ. of Illinois Press, 1980); Marianne Novy, "Demythologizing Shakespeare," *Women's Studies*, 9 (1981), 17–27; French, *Shakespeare's Division;* Garner, "*A Midsummer Night's Dream*"; Susan L. Carlson, "Comic Textures and Female Communities, 1937 and 1977: Clare Boothe and Wendy Wasserstein," *Modern Drama*, 27 (1984), 564–573; and Susan L. Carlson, "Women in Comedy: Problem, Promise, Paradox," in *Drama, Sex, and Politics*, ed. James Redmond (Cambridge: Cambridge Univ. Press, 1985), pp. 159–171.
[26]Synge to Editor, *Irish Times*, 30 January 1907, in *Collected Letters*, I, 286.

resolution. Yet the play's final emphasis on the failure of this resolution, highlighting not Christy's comic triumph but Pegeen's tragic lamentations at losing him, produces a stylistic rupture that points ahead formally to postmodern drama while calling attention thematically to the entrapment of Irish women in the conventions of their time.

5 The Dynamics of Sex and Suffering: Hauptmann's *Rose Bernd*

Gerhart Hauptmann's naturalist drama *Rose Bernd* (1903) is commonly regarded as one of his masterpieces. Critics praise, for example, the richness and verisimilitude of his evocation of the Silesian peasant milieu, and the play's dramatic tautness testifies to the validity of the novelist Theodor Fontane's comparison of Hauptmann with Ibsen.[1] In Germany the play has been frequently staged and has twice been made into a film, and in this country it has been performed with such actresses as Ethel Barrymore in the title role.

Although *Rose Bernd* does not share the world renown of *The Playboy of the Western World*, it bears striking similarities to Synge's drama, and a comparison of the two works offers illuminating insights into the portrayal of women at the turn of the century. In Hauptmann's play, as in Synge's, the power of men in patriarchal societies is dramatized through the depiction of a motherless daughter engaged to a man she does not love who has been chosen by her father; once again the father's authority is reinforced by a sexually and religiously conservative rural environment. Like Pegeen Mike, Rose has become a kind

[1] Theodor Fontane, "Hauptmann: *Vor Sonnenaufgang*," in Fontane, *Aufsätze, Kritiken, Erinnerungen* (Munich: Hanser, 1969), II, 820.

of substitute wife to her widowed father: she has not only taken over the tasks of the household but raised three younger siblings as well. And, as in *The Playboy*, the oedipal constellation of a close father–daughter relationship and an absent mother has created a dichotomous set of character traits in Rose: on the one hand she is a girl of uncommon spirit and vigor; on the other hand she is bound by an unusually strong sense of duty to her father.

Here the similarities end. While Synge's play is suffused with humor, *Rose Bernd*, following the brief idyllic interlude between Rose and her lover, Flamm, at the play's opening, is a study in bleakness. Whereas the arrival of Christy Mahon offers Pegeen at least the chance of an escape from the mismatch her father has urged on her, there is no possible happy ending to *Rose Bernd*, since Flamm makes it clear that he will never divorce his invalid wife. Moreover, Rose is caught between not two men but three: Flamm; her pious and sickly fiancé, Keil; and the brutish machinist Streckmann, who uses his knowledge of her illicit relationship with Flamm to terrorize her and eventually bring about her downfall. More than any of the other writers discussed in this book, Hauptmann is a dramatist of suffering, tirelessly investigating the tragic aspects of human existence. Nowhere is his sense of tragedy more evident than in *Rose Bernd*, where, in contrast to many of his other plays, suffering is not transcended through the intimation of a divine presence.[2] This is not to say, however, as Hans Joachim Schrimpf and others since him have done, that Rose is the victim of an "incomprehensible fate" and that she becomes "no longer a person but rather the mouthpiece of a dark, uncanny power."[3] Neither is it "class distinction" that victimizes her, as one critic wrote several decades ago.[4] Nor does John Osborne's statement about Hauptmann's dramatic oeuvre

[2]See Karl S. Guthke, *Gerhart Hauptmann: Weltbild im Werk*, 2d ed. (Munich: Francke, 1980), pp. 113–115.

[3]Hans Joachim Schrimpf, "Hauptmann: Rose Bernd," in *Das deutsche Drama vom Barock bis zur Gegenwart*, ed. Benno von Wiese (Düsseldorf: Bagel, 1958), II, 173, 182.

[4]L. B. Keefer, "Woman's Mission in Hauptmann's Dramas," *Germanic Review*, 9 (1934), 36.

as a whole apply to this particular play: "It appears . . . that for
Hauptmann, the dramatist, the greater significance lay not with
the question of the validity or non-validity of an interpretation
of the world, but with the simple fact of its existence, and its
consequences for the action of his play."[5] Rather, Rose is quite
clearly a victim not only of paternal domination, as is Synge's
Pegeen, but also of rural machismo and unequal treatment of
the sexes. She is victimized, in other words, not as a "mouthpiece" but as a woman—in her female roles as daughter, lover,
and (unmarried) mother. Although she is depicted as both
daughter and mother in the play, her subordination to her au-
thoritarian father and to other father figures is of such influence
on her life that I have chosen to focus on her position as daughter.

Cowed by the piety of her father and the bookish Keil, impregnated and then abandoned by Flamm, raped by Streckmann, and driven by desperation to strangle her baby at birth,
Rose assumes a place in two venerable traditions in German
literature: the bourgeois tragedy and the infanticide drama. Beginning with Lessing and continuing through Schiller and Hebbel, the bourgeois tragedy is propelled by the conflict between a
father's obsessive concern for his daughter's honor and her attraction to a man of whom he does not approve. The infanticide
drama, which flourished among Sturm und Drang writers, attacks the barbaric social and legal treatment of unmarried mothers and infanticides, who were often publicly humiliated and
subjected to cruel punishments—drowning, torture with heated
pincers, burial alive, impalement.[6] Both traditions fuse and
culminate in *Rose Bernd*. But, clearly influenced by his times,
Hauptmann differs from his predecessors in one significant
way: his drama sets up an ethical hierarchy in which certain
conventionally masculine attributes and behavior patterns are

[5]John Osborne, *The Naturalist Drama in Germany* (Manchester: Manchester
Univ. Press, 1971), p. 150.
[6]See Georg Pilz, *Deutsche Kindesmord–Tragödien: Wagner, Goethe, Hebbel, Hauptmann* (Munich: Oldenbourg, 1982), pp. 11–13.

presented as negative while traditionally feminine qualities are presented as positive, a value system that allies him with feminists of his day and our own. The tragic irony of his play is that feminine behavior is ineffectual or even condemned while masculine behavior, though producing disastrous results, remains unpunished. Thus while Synge calls conventional gender roles into question by blurring them, Hauptmann achieves a similar effect by criticizing a closed-minded, inflexible differentiation in the treatment of men and women. In form Hauptmann's protest is quite different from Synge's. Indeed, the behavior of Pegeen Mike and Rose Bernd can be viewed as paradigmatic of women's actual responses to male oppression at the turn of the century: feminism on the one hand and hysteria on the other. Whereas Pegeen's rebellion against her father, like the feminist movement, is active, outer-directed, emancipatory, and potentially constructive, Rose's subjugation to her father and entrapment from within and without in female roles creates in her a pathological state akin to hysteria in its passivity, inner-directedness, confining nature, and destructiveness (both of herself and of her child). In many ways she is reminiscent of that classic hysteric, Freud's Dora, also an "object of erotic barter."[7] But while Dora manages to free herself from the law of the father—from sexual exploitation by her own father and by Herr K. and from professional exploitation by Freud—Rose is ensnared and condemned by it.

Insofar as Rose's ruination results from the treatment she receives as a female, her fate is a manifestation of hysterization, Foucault's term for the reduction of the woman to her reproductive function, to her femaleness.[8] The forces that bring about Rose's hysterization are all exaggerated facets of conven-

[7]Erik H. Erikson, "Reality and Actuality: An Address," in *In Dora's Case: Freud—Hysteria—Feminism*, ed. Charles Bernheimer and Claire Kahane (New York: Columbia Univ. Press, 1985), p. 49.

[8]Michel Foucault, *The History of Sexuality*, vol. I, *An Introduction*, trans. Robert Hurley (New York: Vintage, 1978), p. 104; cf. p. 11 above.

tional masculinity: aggressive sexuality, male pride, and sexual jealousy. Of these agents of hysterization, sexuality is the most prevalent in the play. In 1922 the critic Paul Fechter called Hauptmann "the true eroticist of modern literature"[9]—quite a label for a writer to have earned in an age in which literary eroticism was so prevalent and palpable. Hauptmann's sense of the importance of sexuality in human life is suggested by a comment he made on the following passage from Ludwig Tieck's romantic novel *William Lovell:* "Nothing but sensuality is the driving cog in our machine, it puts movement into our existence and makes it joyful and lively. . . . All human wishes revolve around this pole, like gnats around a burning candle. A sense for beauty and a feeling for art are simply other dialects and pronunciations, they characterize nothing further than the human inclination to sensual pleasure. I view even religious devotion as a diverted channel for raw sensual instinct." Next to this passage Hauptmann wrote that it was "true . . . and not expressed strongly enough."[10]

Rose Bernd is saturated with sexuality. Like Pegeen Mike, Rose attempts to "return" to her father's choice for her—to break off with Flamm at the play's outset and marry Keil at last—but her intentions are foiled by the virtual personification of male libido run rampant, Arthur Streckmann, who has chanced to witness her farewell tryst with Flamm. As a man whose job takes him traveling through the countryside with his steam-powered threshing machine, he quite literally gets around, and he is used to enjoying easy conquests among the local girls. The attitude of this burly, attractive ladies' man toward women is evident in his lascivious talk of sex in terms of grinding and in his repeated insistence to the reluctant Rose that one man is as good as an-

[9]Paul Fechter, *Gerhart Hauptmann* (Dresden: Sibyllen-Verlag, 1922), p. 101.
[10]Passage from Hauptmann's copy of Heinrich Koerber, *Die Psychoanalyse: Die Freudsche Lehre in ihrer Theorie und Anwendung gemeinverständlich dargestellt* (1924), p. 47, quoted in Karl S. Guthke, "Freud und Hauptmann: Doppelgänger wider Willen?" in Guthke, *Das Abenteuer der Literatur: Studien zum literarischen Leben der deutschsprachigen Länder von der Aufklärung bis zum Exil* (Bern: Francke, 1981), pp. 293–294.

other. Since this rural "real man" explains his wife-beating to Rose by claiming, "A man has to show you women who's the boss,"[11] it is not surprising that he resorts to threats of disclosure and finally rape to have his way with her and thereby assuage his wounded pride at her preference for Flamm over himself.

In *Rose Bernd* male lust knows no class boundaries. Blonde, beautiful, and vigorous, Rose is as hotly pursued by the well-to-do landowner and magistrate Flamm as by the manual laborer Streckmann. While Flamm repeatedly makes such fatalistic statements as "What has to be just has to be" (III, 422) and "explains" his affair with Rose by reminding her that his wife has been confined to her bed or wheelchair for nine years and that a healthy, virile fellow like himself has to take care of his needs somewhere, this naturalistic justification is undermined by Frau Flamm's later revelation to Keil that she has for *twelve* years patiently tolerated "a man that all the women run after" (IV, 437). And, although Flamm is a genial and in many ways likable person, he is nearly as given to egotism and sexual jealousy as Streckmann is. He reveals his selfishness with both Rose and his wife. During his farewell to Rose in the first scene he embraces and kisses her in a rush of passion, throwing caution to the winds—"even if it brings me unhappiness" (I, 382)—only to jump up and disappear when he hears someone coming—the someone being Streckmann, who will bring unhappiness not to Flamm but to Rose. In the second act he commands the maid to wheel his wife out of the room without even consulting her so that he can talk privately to Keil and Bernd. Later, when his wife suggests that they help Rose out, he counters, "One shouldn't get mixed up in other people's affairs. That only brings annoyance and ingratitude" (IV, 430), a dismissal that foreshadows his rejection of Rose when he learns that she has been with Streckmann (but not that he raped her). His use of the same

[11]Gerhart Hauptmann, *Rose Bernd*, Act I, *Gesammelte Werke in sechs Bänden* (Berlin: Fischer, 1913), III, 383; all subsequent quotations are from this edition (translations mine), and are identified in the text by act and page number.

phrase with which Streckmann had slandered Rose—"and whoever else you're carrying on with" ("und mit wem du sonst noch
dei' Gestecke hast," IV, 444)— reflects the same kind of injured
sexual pride the machinist had manifested. And because of his
extensive experience with women, Flamm's jealous repudiation
of Rose leads us to suspect that the reason he threw out the
pregnant maid and her boyfriend mentioned in Act IV is that
Flamm too has been her lover.

The class difference between Flamm and Rose, emphasized
for us by our knowledge that she has been his servant and by her
use of the formal form of address with him whereas he uses the
informal form with her, is not the only aspect of his greater
power and authority; he is also a father figure to her. Nearly
twice her age, he could easily be her father, and in attempting to
explain his affair with her to his wife he points out that he
watched her grow up and that his feelings for her were in part a
displacement of his love for the young son he and Frau Flamm
had lost.

The third man in Rose's life, her perfectly mismatched fiancé,
is also associated with paternal authority. Throughout the play
Keil is paired with Bernd, appearing without him only once.
When Rose begins to waver in her decision to marry him at last,
Keil speaks to her "dictatorially" (II, 400), as her father so often
does. Just as Michael Flaherty favors Shawn Keogh as a fiancé
for Pegeen because of his wealth, Bernd urges Keil on Rose in
large part because he has lost his living quarters and is counting
on moving into the house Keil has just bought. But Keil is far
more than Shawn the deputy of his intended father-in-law, since
in his genuine piety he is a kind of ideal mirror for the preachy
old man. Flamm's exasperated outburst to Rose in the first scene
is only a slight exaggeration: "Then let your father marry August Keil, if he's so infatuated with him. He's practically in love
with the man! It's nearly an obsession with him" (I, 380). Most
significant, Keil and Bernd are linked in Rose's mind. She repeatedly talks of them in one breath, as when she says to Flamm,

"Who knows what I'd do if it weren't for August and Father! I'd
most like to rush out in all directions" (III, 422).

That Rose voices such a wish is not unreasonable. Marriage to
the pale, thin teetotaler would be as confining to her now as life
with her father has always been; as Flamm puts it, "Up to now
you've slaved away for your father—you have no idea what living is" (I, 380). The "clean and very frosty impression" (V, 446)
created by Bernd's parlor, filled as it is with crucifixes, Bibles,
and hymnals, reflects the personality he projects—hard-driving,
self-righteous, and intolerant of faults in others. His self-righteousness belies both his own inclination to take a drink every
now and then and his materialism, indicated early by Streckmann's comment that Bernd won't chide Rose for working on
the Sabbath if there is money to be made from her labors. Like
Synge's Michael Flaherty, then, Bernd is obviously a flawed authority figure, weaker than his paternal counterparts in earlier
bourgeois tragedies. Yet he is an authority figure nonetheless:
he orders Rose to marry Keil when she begins to vacillate again
in the second act, and his impatience with her when she is late in
bringing his supper to him in the field is typical of the imperious
tone he takes with her throughout the drama.

Bernd's power is manifested most clearly in the charge of
slander he files against Streckmann for insulting Rose by claiming
she is "carrying on with everyone" (III, 426). It is ironically appropriate that Bernd's charge helps bring on Rose's ruin—she
perjures herself in court, thus entangling herself all the more
inescapably in the web that entraps her—for it is motivated less
by genuine concern for his daughter than by the fear that he will
lose his position as churchwarden and by his obsession with
honor. When Keil presses him to withdraw his charge against
Streckmann, he replies, "My honor demands it! The honor of
my house and my girl. And yes, your honor too, in the end" (V,
452). This kind of rigid and often crippling notion of honor is
associated throughout the German literary tradition with male
characters: from Tellheim in Lessing's *Minna von Barnhelm*
(1767), whose honor is so injured over an undeserved charge of

misappropriated funds that he considers himself unworthy of the woman he loves, to the fathers of bourgeois tragedy, preoccupied with the honor of their daughters—Galotti in Lessing's *Emilia Galotti* (1772), Miller in Schiller's *Kabale und Liebe* (1784) *(Love and Intrigue)*, and Meister Anton in Hebbel's *Maria Magdalena* (1844).

Yet in Hauptmann's play the father's patriarchal obsession with his daughter's honor is thrown into question by his attitude toward her throughout the play. Bernd's comment to Streckmann about Rose—"That is some girl! [Keil] had better keep a good hold on her" (I, 392)—suggests that she is the object less of his love than of his male pride. This suggestion is confirmed by his repulsed rejection of her when he learns that she has had sexual relations with Streckmann and Flamm, his feelings demonstrated most graphically in his exhortation to her to stay away from her younger sister so as not to "poison" her (V, 457). In the end Rose's desertion by the father takes on even metaphysical dimensions, as she implies in her indirect, raving description of her desperate murder of her newborn infant: "I stared at the stars! I screamed and cried out! No heavenly father budged to help me" (V, 457).

The hysterization of Rose by Streckmann, Flamm, and Bernd, the depersonalizing treatment that reduces her to her biological femininity, is not atypical behavior for these characters; remarks made by all of them reveal their common tendency to view women as interchangeable members of a group rather than to regard them as individuals. After Streckmann finds Rose outside on a Sunday morning, for example, he proclaims, "Womenfolk belong in church" (I, 383). Similarly, in recalling how quickly and quietly Rose had recently agreed to register her engagement to Keil (in contrast to her earlier protests), Bernd tells Keil, "That's just how women are" (III, 409). As for Flamm, Rose's defense of Keil as her prospective husband prompts him to explode, "It's impossible to understand you women! You're an intelligent and determined person, but in this one point you're as stupid as all women, it's amazing—as stupid as a goose in the rain" (I, 381).

In a still crueler vein, when Rose desperately attempts to explain her actions with Streckmann to the jealous Flamm by saying, "He followed me and baited me like a dog" (IV, 445), Flamm bitterly retorts, "You women make dogs of us—today this one, tomorrow that one"—a blatantly ironic statement in light of our knowledge that Streckmann raped Rose. Only Keil sees her primarily as a person rather than as a female, introducing his revelation to Bernd about her actions with the words "Our Rose was a human being like anybody else" (V, 453). Lacking the masculine traits that win out in the world Hauptmann portrays, however, Keil remains as ineffectual as the women characters with whom he sympathizes.

Rose's comment that Streckmann "baited" her points to the most extreme manifestation of her dehumanization in the drama, her treatment as an animal—specifically, a hunted animal. The text abounds in images of hunting and entrapment. Describing her rape, for instance, she rails at Streckmann, "You swooped down on me like a bird of prey!" (III, 425). And it is no accident that Flamm is portrayed as the quintessential hunter. With his hunter's dress, booming hunter's song, and den full of trophies and other trappings of the hunt, he borders on a caricature from *Heidi* or "The Katzenjammer Kids." He repeatedly appears either carrying or cleaning a gun, the implications of which require no elaboration, and he expressly refers to hunting as his salvation: "If one couldn't do a bit of hunting now and then and couldn't put on a gun, well . . . one would have to run away to sea" (IV, 432). Even his state of mind is revealed through the imagery of firearms, as when he unthinkingly picks up and then hurls aside a cartridge pouch in his distraction at learning Rose is pregnant.[12] Such imagery is appropriate for one of the most powerful of Rose's hunters. She describes them

---

[12]Cf. Hans-Wilhelm Schäfer, "Das Motiv der Jagd im Werk Gerhart Hauptmanns," in *Akten des VI. Internationalen Germanisten-Kongresses, Basel 1980,* ed. Heinz Rupp and Hans-Gert Roloff (Bern: Lang, 1980), III, 459n. Schäfer notes that Flamm's loss of balance is reflected in the interruption of his hunting activities.

all as such near the end of the play: "August, they stuck to me like burrs!—I couldn't even cross the street!—Every man was after me!—I hid.—I was afraid! I was so afraid of men!—It didn't help, things only got worse! And then I just went from snare to snare, so that I hardly ever came to my senses again" (V, 458). But the most poignant image in this complex is her metaphorical portrayal of her infanticide: "And then I ran like a mother cat with her kitten in her mouth! But the dogs chased me down and I had to drop it" (V, 459).

Rose's hysterization is thus a twofold process; the outer world's reduction of her to her female status produces in her an inner state of hysteria. Hauptmann traces her inner deterioration with a care that reflects his lack of interest in outer dramatic action, a perspective he repeatedly emphasizes as a principle in his programmatic writings: "Wherever you find that which dramaturgical pests are forever missing, forever seeking, and never recognizing for what it is, namely that which they call 'plot'— whenever you chance to encounter this, take whatever you can find—ax, club, or any old rock that happens to be at hand—and beat it to death"; "'Action' in the drama is either inner action or none at all." Correspondingly, for the dramatist, character is paramount: "First human beings, then the drama"; "What one gives to the plot one takes away from the characters."[13] Hauptmann's practice was consistent with his principles: the real events of *Rose Bernd*—Rose's rape by Streckmann, the birth and murder of her child—occur offstage, between the acts, in strong contrast to, for instance, Heinrich L. Wagner's gruesome play *Die Kindermörderin* (1776) (The infanticide), in which the title figure kills her baby in full view of the audience by running a knitting needle through its temple.

Hauptmann's subordination of plot to character in his dramatic theory and practice reflects an interest in psychology which links him to his contemporary Freud. Karl Guthke has

[13]Hauptmann, *Die Kunst des Dramas: Über Schauspiel und Theater,* ed. Martin Machatzke (Berlin: Propyläen, 1963), pp. 181, 205, 198, 183.

argued convincingly that Hauptmann's expressed reservations about Freud belie the dramatist's sense of an underlying commonality, manifested perhaps most clearly in a similar fascination with psychological instability.[14] Hauptmann's contemporaries were struck by the hysteria-like mixture of religion and sexuality in his *Hannele* (1893) and *Der arme Heinrich* (1902) *(Henry of Auë)* and by the portrayal of Johannes Vockerat in *Einsame Menschen* (1891) *(Lonely Lives)*, which Schnitzler in a now famous characterization called a "tragedy of neurasthenia."[15] Equally impressive in its rendering of psychic pathology is *Rose Bernd*, which is comparable to a dramatic case study in its detailing of Rose's decline, from the "irrepressible laughter" occasioned by her encounter with Flamm at the play's opening to her laughter "with hideously hysterical irony" at its close.

One of the clearest indications of Rose's hysteria is her death wish, expressed early in the play and repeated at intervals. Rose responds to Streckmann's hints of disclosure in the first act by threatening to hang herself from a beam, and confides to Frau Flamm that she has fantasies of drowning herself and that it would have been better if her mother had taken her along with her. Hauptmann is careful, moreover, to reveal her increasing disorientation through her physiognomy, gestures, and actions. The confusion created in her by Streckmann's reiterated threats is evident in the dazed question she repeats to him: "Who are you? Who are you?" (III, 423); after he puts out Keil's eye and insults her in front of Keil, Bernd, and the field workers, she is "as if asleep" and babbles incoherently about having received a doll for Christmas (III, 426). Hereafter, as Keil tells Frau Flamm, Rose hardly dares leave the house and sometimes weeps all day long; on her visit to Frau Flamm she is described as having "peaked features and a sickly glow in her eyes" (IV, 440),

---

[14]Guthke, "Freud und Hauptmann," pp. 277–294.
[15]Arthur Schnitzler, "Gerhart Hauptmann: *Zu den 'Einsamen Menschen'*" (1892), *Neue Rundschau*, 73, nos. 2–3 (1962), 205.

and following the birth and death of her baby she is dizzy and has hallucinations.

The most significant manifestation of Rose's progressive hysterization, however, is her speech, or more accurately, her failure to speak. The kind of misunderstandings and gaps in communication which are responsible for much of the catastrophe in this "tragedy of wordlessness"[16] are found often in Hauptmann's work and, in their anticipation of contemporary drama, constitute one of his major contributions to the development of the theater. But none of the other characters in *Rose Bernd* suffers from the failure to speak to the extent that the heroine does, and the dynamics of this play set up a dichotomy that associates language with male power and silence with female powerlessness. This dichotomy, far from uncommon in literature, is reminiscent of Wedekind's *Earth-Spirit,* where, as we saw, both Lulu's treatment as an animal in the prologue and her pierrot costume point up her silence.

Rose Bernd comes into conflict with two bastions of the patriarchal order, both grounded in language: religious orthodoxy and secular law. Religion, dominated by a heavenly father, is repeatedly associated with her own father, for whom the Bible—the Word—is indeed the last word. The first thing he does on coming home in the evening is to have his youngest daughter take out the Bible for him to read; he even chooses to refresh himself from the hot work of threshing with a bit of the Good Book. Most striking, after learning that Rose has had sexual relations with Flamm and Streckmann, he refuses to look at her, plugs his ears with his thumbs, and buries his head in the Bible. This last image in particular, bordering on caricature, shows that Bernd is guided not by the spirit but by the letter of the book so dear to him—the letter that damns his daughter.

Language is also associated with male power in the figure of Streckmann, who holds over Rose the threat of ruining her by

---

[16]Hans Mayer, *Gerhart Hauptmann* (Velber: Friedrich, 1970), p. 63.

speaking what he knows about her affair with Flamm. As his threats increase, so does her powerlessness, signaled by her decreasing ability to speak. When he first reveals his knowledge to her, her helplessness is expressed in the sounds and gestures, described in the stage directions, which come more and more to supplant her words: "helplessly weeping and moaning and yet working convulsively"; "sobbing and crying out, beside herself"; "She tries beseechingly to grasp his hands, which he withdraws" (I, 387–388). Similarly, when Frau Flamm tries to coax out of her the reason for her unhappiness, Rose can speak only haltingly, in fragments, and discloses her pregnancy not with words but through the gestures and facial expressions with which she responds to Frau Flamm's pantomime with the doll.[17] And as far as the key secret is concerned—the fact that her relations with Streckmann were not voluntary but forced—Rose is unable to utter it to anyone, neither Flamm nor his wife nor Keil nor the court.

The cause of Rose's reticence, which incites her to perjury, punishable by imprisonment, and compels Flamm to reject her, is revealed in the desperate exclamation she screams out repeatedly to the Flamms: "I was ashamed!" (IV, 444). As we saw in Chapter 1, men conventionally associate shame with women, and Rose's shame contrasts markedly with the pride displayed by the male characters. Whereas "a man doesn't lie under oath" (IV, 444), as Flamm says, Rose, in perjuring herself because she is ashamed, obeys not the objective laws set down by men but an inner, subjective, female law. Rose's shame emphasizes her en-

---

[17]There are a number of affinities between Rose Bernd and "Anna O.," or Bertha Pappenheim, the early patient of Josef Breuer whose hysteria also manifested itself in, among other symptoms, linguistic disruption. But whereas Rose's difficulties in speaking demonstrate her helplessness in the face of paternal power, Anna O.'s use of gibberish and gestures signifies a rebellious rejection of the cultural order represented by the father for whom she has to care in his illness. See Dianne Hunter, "Hysteria, Psychoanalysis, and Feminism: The Case of Anna O.," in *The (M)other Tongue: Essays in Feminist Psychoanalytic Interpretation*, ed. Shirley Nelson Garner, Claire Kahane, and Madelon Sprengnether (Ithaca: Cornell Univ. Press, 1985), pp. 89–115.

trapment in her female status not only from without but from within. Thus while Synge questions conventional gender roles by creating a character (Pegeen Mike) who transcends the conventions, Hauptmann challenges gender roles by demonstrating the destructive consequences of imprisonment in these roles. Appropriately, Keil characterizes Rose's final and most horrifying transgression of both religious and secular law—the murder of her child—as "unspeakable" ("unsäglich"; V, 461). Inconceivable to the male imagination, her infanticide is the extreme manifestation of the female powerlessness betokened on so many earlier occasions by her silence.

The gender hierarchy that codes conventionally masculine behavior as ethically negative but effective and feminine behavior as positive but ineffectual is memorably exemplified in Flamm's wife, whose handicapped condition has obvious symbolic significance. The female–female bond represented by her offers of help to Rose—in sharp contrast to the friction between the play's male and female characters—is akin to the female solidarity at the beginnings of the turn-of-the-century feminist movement and further distinguishes Hauptmann's play from earlier infanticide dramas and bourgeois tragedies. For Frau Flamm provides Rose with what she has lost and desperately needs, a mother (figure). One of Hauptmann's many motherless characters, Rose is much more damaged by the lack of her female parent than is Synge's Pegeen Mike. In her dazed state following Streckmann's public defamation of her morals, she stammers, "Maybe a girl really does need a mother" (III, 426), and it has been suggested that she kills her newborn to protect it from growing up without a mother.[18] Although Frau Flamm, having lost her son when he was five, is no longer a mother, she is the quintessential mother figure. Hauptmann describes her as "matronly" (II, 393), and even her husband calls her "Mother," al-

[18]Klaus Dieter Post, "Das Urbild der Mutter in Hauptmanns naturalistischem Frühwerk," in *Mythos und Mythologie in der Literatur des 19. Jahrhunderts*, ed. Helmut Koopmann (Frankfurt: Klostermann, 1979), p. 345.

though she is only a couple of years older than he. Like Flamm, she associates Rose with their dead son, with whom the girl used to play, and having promised Rose's dying mother to keep an eye on her, Frau Flamm has always felt "as if she were half my own child" (IV, 430). In contrast to Evchen Humbrecht's flirtatious, negligent mother in *Die Kindermörderin*, to Luise Miller's silly, bumbling mother in *Love and Intrigue*, and to Gretchen's motherly friend Marthe in Part I of Goethe's *Faust* (1808), who helps couple Gretchen with her seducer, Frau Flamm offers the entrapped Rose comfort and is the only character in the play who does not want something from her. The irony is, of course, that Rose, having betrayed Frau Flamm with her husband, feels unable to confide in her or accept her offers of help, and thus Frau Flamm's kindness only increases her sense of entrapment.

Frau Flamm's sensitivity and magnanimity contrast significantly with the imperceptiveness and egotism of the play's male characters. Unlike Flamm, who fails to notice Rose's pregnancy despite her broad hints in the third act, or Bernd, who in the face of Rose's transgressions longs to be deaf and blind, Frau Flamm not only notices that Rose is pregnant but perceives the changes in her husband after Rose ends her relationship with him. To help Rose out of her difficult situation, she suggests to Flamm that they adopt a (Rose's) child. Most remarkable, even after she learns that her husband is the father of the expected baby, and after he has rejected Rose, Frau Flamm assures her that she and the child will be provided for.

Insofar as Frau Flamm clearly sets the drama's ethical standard, it is worthwhile to look at her pronouncements on men. Echoing and taking one step further Rose's claim to Streckmann in the first act, she tells Rose that "one man is good for just as much as the other, and none of them is worth much of anything" (II, 404). After guessing that her husband has been having an affair with Rose, she observes with resignation, "You make things easy for yourselves, you men" (IV, 437), and following his use of the *Phaedrus* analogy to describe his passion for Rose, she comments, "That's a real pretty story you've told—complete with learned allusions—and when you men do that you always think you're in the right! A poor woman has little chance to get anywhere then" (IV, 439). Then, agreeing despite what she has just learned to speak with Rose, she warns him, "But don't imagine that I can make whole again everything you've broken. You men are like children in that respect" (IV, 440). To be sure, these remarks show Frau Flamm to be guilty of having as monolithic a view of men, seeing them primarily as men rather than as human beings, as Streckmann, Bernd, and Flamm have of women. The difference is that the men are not victimized by this kind of thinking, as Frau Flamm and especially Rose are. For it should not be forgotten that the play's ultimate focus is on Rose's suffering; the final line seems to express the author's own bias: "What this girl must have suffered!" It is no accident that this line is spoken by Keil, the only one of the major male characters who, as we have noted, regards Rose as a person first and a woman second.

But the first feminist movement and the Hauptmann of *Rose Bernd* have more in common than a belief in the ethical superiority of the female-female bond. Whereas Freud's theoretical writings attribute a relatively weak sex drive to women, Hauptmann portrays Rose as a full-fledged sexual being. Her sexuality is in itself healthy and unproblematic; it becomes problematic only because of the prominence it assumes for the men in the play. While the sexuality of several characters is dramatically emphasized, only Rose is victimized because of hers. Flamm's observation about slander suits applies equally to sexual relations: "It's the woman who bears the costs in the end" (IV, 433). The essence of the conflict engendered by Rose's highly sexed nature is captured by a remark her mother had once made to Frau Flamm: "My Rose is born to be a mother! But her blood is a bit too hot!" (II, 405).[19] The play's sympathy for Rose shows that

[19]Precisely this kind of condemnatory view can be found in early criticism of the play, such as the following interpretation by Gerhard Hering: "Rose's hot-bloodedness leads beyond her love for Flamm to her surrender to Streckmann, and from this to wild shame and a defiant attempt to save herself through lies, perjury, and finally infanticide"; Hering, *Porträts und Deutungen: Von Herder zu Hofmannsthal* (Hamburg: Claassen & Goverts, 1948), p. 87.

Hauptmann regards it as unjust that women should not have the same rights to exercise their sexuality as men, should be forced to choose between freely expressed sexuality and motherhood, and should be ostracized and even punished for having children out of wedlock.

These views resemble those advocated by the more radical branches of the German women's movement at the turn of the century. In the 1890s feminist activity in Germany had been dominated by "abolitionism," a movement founded in England by Josephine Butler, which worked to abolish state interference in private morality, especially police control of prostitution. The rationale behind these efforts was the belief that women should not be punished for prostitution while men could hire their services with impunity, and the abolitionists' ideal was to raise the morality of everyone to the level of chastity expected of women. In the middle of the first decade of this century, however, the so-called New Morality *(Neue Ethik)*, a gospel not of moral repression but of moral libertarianism, began to gain popularity. The foremost proponent of this doctrine was the Berlin feminist Helene Stöcker, who campaigned against the stigmatization of illegitimate children and unwed mothers, as well as against the idea that women were inherently chaste, and pleaded for a wider availability of contraceptives.[20] Although Stöcker's position was rejected by more moderate feminists as sexually permissive, it was embraced by radical members of the movement such as Minna Cauer, Anita Augspurg, and Lida Gustava Heymann.

The causes implicitly espoused by *Rose Bernd* link Hauptmann not only to the New Morality of radical feminism but to many female naturalist writers as well. Klara Müller, Margarete

[20]See, e.g., Richard J. Evans, *The Feminist Movement in Germany, 1894–1933* (London: Sage, 1976); Amy Hackett, "Feminism and Liberalism in Wilhelmine Germany, 1890–1918," in *Liberating Women's History: Theoretical and Critical Essays,* ed. Berenice A. Carroll (Urbana: Univ. of Illinois Press, 1976), pp. 127–136; and Herrad Schenk, *Die feministische Herausforderung: 150 Jahre Frauenbewegung in Deutschland,* 2d ed. (Munich: Beck, 1981).

Beutler, and Maria Janitschek, for example, all praise "free" (unwed) motherhood and women's right to the uninhibited satisfaction of their erotic desires.[21] Women writers such as these and the Hauptmann of *Rose Bernd* are thus to be distinguished from the majority of male naturalist writers, who paid lip service to feminist concerns while in fact lacking respect for them. For instance, although both *Die Gesellschaft* (Society) and *Die Freie Bühne* (The free stage), two of the most prominent naturalist periodicals, published articles in favor of women's rights in their first issues, later issues contain clearly antifeminist material. Typical is an 1890 article in *Die Gesellschaft* in which Conrad Alberti suggests that Ibsen's *Doll House* should be retitled *Nora, or the Results of a Silly Method of Educating Women.* Other naturalist writers and journalists scoff at the notion of "free love" and criticize feminists as unfeminine, not "real women."[22]

The young Hauptmann shared these critical views, as the plays he wrote before *Rose Bernd* indicate. In *Vor Sonnenaufgang* (1889) *(Before Dawn)* the protagonist, Loth, has clearly absorbed the lessons of women's emancipation, explaining to his host, Hoffmann, that he would be interested only in the kind of woman who has no inhibitions about demanding what she wants, especially in the area of love; his insistence that he would want a woman to confess her feelings for him openly prompts Hoffmann's sister-in-law Helene to do just that. The sincerity of Loth's open-minded stance is thrown into question, however, by his priggish self-righteousness and his fanatical belief in heredity, which lead him to abandon Helene in a flash, driving her to suicide, when he learns that her father and sister are alcoholics. Similarly, it has often been noted that the student Anna Mahr in *Lonely Lives,* in whom Hauptmann intended to depict the "emancipated woman" par excellence, brings misery to every character

[21]Richard Hamann and Jost Hermand, *Naturalismus* (Munich: Nymphenburg, 1972), pp. 103–104.

[22]Dieter Bänsch, "Naturalismus und Frauenbewegung," in *Naturalismus: Bürgerliche Dichtung und soziales Engagement,* ed. Helmut Scheuer (Stuttgart: Kohlhammer, 1974), pp. 122–149.

in the play except herself, and more recently critics have observed that she is so full of inconsistencies and contradictions that what she actually demonstrates is Hauptmann's inability to portray an emancipated woman.[23]

The greater understanding of and sympathy with issues central to the feminist movement demonstrated by *Rose Bernd* surely originated in part in Hauptmann's own experiences. By the time of the play's conception he had already left his wife, Marie, for Margarete Marschalk and had had a child by her out of wedlock, since Marie had not yet granted him a divorce. Through Margarete he came to know the stigmatization endured by unmarried mothers.[24] But the immediate inspiration for the drama was his service in 1903 as a juror in the infanticide trial of a twenty-five-year-old peasant girl, whose acquittal he supported. Hauptmann's interest in these feminist problems persisted beyond *Rose Bernd.* The notes for his satiric dramatic fragment *Mutterschaft* (Motherhood) of 1905 sketch the story of a woman physician who, moved by the plight of the pregnant and unmarried daughter of a pastor, formulates plans for a home for unwed mothers. The community is so shocked by her idea that they have her committed to a mental institution, but after her release a few years later she speaks out again on behalf of single mothers, bringing out her own well-mannered and attractive young son to prove her point.

Hauptmann takes up this theme again in the massive novel *Die Insel der Großen Mutter oder Das Wunder von Île des Dames: Eine*

[23]For the first position see, e.g., Jenny C. Hortenbach, *Freiheitsstreben und Destruktivität: Frauen in den Dramen August Strindbergs und Gerhart Hauptmanns* (Oslo: Universitetsforlaget, 1965), p. 91; for the second, see Sabine Schroeder, "Anna Mahr in Gerhart Hauptmann's *Einsame Menschen:* The 'Emancipated Woman' Re-examined," *Germanic Review,* 54 (1979), 125–130, and Naomi Stephan, "Die Frauenfiguren in Gerhart Hauptmanns *Einsame Menschen* und Ulrika Woerners *Vorfrühling:* Universal oder trivial?" in *Die Frau als Heldin und Autorin: Neue kritische Ansätze zur deutschen Literatur,* ed. Wolfgang Paulsen (Bern: Francke, 1979), pp. 190–200.

[24]For a concise and lively account of the major women in Hauptmann's life, see Evelyn Weber, "Gerhart Hauptmann und die Frau," *Neue Deutsche Hefte,* 31, no. 1 (1984), 76–96.

Geschichte aus dem utopischen Archipelagus (1924) *(The Island of the Great Mother, or The Miracle of Île des Dames: A Story from the Utopian Archipelago)*, the story of a paradisaic colony organized by a group of women shipwrecked on a tropical island. Although the only male present is a young boy, the women suddenly begin to give birth and are consequently inspired to celebrate the dispensability of the men who control the civilization they have left behind. Much in Hauptmann's book, particularly the element of parthenogenesis, is reminiscent of Charlotte Perkins Gilman's feminist utopian novel *Herland* (1915), and the establishment of homes for single mothers was one of the primary goals of the League for the Protection of Motherhood and Sexual Reform, a German feminist organization founded in 1904. Yet the fact that Hauptmann was unable to complete *Mutterschaft*, a realistic depiction of the problem of unmarried mothers, and transferred it to the mythical, mystical setting and treatment of *The Island of the Great Mother*, reflects the kind of ambivalence toward feminism that, as we have seen, characterizes most of the dramatists represented in this book. Ultimately Hauptmann's novel seems to constitute less an argument for female autonomy than a glorification of what he describes in 1924 as woman's essence, motherhood: "In order to gain a full consciousness of her worth, woman need do nothing more than realize what she is: namely, the mother of all men who have ever lived, acted, thought, and written. . . . The maternal function is fertile and rich: a mother is formed in soul and body around the source of life."[25] Even at the turn of the century, feminists would have been disturbed by the limitations this view imposes on women.

But such matters are not at issue in *Rose Bernd*. In the light that Hauptmann's statement about motherhood retrospectively casts on *Rose Bernd*, we might see the play as a dramatization of the forces that *prevent* Rose from becoming what she is naturally

---

[25]Hauptmann, "Vom Mann und vom Weib," in *Ausblicke* (Berlin: Fischer, 1924), p. 64.

55

destined to be—a mother. If the play is seen as the clash between "mother-power" and "father-power," it is clearly the mothers who lose; both Rose and Frau Flamm—handicapped, bereft of her son, and deceived by her husband—are "blessed with sorrows," as Frau Flamm says all mothers are (II, 405). Little wonder that Goebbels banned a film version of *Rose Bernd* scheduled for production under the Nazi regime, claiming that "it is the duty of German mothers to give birth joyfully."[26] As we have seen, it is not the plight of the mother but rather the daughter's subjugation to the father that dominates the play. Yet in its treatment of a would-be mother, *Rose Bernd* serves as a transition to the remaining chapters of this book, which examine more closely dramatic portrayals of maternity.

[26]Quoted in Roy C. Cowen, *Hauptmann-Kommentar: Zum dramatischen Werk* (Munich: Winkler, 1980), p. 137.

PART IV

Mothers in Spite
of Themselves

Although scholars disagree as to whether patriarchal social structures were preceded by matriarchal forms, it is certain that virtually all primitive peoples worshiped a mother goddess. Recognized as the source of life and thus the embodiment of fertility, the mother eventually came to represent the archetypal feminine. Erich Neumann describes this development in his study of the Great Mother archetype:

> It is only relatively late in the history of mankind that we find the Archetypal Feminine designated as Magna Mater. But it was worshiped and portrayed many thousands of years before the appearance of the term. . . . [A] wreath of symbolic images, however, surrounds not only *one* figure but a great number of figures, of Great Mothers who, as goddesses and fairies, female demons and nymphs, friendly and unfriendly, manifest the one Great Unknown, the Great Mother as the central aspect of the Archetypal Feminine, in the rites and myths, the religions and legends, of mankind.[1]

[1]Erich Neumann, *The Great Mother: An Analysis of the Archetype,* trans. Ralph Manheim, 2d ed. (Princeton: Princeton Univ. Press, 1963), pp. 11–12.

The archetype of the mother or Great Mother has continued to captivate the human imagination in a wide variety of incarnations.[2] What might be called the cult of the mother reached the height of its influence in the nineteenth century, when the rigid sexual division of spheres produced an isolated domestic realm over which the mother reigned supreme; as Nancy Chodorow and Susan Contratto observe, "At a time when everyone's life was being affected by the frenzied growth of developing industrial capitalism, somehow mothers were seen as having total control and unlimited power in the creation of their children."[3]

In larger social terms, however, maternity and mother-dominated child-raising are potentially the root of female oppression, insofar as they can serve to confine women to the home. Indeed, Julia Kristeva asserts that it is not woman as such who is repressed in patriarchal society, but the mother.[4] Accordingly, both the old and the new feminist movements have made motherhood and related issues their central concerns. Twentieth-century feminists echoed the calls of turn-of-the-century women for the distribution of safe and dependable methods of contraception, and added the demand for legalized abortion. In her landmark book *The Second Sex* Simone de Beauvoir singles out woman's biological destiny as mother as her "misfortune," and as late as 1977 we find her claiming that "child-bearing, at the moment, is real slavery."[5] Shulamith Firestone goes so far as to argue for the wholesale replacement of biological motherhood by artificial

[2]See, e.g., in addition to Neumann, C. G. Jung, *Four Archetypes: Mother/Rebirth/Spirit/Trickster*, trans. R. F. C. Hull (Princeton: Princeton Univ. Press, 1959), pp. 7–44.
[3]Nancy Chodorow and Susan Contratto, "The Fantasy of the Perfect Mother," in *Rethinking the Family: Some Feminist Questions*, ed. Barrie Thorne with Marilyn Yalom (New York: Longman, 1982), p. 64.
[4]Julia Kristeva, *La Révolution du langage poétique* (Paris: Seuil, 1974), p. 453.
[5]Simone de Beauvoir, *The Second Sex*, trans. and ed. H. M. Parshley (1952; New York: Vintage, 1974), p. 72; "Talking to Simone de Beauvoir," *Spare Rib*, no. 56 (March 1977), 8 (quoted in Jeffner Allen, "Motherhood: The Annihilation of Women," in *Mothering: Essays in Feminist Theory*, ed. Joyce Trebilcot [Totowa, N.J.: Rowman & Allanheld, 1983], p. 315).

methods.[6] More recent feminist positions have been less radical, concentrating on such matters as the manipulation of the institution of motherhood to serve male purposes[7] or arguing that the raising of children by women alone reproduces traditional sex-typed patterns of behavior in both boys and girls and that child-rearing should therefore be equally shared by men and women.[8] Whatever their precise orientation, however, feminists of all eras have felt compelled to take a stand on maternity.

It is thus not surprising that at the turn of the century play-wrights became fascinated by mother figures, for it was precisely at this time that the cult of the mother clashed with the burgeoning of the first feminist movement, which was calling into question the idea that motherhood was woman's inevitable and single vocation. In their attention to the mother these dramatists go further than Freud, who, while recognizing her role in human development as central, does not examine it closely, concentrating instead on the child's oedipal relationship with the father. Henrik Ibsen and Hugo von Hofmannsthal offer two quite different dramatic portrayals of resistance to motherhood in *Hedda Gabler* and *The Woman without a Shadow*. Since the former play ends tragically and the latter with an apparently harmonious resolution, they serve especially well as paradigmatic illustrations of the phenomenon. Although both Hedda Gabler and Hofmannsthal's Dyer's Wife are daughters and wives as well as would-be mothers, the maternal role is the major source of their victimization and will hence be the focus of attention here.

Treating a similar female problem in essentially opposite ways, these two plays represent a distinction analogous to the

[6]Shulamith Firestone, *The Dialectic of Sex: The Case for Feminist Revolution* (New York: Morrow, 1970).

[7]Adrienne Rich, *Of Woman Born: Motherhood as Experience and Institution* (New York: Norton, 1976).

[8]See, e.g., Dorothy Dinnerstein, *The Mermaid and the Minotaur: Sexual Arrangements and Human Malaise* (New York: Harper & Row, 1976), and Nancy Chodorow, *The Reproduction of Mothering: Psychoanalysis and the Sociology of Gender* (Berkeley: Univ. of California Press, 1978).

one introduced by Nancy Miller to talk about "heroine's texts" in eighteenth-century fiction. Miller distinguishes between novels with a "dysphoric" plot, which close with the heroine's death in the prime of youth, and those with a "euphoric" plot, which describe the heroine's ascent and end with her integration into society.[9] If one substitutes pregnancy for the marriage in which the euphoric text typically culminates, the plays by Ibsen and Hofmannsthal fit Miller's dual pattern closely, a parallel that reinforces their paradigmatic character.

[9]Nancy Miller, *The Heroine's Text: Readings in the French and English Novel, 1722–1782* (New York: Columbia Univ. Press, 1980).

6 Maternity and Hysteria: Ibsen's *Hedda Gabler*

No book on the relation of turn-of-the century European dramatists to feminism would be complete without Ibsen. The American Ibsen actress Elizabeth Robins speaks for many of her colleagues when she says that "no dramatist has ever meant so much to the women of the stage as Henrik Ibsen."[1] Few moments in the history of the theater are so famous as Nora Helmer's defiant slamming of the door of her home at the end of *A Doll House* (1879), a gesture widely credited with announcing the sexual revolution. Despite Ibsen's often cited claim in his speech to the Norwegian Women's Rights League in 1898 that he was not sure what women's emancipation really was and that his concern had been with the emancipation of human beings, there is no denying the overwhelming reception accorded *A Doll House* in its day. Feminists regarded the play as something of a miracle. Its powerfully subversive potential is captured by the condemnation of the new, emancipated woman issued by the contemporary pastor M. J. Faerden:

> Just as Nora appears in the final scene, free and unfettered by any bond, divine or human, without commitment or obligation to the man whom she has given her promise or to the children she has brought into this world—likewise we will find the wife in the

[1]Elizabeth Robins, *Ibsen and the Actress* (1928; New York: Haskell House, 1973), p. 55.

modern marriage, from beginning to end. In the future her place will not be in the innermost sanctuary of the home, like a priestess at its hearth and altar. The emancipated woman has taken her place at the door, always ready to depart, with her suitcase in her hand. The suitcase—and not, as before, the ring of fidelity—will be the symbol of her role in marriage.[2]

The play, in fact, did much to bring about reforms in the condition of women in Scandinavia, thus realizing in part Ibsen's hopes that women would gain greater political influence. He knew and was influenced by leading Norwegian feminists such as Camilla Collett, who helped make the women's movement in Scandinavia the most successful in Europe before World War I. His comment about why women and not men should be consulted about the married women's property bill is characteristic of his awareness that his society was controlled by men: "To consult men on such a matter is like asking wolves if they desire better protection for the sheep."[3]

Concerned as he was with women as a group, Ibsen also expressed opinions on the specific issue of motherhood. His remarks on the subject in his speech to the Norwegian Women's Rights League have been construed as evidence that his belief in the importance of personal freedom was restricted to men: "It is for the *mothers*, by strenuous and sustained labour, to awaken a conscious feeling of culture and discipline. This feeling must be awakened before it will be possible to lift the people to a higher plane. It is the women who shall solve the human problem. As mothers they shall solve it. And only in that capacity can they solve it. Here lies a great task for women."[4] Yet these remarks take on a rather different significance when juxtaposed to

[2]Translated and quoted by Katherine Hanson, "Ibsen's Women Characters and Their Feminist Contemporaries," *Theatre History Studies*, 2 (1982), 86–87.

[3]Quoted in Katherine M. Rogers, "A Woman Appreciates Ibsen," *Centennial Review*, 18 (1974), 103.

[4]The idea that Ibsen was thinking only of men when he demonstrated the importance of personal freedom is argued by, e.g., Roslyn Belkin, who quotes this passage in "Prisoners of Convention: Ibsen's 'Other' Women," *Journal of Women's Studies in Literature*, 1 (1979), 144.

Ibsen's comparison, in the notes to *A Doll House,* of a mother in modern society to "certain insects who go away and die when she has done her duty in the propagation of the race."[5] He thus appears to be saying not that motherhood *should* be women's only vocation, but rather that the society of his day offers them little else.

It is against this complex background that we should view Ibsen's subsequent dramatic treatment of maternity. It is customary to regard *Ghosts* (1881), in which we learn that Mrs. Alving has sacrificed her personal happiness and endured untold misery with her profligate husband for the sake of her son Oswald, as a response to *A Doll House,* in which Nora abandons her children to realize herself. But *Ghosts* is not Ibsen's last word on motherhood. I would like to focus here on his later play *Hedda Gabler* (1890), in which the title character resists maternity from the outset. Looking at Ibsen's dramatic oeuvre as a totality, we can see that if motherhood as portrayed in *Ghosts* is regarded as the status quo for his era, then *A Doll House* and *Hedda Gabler* represent two differing reactions against it, the former successful, the latter tragic. For Hedda Gabler, like Hauptmann's Rose Bernd, can be seen as the personification of the hysterization of the female body, or the reduction of the woman to her status as female, and it is this process that brings about her downfall. This perspective casts into a somewhat different light the conventional view of Hedda as gratuitous termagant, typified by Henry James's characterization of her as "a wicked, diseased, disagreeable woman."[6]

Not only Hedda but the other two major female characters in the play may be defined vis-à-vis literal or metaphoric maternity. The unmarried Juliane Tesman has missed what seems to have been her life's calling; kind, good-natured, and self-sacrificing, she was born for motherhood. She is the embodiment of

[5]*Playwrights on Playwriting: The Meaning and Making of Modern Drama from Ibsen to Ionesco,* ed. Toby Cole (New York: Hill & Wang, 1960), p. 152.

[6]Henry James, "On the Occasion of *Hedda Gabler*" (1891), in *Discussions of Henrik Ibsen,* ed. James W. McFarlane (Boston: Heath, 1962), p. 58.

caretaking, occupying her days with the nursing of her bedrid-
den sister; the hope she discloses to her nephew Tesman near
the beginning of the play—that her sister be allowed to live a bit
longer, as otherwise she will have nothing to fill her life—is a
poignant capsulization of her existence. Having been both "father and mother"[7] to the orphaned Tesman, she continues to
look after him as an adult, taking out a mortgage for his house
on her pension. Still given to mothering him, she comes to check
on him the morning after he returns from his honeymoon even
though she has just welcomed him home the night before. Even
now she refers to him as her brother's "little boy" (I, 697), clearly
demonstrating Testman's role as her surrogate child. Yet her
infantilization of him is not unjustified. Insofar as the assumption of paternity is a conventional signpost in literature for a
man's achievement of maturity, Tesman's reaction to Aunt
Julie's hints about his imminent fatherhood is telling: when she
presses him about his "expectations," he responds that he has
"every expectation in the world of becoming a professor shortly"
(I, 699). Similarly, when his aunt suggests that he will soon find a
use for the two extra rooms in the house, Tesman assumes that
she is referring to his growing library.

Tesman's latter remark introduces the thematic analogy between children and books on which Thea Elvsted's metaphorical
maternity rests. The symbolism marking Thea and Løvborg's
manuscript as their "child" is impossible to miss; indeed, it is
overdetermined by their repeated references to it. Løvborg emphasizes that the manuscript was a joint creation: "My book and
Thea's—for that's what it is"; "Thea's pure soul was in that book"
(III, 759, 761). Similarly, Thea tells Hedda that "whenever
[Løvborg] wrote anything, we'd always work on it together" (I,
715), and Tesman's observation that Løvborg has "never written
like this before" (II, 727) attests to Thea's role in the venture.

[7]Henrik Ibsen, *Hedda Gabler*, in *The Complete Major Prose Plays*, trans. Rolf
Fjelde (New York: Farrar, Straus & Giroux, 1965), Act I, p. 698; subsequent
quotations from *Hedda Gabler* and *A Doll House* are identified in the text by act
and page number.

When Løvborg tries to conceal his negligence in losing the manuscript by telling Thea that he has torn it into a thousand pieces, she screams and compares his action to the murder of a child: "But how could you do it—! It was my child too" (III, 760). Confiding the truth about the book to Hedda, Løvborg admits, "But killing his child—that's not the worst thing a father can do. . . . I lost the child" (III, 761).[8] As Miss Tesman has done, first with her nephew and then with her sister, Thea has structured her existence around the care of her surrogate child. When Løvborg tells her that he has no more use for her now that he plans to stop writing, she responds with despair: "Then what will I do with my life?" (III, 759).

Thea's disconsolate cry reveals that her metaphorical maternity is in fact only midwifery; were she genuinely creative, she could undertake to write a book on her own. For what is actually being invoked here is the common metaphor of literary *paternity*, not maternity, coupled with the conventional topos of female inspiration. Thea's status may be illuminated by the remarks of recent feminist critics who explore the significance of this metaphor for writing by women. In *The Madwoman in the Attic*, Sandra Gilbert and Susan Gubar survey the history of the analogy between pen and penis, noting, for example, that "Renoir 'is supposed to have said that he painted his paintings with his prick.'"[9] They cite Edward Said's observation that the metaphor of literary paternity is "built into the very word, *author*, with which

---

[8]Oscar Wilde provides a comic variation on the symbolic equivalence between child and manuscript in *The Importance of Being Earnest*, in which the hapless governess Miss Prism admits that, years before, she had "lost" her infant charge by mixing him up with the manuscript of a piece of fiction she had been working on, placing the manuscript in a basinette and the baby in the handbag, which she then left at Victoria Station. These two examples seem to suggest deep-seated paternal guilt or filial resentment on the part of both Ibsen and Wilde, or perhaps simply a generalized Victorian sense of parental negligence. The symbolism associating children with works of art recurs in Ibsen's last play, *When We Dead Awaken*, in which the sculptor Rubek and his former model Irene refer to his statue of her as their child.

[9]Quoted in Sandra M. Gilbert and Susan Gubar, *The Madwoman in the Attic: The Woman Writer and the Nineteenth-Century Literary Imagination* (New Haven: Yale Univ. Press, 1979), p. 6. Subsequent page references appear in the text.

writer, deity, and *pater familias* are identified" (4). Barbara Johnson points out the perhaps obvious reason motivating the metaphor: men are unable to bear actual children.[10] Both she and Gilbert and Gubar note that the metaphor of literary paternity establishes a clear-cut division of labor which assigns biological creation to women, artistic creation to men, and dictates that the female appropriation of art can only interfere with women's proper role as mothers; it was against this bias that nineteenth-century women writers had to struggle. Susan Suleiman elaborates on the dichotomy: "Whereas the male writer, in comparing his books to tenderly loved children . . . , could see his metaphorical maternity as something *added* to his male qualities, the childless woman whose books 'replaced' real children too often thought (was made to feel) that she had less, not more."[11] This dichotomy between literary paternity and biological maternity, as well as its subversion by women writers, illuminates Thea's situation: she is neither biological mother nor literary creator but instead is relegated to the role of muse.

With an irony typical of Ibsen, the only actual mother (or mother-to-be) in the play is the least maternal. In contrast to Miss Tesman and Thea, Hedda Gabler has an antipathy to both metaphorical and literal children. Her attitude toward books is announced by her comment to Brack that "there's nothing [Tesman] likes better than grubbing around in libraries and copying out old parchments, or whatever you call them" (II, 724). She is unutterably bored by talk of the subject that fascinates both Tesman and Løvborg, the history of civilization, and

[10]Barbara Johnson, "Apostrophe, Animation, and Abortion," *Diacritics*, 16 (Spring 1986), 38.
[11]Susan R. Suleiman, "Writing and Motherhood," in *The (M)other Tongue: Essays in Feminist Psychoanalytic Interpretation*, ed. Shirley Nelson Garner, Claire Kahane, and Madelon Sprengnether (Ithaca: Cornell Univ. Press, 1985), pp. 359–360. On this subject see also Susan Gubar, "'The Blank Page' and the Issues of Female Creativity," in *Writing and Sexual Difference*, ed. Elizabeth Abel (Chicago: Univ. of Chicago Press, 1982), pp. 73–93; and, on combining writing and motherhood in the nineteenth century, Margaret Homans, *Bearing the Word: Language and Female Experience in Nineteenth-Century Woman's Writing* (Chicago: Univ. of Chicago Press, 1986), esp. pp. 153–188.

is interested neither in Løvborg's recently published book on the topic nor in his new manuscript. Her response to Løvborg's frantic ravings about his lost manuscript—"Well—but when all's said and done—it was only a book" (III, 761)—foreshadows the ease with which she will burn it, thus destroying the metaphorical child in lieu of the actual embryo she is unable to do away with.

As Janet Suzman has observed, recalling her own experience as an actress in the role of Hedda Gabler, Hedda's pregnancy draws together every strand of the play.[12] Though never mentioned explicitly, her condition is hinted at many times, and these intimations tell us much about Hedda's attitude toward maternity. When Tesman points out to his aunt that Hedda has "filled out" on their wedding trip, for example, she immediately shuts him up and insists that she is exactly as she was when she left (I, 704). Similarly, when Tesman praises her "flourishing" condition to Brack, she interrupts him with the exhortation to "leave me out of it!" (I, 716). When Tesman responds to her comment about how yellow and withered the leaves are by saying that it is already September, she becomes "restless" (I, 705), the passage of time doubtless reminding her of the unstoppable progression taking place within her. Her reply to Brack's allusion to her "most solemn responsibility" is significant: "I have no talent for such things, Judge. I won't have responsibilities!" (II, 730). She is not even able to bring herself to tell Tesman about her condition, urging him to ask his aunt instead. But most revealing of all is her desperate response to Tesman's joy when he guesses the news: "Oh, I'll die—I'll die of all this!" (IV, 767).

Hedda's resistance to the female roles of muse and mother is characteristic of her consistent rebellion against the conventional turn-of-the-century view of woman's place. Inasmuch as we can talk about the psychology of a literary character, we can

---

[12]Janet Suzman, *"Hedda Gabler:* The Play in Performance," in *Ibsen and the Theatre: The Dramatist in Production,* ed. Errol Durbach (New York: New York Univ. Press, 1980), p. 89.

surely trace Hedda's partial rejection of femininity to the influence of her upbringing. Because Hedda, like Wedekind's Lulu,
Synge's Pegeen Mike, and Hauptmann's Rose Bernd, has grown
up without a mother, she has developed into a woman of unusual independence and strength of will. It is no accident that
we meet Hedda's father before encountering her: the introductory stage directions mention a "portrait of a handsome, elderly
man in a general's uniform" (I, 695), identified soon after by
Miss Tesman's description of Hedda as "General Gabler's
daughter" (I, 696). Ibsen explains that he called the play *Hedda
Gabler* because he "intended to indicate thereby that as a personality she is to be regarded rather as her father's daughter than as
her husband's wife,"[13] an explanation that of course says as
much about Hedda's marriage as it does about her relationship
with her father. In the opinion of the avant-garde director
Charles Marowitz, "the central character in *Hedda Gabler* has
always been General Gabler,"[14] and in his 1978 production of
the play, in which everything is seen from Hedda's point of view,
the general even takes part in the action. As Elizabeth Hardwick
notes, the man Hedda marries is "much more of a girl than she
is," for while she was being raised by a general on pistols and
horses, he was being reared by two maiden aunts.[15] Thus Hedda's position as daughter seems to offer her a freedom that her
roles of wife and especially mother later deny her.

[13]Ibsen to Count Moritz Prozor, 4 December 1890, in *The Oxford Ibsen*, ed.
James W. McFarlane (London: Oxford Univ. Press, 1966), VII, 500. The importance of General Gabler for Hedda recalls the even more significant role of Dr.
West in *Rosmersholm*: he never appears in the play but his shadow hangs over the
life of his supposed adoptive daughter, Rebecca West. Indeed, Freud deduces,
on the basis of Rebecca's refusal of Rosmer and her agitated reaction to Kroll's
disclosure, that she is in fact West's biological daughter, and that she has had a
sexual relationship with him. See Freud, "Some Character-Types Met with in
Psycho-Analytic Work" ("Einige Charaktertypen aus der psychoanalytischen Ar-
beit," 1916), *SE*, XIV, 324–331.
[14]Quoted in Kathleen Dacre, "Charles Marowitz's *Hedda* (And *An Enemy of the
People*)," *Drama Review*, 25 (Summer 1981), 5.
[15]Elizabeth Hardwick, *Seduction and Betrayal: Women and Literature* (New York:
Random House, 1970), p. 57.

Yet if Hedda wants to live a man's life, as her creator says she does,[16] she is also aware that the aspects open to her are limited to riding and shooting. Her solution has been to live a masculine existence vicariously. Thus she sat in her father's home with Løvborg, the General's back to them, urging him to tell her about those thing "that she's forbidden to know anything about" (II, 739); his trivial adventures with women and alcohol satisfied her curiosity, deprived as she was, as a middle-class young lady, of any contact with such things. And thus she tells Brack that she wishes she could be at his drinking party, invisible, "to hear a little of your unadulterated liveliness" (II, 745); failing that, she presses Tesman afterward for details. It seems it is her hunger for the aspects of life forbidden to her that is the source of her obsession with the image of vine leaves; she projects her own desire for "fieryness and boldness" onto Løvborg. But perhaps the most graphic demonstration of her vicarious existence through men occurs in a conversation she has with Brack:

Brack: But couldn't you find some goal in life to work toward? Others do, Mrs. Hedda.
Hedda: A goal—that would really absorb me?
Brack: Yes, preferably.
Hedda: God only knows what that could be. I often wonder if— (*Breaks off.*) But that's impossible too.
Brack: Who knows? Tell me.
Hedda: I was thinking—if I could get Tesman to go into politics. [II, 729]

Hedda's attitude toward Løvborg as he goes off to Brack's drinking party is revealing: "For once in my life, I want to have power over a human being" (II, 745). For she has never had power herself, neither in the social world nor now, most immediately, over her own body.

Nor surprisingly, it is this aspect of Hedda's situation that won a good deal of support for the drama from turn-of-the-century

[16]Cole, *Playwrights on Playwriting*, p. 166.

feminists. The remarks of Elizabeth Robins, the American actress whose first contribution to the Ibsen movement was her determination to stage the play accurately despite vehement opposition,[17] are typical of the feminist stance:

> Mr. Clement Scott understand Hedda?—any man except that wizard Ibsen really understand her? Of course not. That was the tremendous part of it. How should men understand Hedda on the stage when they didn't understand her in the persons of their wives, their daughters, their women friends? One lady of our acquaintance, married and not noticeably unhappy, said laughing, "Hedda is all of us."
>
> Hedda was not all of us, but she was a good many of us. . . . Anyway, she was a bundle of unused possibilities, educated to fear life; too much opportunity to develop her weakness; no opportunity at all to use her best powers.[18]

Such sentiments, however, have been more than outweighed by unsympathetic responses to Hedda over the decades.[19]

It is fitting that the one thing Hedda has left "to amuse myself with" (I, 721) are her father's pistols. For, as Nancy Huston has shown, there is a symbolic equivalence between childbirth and war; in short, "men make war *because* women have children."[20] Hedda's assumption of this quintessentially masculine activity parallels her rejection of its feminine counterpart. And yet until the end of the play neither is effective. She does not actually hunt or hit her would-be targets, Løvborg and Brack, but is merely "shooting into the sky" (II, 722); not for nothing did Lou Andreas-Salomé single out this phrase as Hedda's "motto."[21] Nor can she escape her pregnancy, except in death—the one

[17]Joanne E. Gates, "Elizabeth Robins and the 1891 Production of *Hedda Gabler*," *Modern Drama*, 28 (1985), 617.

[18]Robins, *Ibsen and the Actress*, pp. 18–19.

[19]See, e.g., Hardwick, *Seduction and Betrayal*, pp. 49–68.

[20]Nancy Huston, "The Matrix of War: Mothers and Heroes," 1985; rpt. in *The Female Body in Western Culture: Contemporary Perspectives*, ed. Susan R. Suleiman (Cambridge: Harvard Univ. Press, 1986), p. 119.

[21]Lou Andreas-Salomé, *Ibsen's Heroines* (1892), trans. Siegfried Mandel (Redding Ridge, Conn.: Black Swan, 1985), p. 130.

time she hits her target, as it were. The moment is doubly significant as a masculine act, since in shooting herself in the temple Hedda, in contrast to Løvborg, dies a man's death. Appropriately, the symbol of her unsuccessful desire for male power becomes the agent of her self-destruction.

At its extreme, a mixture of masculine and feminine tendencies such as Hedda possesses would be labeled androgynous or bisexual. While there seems to be little point in pursuing this line of thought in and of itself, it is worth observing that bisexuality is often associated with hysteria. In her influential discussion of the sorceress and the hysteric, for example, Catherine Clément observes that "the other, the *hysteric,* incarnates somewhere an incompatible synthesis—bisexuality. . . . In severe hysterical attacks, she is simultaneously 'woman' and 'man,' says Freud: 'the patient with one hand holds her dress tightly against her body (as a woman) while with the other hand she is trying (as a man) to rip it off' *(The Relation of Hysterical Fantasies to Bisexuality).* She plays the role of 'woman' and of 'man': man the aggressor, woman keeping her dress on."[22] In his notes to the play Ibsen writes of Hedda's "hysteria," indicating his interest in the unconscious psychology of the day,[23] and much in her behavior anticipates Freud's case histories of the hysterical female patients he treated in the late 1880s and 1890s. Her extreme nervousness, for instance, is difficult to overlook: she is constantly pacing the floor, crossing the room needlessly, drumming her fingers, clenching her fists "as if in a frenzy" (I, 705). Her "flinging back" the curtains (I, 705) suggests a sense of confinement, of intolerable pressure, such as plagues all the

[22]Hélène Cixous and Catherine Clément, *The Newly Born Woman,* trans. Betsy Wing (Minneapolis: Univ. of Minnesota Press, 1986), pp. 8, 56. Subsequent references appear in the text.

[23]Cole, *Playwrights on Playwriting,* p. 166. In *Ibsen: The Intellectual Background* (1946; New York: Octagon, 1978), p. 180, Brian Downs notes that "Ibsen, like many other laymen of his time, followed intently the researches and theories in unconscious psychology which, so commonly believed to be a discovery of the twentieth century, were in fact advanced with great boldness and success during the preceding generation."

hysterics described in Freud's *Studies on Hysteria (The Newly Born Woman,* 43). Hedda's physical abuse of Thea—pinching her, slapping her, dragging her across the room, threatening to burn off her hair—may likewise be viewed as hysterical behavior. These "symptoms" are of course mild by comparison with those of Emmy von N. and Elisabeth von R., patients of Freud's who suffered actual and debilitating pain; Hedda's condition might best be characterized as mild hysteria. Her state of mind is symbolically announced by Miss Tesman's description of the young Hedda "in that long black riding outfit, with a feather in her hat" (I, 696), the feather subtly intimating the abnormality or unconventionality yet to be revealed.[24] But she manifests other striking similarities to Freud's hysterics. The obsessive memory of vine leaves that she repeatedly links with Løvborg, for example, anticipates Freud's use of the metaphor of hysteria as a "museum of monuments" to "hyperaesthetic memories."[25] And her antipathy to sex—evident in her outraged reaction to Løvborg's sexual overture years before, in her coldness toward Tesman, and in her assurances to both Brack and Løvborg that she intends to remain faithful (despite her lack of feeling for her husband)—is akin to the disgust with the genitals of the opposite sex which Freud views as "one of the characteristics of all hysterics, and especially of hysterical women."[26]

The important difference between Freud's conception of hysteria and the one Ibsen appears to be presenting concerns the source of the malady. It is Freud's opinion that hysteria is caused by a traumatic incident or series of incidents; according to his theory, once the disturbing incident is verbally recalled and its accompanying affect put into words, the hysterical symptoms will disappear. He eventually came to believe that the traumatic

[24]For this insight into the "hysterical feather" (as the only flamboyant element of Hedda's somber outfit) I am indebted to John Hoberman.

[25]See Dianne Hunter, "Hysteria, Psychoanalysis, and Feminism: The Case of Anna O.," in *(M)other Tongue*, pp. 92, 109.

[26]Sigmund Freud, *Three Essays on the Theory of Sexuality (Drei Abhandlungen zur Sexualtheorie,* 1905), *SE,* VII, 152.

event is usually sexual in nature and that hysteria is the expression of secret sexual desires. Hence he concludes that his patient Katharina's shortness of breath stems from her memories of witnessing her uncle having sex with her cousin Franziska as well as from recollections of the uncle's advances toward Katharina herself, and that Dora's hysterical symptoms are the result of her repressed desire for her father, for his mistress, Frau K., and for the mistress's husband, Herr K. By contrast, Ibsen depicts Hedda's mild hysteria as the reaction to her entrapment in female roles to which she is unsuited, epitomized by her unwanted pregnancy; careful analysis of the text reveals that the stage directions describing her gestures of nervousness or suffocation nearly always follow indirect references to her incipient maternity. In other words, as in the case of Rose Bernd, Hedda's hysteria is the response to her hysterization, or to the reduction of her to her femaleness.

Hedda's situation may be illuminated by contrast with that of Nora Helmer in *A Doll House*, who responds to similar limitations in a different way. Like Hedda, she is trapped by conventional expectations of female roles: the second act finds her in terror that her husband will discover the letter revealing that she borrowed money years before on his behalf and signed for her father, an action she is sure Helmer will find reprehensible in a wife. The result is her frenzied tarantella, which she performs with her hair loosening and falling over her shoulders and as if deaf to the world, a dance that Helmer characterizes as "pure madness" (*A Doll House*, II, 174); foreshadowing Hedda, she contemplates suicide, and dances "as if [her] life were at stake" (II, 174). Following her dance, Helmer admonishes her: "Now, now, now—no hysterics" (II, 175), thus putting a label on the condition her dance has so graphically portrayed. For as Clément demonstrates, the tarantella, as performed by women in southern Italy who have supposedly been bitten by the spider (in fact the tarantula does not exist in this region), is a form of hysterical catharsis. She quotes an account of the ritual: "Around ten o'clock, at the musicians' first notes, the woman bitten by the tarantula lay motionless on her bed but as soon as they lit into the tarantella, she shrieked sharply and her body arched, thus marking the opening of the ritual day. It was the classic hysterical arc" (*The Newly Born Woman*, 20). At the end of the dance the woman is "cured":

> Returning to social life, leaving the "natural" mode, the marvelous freedom that is animal and desiring, leaving music and dance and their specific tempo is, surely, to leave the deadly proximity of suicide, which is always there and always possible; it is certainly to leave risk behind—the danger of the body that is finally unleashed; it is to settle down again under a roof, in a house, in the family circle of kinship and marriage; and it is to return to the men's world: the celebration is indeed over. [22]

Analogously, Nora returns after her dance to her role as wife and mother, but only for a time. Her ultimate break with Helmer and her children allies her hysterical dance with the definition provided by Declan Kiberd: "In the mythologies of the world, the tarantella is a dance of androgynes, after which women behave like men."[27]

The distinction between Nora Helmer and Hedda Gabler is clear. While Nora moves from hysteria and the consideration of suicide to feminism, Hedda remains caught in hysteria, her suicide following immediately on the "wild dance melody" (IV, 777) she plays on the piano. And, demonstrating Cixous's claim that "there is no place for the hysteric," that "hysteria is necessarily an element that disturbs arrangements" (*The Newly Born Woman*, 156), Hedda's death restores the proper coupling: Tesman is reunited with Thea, the "old flame" (I, 706) to whom he is much more suited, leaving us with the expectation that not only Løvborg's manuscript or metaphorical child but also Tesman's literal child will be resurrected—with Thea as its new mother. Like Snyge's Pegeen Mike and Hauptmann's Rose Bernd, then,

---

[27]Declan Kiberd, *Men and Feminism in Modern Literature* (London: Macmillan, 1985), p. 69.

Nora and Hedda exemplify mild forms of the two major female responses to women's oppression at the turn of the century—feminism and hysteria.[28] Hedda's failure to move from hysteria to feminism can be attributed to the conventional feminine traits she retains despite her rebellion against certain female roles. To reevoke Freud's image of the hysteric's dual sexuality, the "female" hand with which Hedda holds her dress tightly against her body wins out over the "male" hand trying to rip it off. From the beginning of the play, for example, she appears as an illustration of what Thorstein Veblen was to call the "conspicuous consumer," the well-appointed woman of leisure who functions as the symbol of her husband's wealth.[29] The first descriptive detail provided about Hedda is the maid's comment that the bride had a lot to unpack on returning from her honeymoon; Tesman elaborates by mentioning "all those boxes" she brought back (I, 698). Her desire for a new piano, a horse, and even a butler parallels her scornful observation to Thea that it is "stupid" of her to be inexpensive (I, 713). Hedda also demonstrates the stereotypically female quality of vanity. She spends hours dressing, and her jealousy of Thea and her "irritating" hair (I, 706) reflects her wish for the capacity to charm men in a traditionally feminine way. Similarly, she divulges to Brack that she married Tesman because she "had danced [her]self out," because her "time was up" (II, 725); in other words, because she was afraid of becoming an old maid. The value she places on social conventions is evident in the "bargain" she made with Tesman—if she married him they would live "in society" and "keep a great house" (I, 720)—and in the fact that while on their honeymoon she missed contact with their "circle," with anyone who could talk "about

---

[28]For an analysis detailing not the differences but the similarities between *A Doll House* and *Hedda Gabler*, see Arthur Ganz, "Miracle and Vine Leaves: An Ibsen Play Rewrought," *PMLA*, 94 (1979), 9–21.

[29]Thorstein Veblen, *The Theory of the Leisure Class* (1899; New York: Sentry, 1965), pp. 68–101.

our kind of things" (II, 724). Her corresponding hatred of im-
propriety manifests itself frequently, as in her complaint that
leaving one's hat in the drawing room is "just not proper" (I,
705) and in her fear that the maid will hear Tesman shouting as
he reacts to her burning of Løvborg's manuscript.

But the most significant aspect of Hedda's conventional femininity is her dread of scandal. When Thea leaves her husband to
pursue Løvborg, it is Hedda, not Thea, who worries about what
people will say. And finally, when Brack threatens to expose
Hedda's role in Løvborg's death if she does not become his
mistress, there is only one answer for her. Unlike her successor
Dora, she cannot accept the part of sexual pawn; unlike Thea
and her predecessor Nora, she cannot face the scandal that
walking out the door would unleash, since she lacks the courage
that would make life "bearable" (II, 741). Her suicide is thus the
result of a triple hysterization: her simultaneous entrapment in
impending maternity, in feminine propriety, and in her role as
an object of sexual blackmail. As such, her death differs
markedly from the typical nineteenth-century literary suicide,
which is motivated by love.[30]

It is worthwhile to consider a few similarities between *Hedda
Gabler* and a play set in a very different milieu, *The Playboy of the
Western World*. Both dramas feature heroines divided by the conflict between their masculine and feminine inclinations; both
heroines live out their male-oriented desires vicariously, through
an idealized man; both vie for his favor with another female
figure who ultimately shows herself to be less bound by social
convention than they; one heroine provides her man with the
means of his literal destruction, the other kills him off metaphorically in rejecting the masculine impulses in herself; both
plays end unhappily, one with the heroine's suicide, the other
with her lamentations over the loss she has suffered. Given that

[30]Cf. Margaret Higonnet, "Speaking Silences: Women's Suicide," 1985; rpt. in
Suleiman, *Female Body in Western Culture*, pp. 68–83.

one drama takes place in a middle-class drawing room in Scandinavia and the other depicts an out-of-the-way Irish peasant community, the parallels between them point to an overriding awareness in turn-of-the-century dramatists of the tensions in women during an era when traditional female roles were being called into question and little was available to put in their place.

7 Humanism and Patriarchy: Hofmannsthal's *Woman without a Shadow*

On the surface, few plays could be further removed from the realistic, drawing-room sphere of *Hedda Gabler* than Hugo von Hofmannsthal's *Die Frau ohne Schatten* (*The Woman without a Shadow,* 1919). The fourth of six librettos by Hugo von Hofmannsthal which Richard Strauss set to music, the text is a fairy tale, taking us into the world of magic and make-believe. Indebted to sources ranging from the *Arabian Nights* to a Swedish tale retold by the nineteenth-century Austrian poet Nikolaus Lenau to Goethe's *Faust* and "Märchen" ("A Fairy Tale") to the fairy tales in Novalis's *Heinrich von Ofterdingen* to Chamisso's "Peter Schlemihls wundersame Geschichte" ("The Strange Story of Peter Schlemihl") to Vienna's cosmic Theater of the World, the plot of the opera has aptly been labeled "byzantine."[1] Yet the

[1]Matthew Gurewitsch, "In the Mazes of Light and Shadow: A Thematic Comparison of *The Magic Flute* and *Die Frau ohne Schatten,*" *Opera Quarterly,* 1 (Summer 1983), 16. On the sources of the plot see, e.g., Wolfgang Köhler, *Hugo von Hofmannsthal und "Tausendundeine Nacht": Untersuchungen zur Rezeption des Orients im epischen und essayistischen Werk* (Bern: Lang, 1972), pp. 125–152; Kurt Oppens, "Die Frau ohne Schatten blickt in den Spiegel: Strauss' Oper und ihre Quellen in der Literatur," in *Oper (Jahrbuch der Zeitschrift "Opernwelt"): Bilanzen und Pläne, Resultate und Probleme* (Velber: Friedrich, 1967), pp. 37–43; and Walter Naumann, "Die Quelle von Hofmannsthals *Frau ohne Schatten,*" *MLN,* 59 (1944), 385–386. Aware of the libretto's complexities, Hofmannsthal developed its characters and imagery more fully in a prose version that he hoped would

feelings of both Strauss and Hofmannsthal for *The Woman without a Shadow* can hardly be overestimated. It was Strauss's favorite opera, and Hofmannsthal considered it the magnum opus of both himself and his collaborator, often comparing it to Mozart's *Magic Flute*.[2] Still, both men proved correct in their suspicion that it would be over the heads of the Viennese opera-going public. The opera's reception was not helped by the fact that it premiered in October 1919, when Vienna was reeling from the effects of a devastating world war that had destroyed the old Austro-Hungarian empire. In marked contrast to *Hedda Gabler,* which is still one of Ibsen's most frequently performed dramas, *The Woman without a Shadow* has never enjoyed widespread popularity, undoubtedly because of its philosophically abstruse text.

But such superficial differences between the two works belie fundamental similarities. Hofmannsthal repeatedly referred to *The Woman without a Shadow* as a play or drama, a reflection of the strong connection in the Austrian theatrical tradition since the Baroque between sung and spoken drama. More important, the issue of resistance to maternity is as central to *The Woman without a Shadow* as to *Hedda Gabler.* This libretto, in which the Dyer's Wife sells her shadow (symbolizing the ability to bear

---

help clarify the opera. My discussion will focus on the libretto. For a detailed comparison of libretto and tale see Belma Cakmur, *Hofmannsthals Erzählung "Die Frau ohne Schatten": Studien zu Werk und Innenwelt des Dichters* (Ankara: Basimevi, 1952), pp. 13–39.

[2] On Strauss's preference see Karl Böhm, "Apropos 'Frau ohne Schatten,'" *Österreichische Musikzeitschrift,* 29 (1974), 326; for Hofmannsthal's comparisons of the opera to *The Magic Flute* see, e.g., his letters of 20 March 1911 and 1 August 1916, in *The Correspondence between Richard Strauss and Hugo von Hofmannsthal,* trans. Hanns Hammelmann and Ewald Osers (1961; Cambridge: Cambridge Univ. Press, 1980), pp. 76 and 260, as well as his "Zur Entstehungsgeschichte der 'Frau ohne Schatten,'" in Hugo von Hofmannsthal, *Gesammelte Werke in Einzelausgaben,* ed. Herbert Steiner: *Prosa III* (Frankfurt: Fischer, 1952), p. 451. For additional comparisons between the two operas see Gloria J. Ascher, *"Die Zauberflöte" und "Die Frau ohne Schatten": Ein Vergleich zwischen zwei Operndichtungen der Humanität* (Bern: Francke, 1972); Gernot Gruber, "Das Vorbild der 'Zauberflöte' für die 'Frau ohne Schatten,'" in *Hofmannsthal und das Theater: Die Vorträge des Hofmannsthal Symposiums, Wien, 1979* (Vienna: Halosar, 1981), pp. 51–63; and Gurewitsch, "Mazes of Light and Shadow."

children) to the supernatural and infertile Empress in exchange for entrance into the world of art, magic, and adultery, presents an operatic variation on the theme that dominated all of Hofmannsthal's oeuvre: the conflict between self-involved aestheticism and a commitment to social engagement. The mythical timelessness of fairy tale does not obscure the question at the heart of *The Woman without a Shadow:* to be or not to be a mother. Although at the turn of the century the answer to this question was by no means a given, Hofmannsthal resolves the issue as though it were, offering a positive, "euphoric" counterpart to the "dysphoric" plot of *Hedda Gabler:* the Dyer's Wife ultimately resumes her identity as a mother, and the two couples (Dyer and Wife, Empress and Emperor) are rejoined in a double apotheosis of maternity. As we shall see, however, Hofmannsthal's resolution is harmonious only from the perspective of classical humanism, with its foundation in patriarchal values; a feminist reading that "resists" his text produces a very different interpretation.

The critical responses to *The Woman without a Shadow* provide an exemplary illustration of Stanley Fish's notion of interpretive communities as modified by Patrocinio Schweickart. Schweickart writes:

> The feminist reader agrees with Stanley Fish that the production of the meaning of a text is mediated by the interpretive community in which the act of reading is situated: the meaning of the text depends on the interpretive strategy one applies to it, and the choice of strategy is regulated (explicitly or implicitly) by the canons of acceptability that govern the interpretive community. However, unlike Fish, the feminist reader is also aware that the ruling interpretive communities are androcentric, and that this androcentricity is deeply etched in the strategies and modes of thought that have been introjected by all readers, women as well as men.[3]

[3]Patrocinio P. Schweickart, "Reading Ourselves: Toward a Feminist Theory of Reading," in *Gender and Reading: Essays on Readers, Texts, and Contexts,* ed. Elizabeth A. Flynn and Schweickart (Baltimore: Johns Hopkins Univ. Press, 1986), p. 50.

A representative selection of critical views on *The Woman without a Shadow* clearly conveys the bias shared by most interpreters of the work. In accordance with Hofmannsthal's own ultimate designation of the Empress as the central figure in the opera, most critics regard her search for a shadow—that is, her relinquishment of her supernatural status in favor of complete humanity and thus fertility—as the main thread of the plot. Similarly, Hofmannsthal describes as the opera's "essential core"[4] the scene in the temple in which the Empress, faced with the dilemma of whether to accept the Wife's shadow and thus bring the petrified Emperor back to life or to reject it in order to preserve the fertility of the Dyer and his wife, unselfishly opts for the latter—thereby unwittingly winning her own shadow. Her act of sacrifice is the most graphic manifestation of the "triumph of the allomatic element" that the author saw the opera as representing,[5] "allomatic" stemming from the Greek *allos* or "other" and pointing to the role in the work of self-mastery for the sake of the other. Most critics of the opera and tale praise the Empress's decision, the celebration of her selfessness finding its extreme formulation in Karl Naef's statement that "the greatest deed a woman can perform is an act of sacrifice."[6]

Correspondingly, the libretto's glorification of marriage and children (in the voices of the watchmen at the end of the first act and in those of the unborn children at the opera's close) has elicited these critical opinions: "Through marriage both couples find their true destiny and are blessed with the highest gift life has to offer"; "But the primary motif of the opera is that of life's fulfillment in the child"; "The continuation of the human race hinges on the mystery of maternity. The difficulty of existence guarantees the chain of fate that binds together father, mother,

[4]Hofmannsthal to Strauss, early April 1915, in *Strauss–Hofmannsthal Correspondence*, p. 220.
[5]Hofmannsthal, "Ad me ipsum," in *Gesammelte Werke: Aufzeichnungen* (1959), p. 218.
[6]Karl J. Naef, *Hugo von Hofmannsthals Wesen und Werk* (Zurich: Niehans, 1938), p. 186.

and child. Throughout his entire life Hofmannsthal pondered this realization and tried one solution to it after another"; "In this fairy tale the poet wants in particular to portray the eternal feminine, namely the timeless as well as the topical problematic of the female, which is in essence nothing but the denial or the affirmation of fertility and thus of complete feminine humanity."[7] For such critics, the Nurse, who is completely a creature of the supernatural realm from which the Empress originates and who encourages the Dyer's Wife to sell her shadow (renounce fertility), is an evil, demonic figure and the Wife is utterly wrongheaded in her rejection of maternity. Herbert Steiner's characterization of the Wife—as "the woman who is nearly lost, who wants to renounce her womanhood and selfishly squander the crown of life"[8]—is typical. One critic acknowledges that the Wife's situation demonstrates well-known psychological difficulties experienced by women in the era of female emancipation in which the opera was composed, but he goes on to conjecture that motherhood might have given her life the meaning she was seeking.[9]

To return to the modification of Fish by Schweickart quoted earlier, the philosophy informing the interpretive community represented by the critics cited here is epitomized by the couplet from Goethe's fragmentary epic *Die Geheimnisse* (The mysteries, 1784/85) which Hofmannsthal invokes to describe the gist of *The Woman without a Shadow:* "The man who vanquishes himself liberates himself from the law that constrains all living things."[10] For advocacy of renunciation and self-restraint is of course

[7]Edgar Hederer, *Hugo von Hofmannsthal* (Frankfurt: Fischer, 1960), p. 247; Erich Graf, "Zur Thematik der 'Frau ohne Schatten,'" *Österreichische Musikzeitschrift,* 19 (1964), 231; Walter Ritzer, *"Die Frau ohne Schatten:* Gedanken zum Libretto," *Österreichische Musikzeitschrift,* 29 (1974), 339; Hugo Wyss, *Die Frau in der Dichtung Hofmannsthals: Eine Studie zum dionysischen Welterlebnis* (Zurich: Niehans, 1954), pp. 117–118.
[8]Herbert Steiner, "'Die Frau ohne Schatten,'" *Monatshefte,* 37 (1945), 100.
[9]Wilfried Kuckartz, *Hugo von Hofmannsthal als Erzieher* (Fellbach-Oeffingen: Adolf Bonz, 1981), p. 155.
[10]Hofmannsthal to Strauss, early April 1915, in *Strauss–Hofmannsthal Correspondence,* p. 220.

central to German classical humanism. Yet given that the opera's major characters are female, it is important to consider the role of women in this doctrine as a whole. Julie Prandi offers an insightful summary of the issue. Her work on Goethe, Schiller, and Kleist shows that in the age of German classical humanism women were clearly subordinate to men and were expected to limit their activities to the family. Since women were restricted to the domestic realm, the classical ideal of *Bildung* or self-development and personal education applied to men only. For Goethe the feminine is typically associated with the ideal; Schiller celebrates a traditional division of masculine and feminine characteristics; for Kleist, women are predestined to become wives and mothers. The gender norms of the era in general associated passivity, obedience, emotionality, domesticity, and altruistic love with women; and public life, activity, and rationality with men. Moreover, while the concept of humanity *(Menschlichkeit)* is often connected with women, since it embodies such "private" virtues as compassion and altruism, only men represent the genre of human being *(Mensch)*.[11]

In *The Woman without a Shadow* Hofmannsthal shows himself to be as firmly entrenched in this sexually hierarchical tradition as his contemporary and compatriot Freud.[12] For while female characters predominate in the opera, they are not genuine human beings according to Prandi's definition—"subjects who need and desire freedom to determine themselves and realize themselves in the world (which involves definite activity as op-

[11]Julie D. Prandi, *Spirited Women Heroes: Major Female Characters in the Dramas of Goethe, Schiller, and Kleist* (New York: Lang, 1983), pp. 1–22; subsequent page references appear in the text.

[12]Hofmannsthal was familiar with many of Freud's works. On his reaction to them see, e.g., Heinz Politzer, "Hugo von Hofmannsthals 'Elektra': Geburt der Tragödie aus dem Geiste der Psychopathologie," in Politzer, *Hatte Ödipus einen Ödipus-Komplex?: Versuche zum Thema Psychoanalyse und Literatur* (Munich: Piper, 1974), pp. 78–105; Bernd Urban, *Hofmannsthal, Freud und die Psychoanalyse: Quellenkundliche Untersuchungen* (Frankfurt: Lang, 1978); and Michael Worbs, *Nervenkunst: Literatur und Psychoanalyse im Wien der Jahrhundertwende* (Frankfurt: Europäische Verlagsanstalt, 1983), pp. 259–342. None of these critics focuses on Hofmannsthal's attitude toward Freudian views of women per se.

posed to mere existence)" (9–10)—since their choices are confined to the private domain: the Dyer's Wife is lured away from
marriage and motherhood not by the opportunity for action in
the world but by typically feminine pleasures (jewels, beautiful
clothes, servants, and the promise of a lover), and for the Empress the alternative to maternity is an isolated life with the
Emperor alone, on his estate in an intermediate sphere sus-
pended between the supernatural and earthly realms. In essence, then, the behavior of these women characters still conforms to the gender norms of German classical humanism.

Yet recent critical approaches of the kind espoused by Schweickart and born of the marriage between reader response criticism
and feminism open up other ways of seeing Hofmannsthal's
libretto, approaches perhaps more in keeping with the new possibilities suggested by the women's movements of the turn of the
century and the 1960s than the critical views cited earlier. An
observation made by Nancy Miller points to the particular ap-
propriateness of a feminist reader-oriented approach for a work
like *The Woman without a Shadow:* "To reread as a woman is at
least to imagine the lady's place; to imagine while reading the
place of a woman's body; to read reminded that her identity is
also re-membered in stories of the body."[13] For in few texts does
the female body figure so significantly, if indirectly, as in this
libretto, concerned as it is with the sterility or fertility of two
women characters. The ending of the work is harmonious only
if one assumes an implied reader/viewer who believes (or hopes)
that motherhood is a woman's proper and even highest function
and that women rejoice in renunciation. As we have seen, the
libretto has found many actual readers of this kind among its
critics, who regard as still viable the patriarchally based gender
roles characteristic of German classical humanism from Goethe
to Hofmannsthal. But when one recalls that the years of the
libretto's conception and composition—1911 to 1915—coincide

---

[13]Nancy K. Miller, "Rereading as a Woman: The Body in Practice," 1985; rpt.
in *The Female Body in Western Culture: Contemporary Perspectives,* ed. Susan R.
Suleiman (Cambridge: Harvard Univ. Press, 1986), p. 355.

with the culmination of the European women's movement, which fought for women's autonomy, including control of their own bodies, it seems especially fitting here to postulate a female reader/viewer and to reexamine the text from her particular perspective. I am not implying that the libretto's commentators to date have been exclusively male, since the work has obviously drawn the attention of female critics as well. Rather, I am proposing a reading that "resists" the text by uncovering and challenging the patriarchal values that inform both it and the bulk of the secondary material about it—in short, a feminist reading.

Such a reading would foreground not the Empress—the woman without a shadow—but the Dyer's Wife, the character who in her conflict over whether to accept or reject maternity is more psychologically complex than any other figure in the opera. Indeed, in an early letter to Strauss, Hofmannsthal writes of her as the "principal character,"[14] a designation that was later to cause Strauss difficulties in balancing her part in the musical score. The Wife's confusion over the prospect of maternity arises from her dissatisfaction with her husband, Barak the Dyer. His dominant trait—a seemingly boundless good nature—is intimated even by his name (he is the only named character to appear in the opera), for, among the Berbers, "Baraka" indicates saintliness.[15] Both his benevolence and his enormous physical strength are summed up in the refrain with which he explains his refusal to use a donkey in his work: "If I carry the goods to market myself, / I spare the donkey who would drag them for me!"[16] As these lines suggest, however, he is often too

[14]Hofmannsthal to Strauss, 20 March 1911, in *Strauss–Hofmannsthal Correspondence*, p. 76.

[15]Sherrill Hahn Pantle, *"Die Frau ohne Schatten" by Hugo von Hofmannsthal and Richard Strauss: An Analysis of Text, Music, and Their Relationship* (Bern: Lang, 1978), p. 78.

[16]Hofmannsthal, *Die Frau ohne Schatten*, translation adapted from *The Woman without a Shadow*, trans. Adolf Furstner (London: Boosey & Hawkes, 1943), Act I, pp. 4ff. Subsequent quotations are identified in the text by act and page number of the bilingual libretto.

good to be true; Heinz Politzer remarks that he is "compliant to the limits of his wife's (and the spectators') endurance."[17]

Barak's obsession in life is his desire for children, which two and a half years of marriage have failed to bring him. Lacking children of his own, he is eminently paternal toward his three handicapped brothers and even toward the local beggar children, all of whom revere him as the "father of us all" (II, 8). The following plea to his wife dramatizes his longing for offspring: "If you give me children, children who crouch around / their bowls in the evening, / none will get up from the table hungry. . . . When will you give me / these children?" (I, 4). For Barak, his wife exists only in relation to himself, in the role of potential mother of his offspring, rather than as an individual, to be loved and appreciated for her own qualities. Her designation in the opera is as significant as his: "the Wife" bespeaks her lack of autonomy.

Little wonder, then, that the Wife describes her soul as "satiated with motherhood / before it has tasted it" (I, 5). In this portrait of an ailing marriage, she drags herself through her daily tasks without enthusiasm and, in a manner reminiscent of Hedda Gabler, takes every opportunity to mock and belittle her husband. His simplicity and his insensitivity to her render him animal-like in her eyes. She tells him:

> There are people who always remain calm,
> and no matter what happens, no one will ever
> see their faces change.
> Day in, day out
> they proceed like cattle
> from bed to feed,
> from feed to bed,
> and don't know what has happened,
> or what its purpose was. [II, 11]

Such lines, along with allusions to the Wife's youth and Barak's greater age, suggest that sexual dissatisfaction makes up a not

[17]Heinz Politzer, "On the Genesis of Hugo von Hofmannsthal's *Die Frau ohne Schatten*," trans. Caroline Newman, unpublished paper, p. 4.

insignificant element of her discontent. Moreover, because of the way he commands her, she feels that she is merely another of his possessions, and lists herself along with his "house and hearth and bed" (II, 9).

As the opera opens, the Wife has nearly reached the breaking point:

> *My husband* stands before me! Oh yes, my husband,
> I know, oh yes, I know what that means!
> I'm bought and paid to know it,
> and kept in the house
> and sheltered and fed
> so that I know it,
> and from this day forth I don't want to know it,
> I forswear the word and the thing!   [I, 4; emphasis mine]

Thus she is ripe for the arrival of the Empress and the Nurse, who can on one level be seen as the externalization of her unconscious desires. Divining that there is a shadow to be won here, the Nurse wastes no time in evoking the delights that await the Wife if she enters into their deal. It is not accidental that "beauty" is the first word the Nurse utters in her presence, since beauty is the hallmark of all the images the Nurse conjures up to tempt the Wife to renounce motherhood: slave girls in colorful clothing, luxurious garments, pearls and other jewels, houses, fountains, gardens, young lovers, and eternal youth.

Although many of these pleasures belong to the feminine sphere, the realm evoked here, unlike the role to which the Wife would otherwise be limited, is not gender-bound. For it is in essence the romantic world of imagination and aestheticism which so often in Hofmannsthal's works opposes social activity. The ornately decorated late-Renaissance estate where Andrea isolates himself in his attempt to lead a life focused on sensory impressions and self-reflection in *Gestern* (1891) (Yesterday); the richly furnished rooms and fragrant gardens of Titian's villa, where his disciples seal themselves off from the noisy city below to dedicate themselves to art in *Der Tod des Tizian* (1892) *(The Death of Titian);* the "lumber room" full of the artificial objects in which Claudio loses himself, preferring aesthetic experience to interaction with other human beings, in *Der Tor und der Tod* (1893) *(Death and the Fool);* the magical, shimmering cavern to which the Queen of the Mountain lures Elis Fröbom, away from everyday domestic life and his bride, in *Das Bergwerk zu Falun* (1906) *(The Mine at Falun)*—these places, akin to the fantastic realm the Nurse fabricates for the Wife in *The Woman without a Shadow,* indicate that for Hofmannsthal aestheticism is open to both sexes, offering as in *Hedda Gabler* a tempting alternative to such biologically determined functions as motherhood.

Just as in these other plays by Hofmannsthal, in *The Woman without a Shadow* aestheticism is associated with narcissism, reflected in the Wife's acquisition of her first mirror. But the mirror image with which she suddenly becomes acquainted seems also to signify self-realization. No longer powerless, the Wife now has within reach not only control over her own body but the "boundless power over men" (I, 5) which the Nurse promises her. And yet, illustrating Adrienne Rich's contention that women who refuse motherhood are perceived as dangerous,[18] Hofmannsthal does not allow the Wife to fulfill her dreams of autonomy. Her guilt over the deception she is contemplating, symbolized early on in the "childrens' voices" she thinks she hears beseeching her as their "mother" to let them in from the fearful darkness outside (I, 6), anticipates the pangs of conscience that later prevent her from consummating her desire for the young man conjured up by the Nurse. At the threshold of liberation from conventional female roles she moves to the height of self-sacrifice, addressing the Dyer as "mighty Barak, / stern judge, / noble husband" and begging him to kill her (II, 12). However, unlike the jealous husbands in Hofmannsthal's earlier plays *Idylle* (1893) *(Idyll)* and *Die Frau im Fenster* (1897) *(Madonna Dianora)*—men who murder their wives for actual acts of abandonment or infidelity—Barak is restrained

[18]Adrienne Rich, *Of Woman Born: Motherhood as Experience and Institution* (New York: Norton, 1976).

from destroying his wife, and her death wish is transformed into a fervent hymn to female subordination: "Serving, loving, to bow to you: / to behold you! / to breathe, to live! / To give you, dear man, children!" (II, 12). A harmonious resolution, to be sure—yet the "resisting" reader/viewer cannot help seeing that such a vision is harmonious only from the patriarchal perspective of classical humanism.

The situation of the Wife vis-à-vis Barak is further illuminated by the relationship between the Emperor and the Empress, which in many ways parallels it.[19] Having been drawn to the Empress in the form of a white gazelle that turned into a woman as he was about to kill it, the Emperor talks of her as his booty *(Beute)*—"For my soul / and for my eyes / and for my hands / and for my heart / She is the booty / of all booty / without end!" (I, 2). The repetition of "my" clearly indicates that he regards the Empress as his possession—as Barak does his wife—for his use only. By his use of the word *Beute*, which also means "prey," he reveals that hunting and love are parallel activities for him; as the Nurse puts it, "He is a hunter / and a lover, / otherwise he's nothing!" (I, 1). Indeed in his commentary on the tale Hofmannsthal's contemporary Franz Werfel sees the Emperor as representing "man as rapist."[20] Like any other rapist, the Emperor cannot "loosen the knots of [the Empress's] heart" (I, 1), a state of affairs evident in her lack of a shadow; with her crystal body, designating her in-between status as no longer fully fairy but not yet human being, the Empress resembles other beautiful objects kept by the Emperor for his pleasure. Holding her a virtual prisoner in his castle by day while he hunts and by night as his bedmate, the Emperor seems to appreciate her only functionally, as she exists in relation to him, again just as Barak regards his wife. And just as Barak is dominated by his work

[19]Thomas A. Kovach notes the similarities of both the Wife and the Empress to Mallarmé's Hérodiade in *Hofmannsthal and Symbolism: Art and Life in the Work of a Modern Poet* (New York: Lang, 1985), pp. 211–220.

[20]Franz Werfel, *Zwischen oben und unten: Prosa, Tagebücher, Aphorismen, literarische Nachträge* (Munich: Langen-Müller, 1975), p. 656.

ethic and his need for paternity, the Emperor is dominated by sensuality; neither man has much room in his life for a genuinely mutual relationship with a woman.

In view of these similarities between the two male figures, it is appropriate that the curse on the Emperor affects Barak as well: the god of the spirit realm decrees that if the Empress does not acquire a shadow within three days, the Emperor will turn permanently to stone (a fate in keeping with his cold and isolated way of life), and because the Emperor's salvation depends on the Wife's loss of *her* shadow, Barak will of course be robbed of the children he longs for. Like the Dyer's Wife, the Empress is forced into the maternal role for the sake of her husband, since without the threat to him she would happily remain a semi-supernatural being; like the Wife and Hedda Gabler, she is reduced to her reproductive function. Whereas Hedda Gabler and the Wife are victimized by their hysterization, however, the Empress accepts this status willingly, and her search for motherhood parallels and is aided by the Wife's rejection of it. The Empress's campaign to win a shadow makes her feel as guilty as the Wife does in her attempt to cast her shadow off; in the Empress's words, "Here and there / everything is my fault— / No help for the one, / ruin for the other— / Barak, alas! / Whatever I touch / I kill!" (II, 11). The Empress's assumption of guilt, like that of the Wife, culminates in a death wish, in anticipation of the self-erasure manifested in her renunciation of the shadow once it is within her grasp—precisely the move that *endows* her with a shadow. The Emperor's words to her at this point—"You have vanquished yourself" (III, 16)—sum up the principle of self-denial at the heart of the humanistic ideal celebrated here. Like the Wife, the Empress renounces the world of magic in favor of the world of humanity. But whereas the humanity that male characters achieve in classical literature through renunciation and self- denial is typically associated with freedom and individualism, for Hofmannsthal's Wife and Empress humanity means not autonomy but motherhood.

Even more light is shed on the situation of the Dyer's Wife by the Nurse, who has been the caretaker of the Empress as a fairy in the spirit realm and thus accompanies her to the Emperor's estate in an intermediate sphere as well as to Barak's dwelling on earth. Whereas the Empress can be seen as the externalization of the side of the Wife that moves toward reconciliation with marriage, maternity, and humanity, the Nurse seems to represent the side of her that moves away from these things. The Nurse makes no attempt to hide her antipathy toward the world of human beings, graphically admonishing the Empress, "The air of mankind / breathes death for us. / Its purity smells to us / of rusty iron / and coagulated blood / and of long-dead corpses!" (I, 3), and associating human life with "eternal striving, / forward into the void, / greedy madness mingled with anguish" (III, 14). Accordingly, the Nurse opposes the Emperor from the beginning, urging the Empress to return with her to the spirit realm; failing to persuade her, she delights in playing tricks on human beings whenever possible. Her opposition to marriage is clear throughout her stay with the Empress at the house of Barak and his wife, where she rejoices in the Wife's mocking treatment of her husband, moves their beds apart, incites the Wife to adultery, and otherwise attempts to stir up strife between the couple.

Most significant for our purposes is the Nurse's contempt for maternity, evident in the arguments she uses with the Wife to win her shadow for the Empress:

> Has it cost you bloody tears
> that you have borne no children to that imperious man?
> And does your heart yearn day and night
> that through you many little dyers might come into this world?
> Should your body become a highway,
> and your slenderness a trampled path?
> And should your breasts shrivel up,
> And their splendor soon fade? [I, 5]

It is in her role as antimother that the Nurse most fully lives up to her identity as a witch, one of the labels given her by Hofmannsthal in his synopsis of the plot of the opera.[21] Her resistance to maternity links her with the beautiful witch in Hofmannsthal's *Der Kaiser und die Hexe* (1897) *(The Emperor and the Witch)*, who remains notably childless throughout the entire course of the extramarital affair the Emperor carries on with her, while his wife bears him children. As Catherine Clément and others have pointed out, witches or sorceresses have traditionally been associated with infertility. The sorceress, Clément writes, is above all the abortionist, and "the witches' sabbat is the one place where the sexual act does not result in reproduction. Witches employ effective contraceptive methods."[22] It is not surprising that men have condemned as witches and destroyed women who have possessed this kind of power over the female body, since such rebellion against conventional female roles is a harbinger of social and economic power as well. Accordingly, in *The Woman without a Shadow,* where the glorification of maternity goes hand in hand with feminine subordination, the Nurse is ejected from the picture: she is sent off screaming in a boat.

Given the Wife's comment to Barak that the things he has eaten to increase his fertility "have no power over my soul" (I, 4), we can justifiably speak of the Nurse's campaign as a struggle with Barak for the soul of his wife. Indeed, Hofmannsthal's synopsis describes the Nurse not only as a witch but as a "being of the Mephistophelian kind" (480), indicating a theme we might usefully pursue to understand more clearly her importance for the Wife. A comparison of the Nurse with Goethe's Mephis-

[21]Hofmannsthal, *"Die Frau ohne Schatten:* Die Handlung," in *Gesammelte Werke: Dramen III* (1957), p. 481. Subsequent page references appear in the text.

[22]Hélène Cixous and Catherine Clément, *The Newly Born Woman,* trans. Betsy Wing (Minneapolis: Univ. of Minnesota Press, 1986), pp. 8, 31. Clément's discussion of witches relies heavily on Jules Michelet, *La Sorcière,* published in English as *Satanism and Witchcraft: A Study in Medieval Superstition,* trans. A. R. Allinson (New York: Walden, 1939), and on the *Malleus maleficarum* (1486) of Heinrich Krämer and Jacob Sprenger, published in English as *The Witches' Hammer,* trans. Montague Summers (New York: Dover, 1971). See also, e.g., Barbara Ehrenreich and Deirdre English, *Witches, Midwives, and Nurses: A History of Women Healers* (Old Westbury, N.Y.: Feminist Press, 1973), and Joseph Klaits, *Servants of Satan: The Age of the Witch Hunts* (Bloomington: Indiana Univ. Press, 1985).

topheles reveals many similarities between the two characters. Most essentially, the Nurse's pact with the Wife, whereby the Wife is to receive countless delights in return for her shadow, echoes the bet Mephistopheles makes with Faust, according to which Faust is to lose his soul if he should ever appear content with the pleasures Mephistopheles offers. Moreover, both the Nurse and Mephistopheles are associated with the devil in the form of a snake; both oppose mankind and seek to thwart human endeavor; the Nurse, along with the Empress, serves the Dyer's Wife in disguise, just as Mephistopheles serves Faust; the jewels and other luxurious articles that the Nurse conjures up to tempt the Wife remind us of the box of jewels Mephistopheles provides Faust for Gretchen; just as Mephistopheles facilitates Faust's seduction of Gretchen, so the Nurse arouses the Wife's interest in the (phantom of) the young man; similarly, the sleeping potion the Nurse slips into Barak's drink to clear the way for his wife's rendezvous with the youth recalls the sleeping potion Mephistopheles gives Faust for Gretchen's mother. Most obviously, the Nurse "quotes" Mephistopheles with her command to the Empress, "Hither to me!" (II, 12), at the end of the second act.

And yet these tangential parallels bring into relief basic differences between Faust and the Dyer's Wife. Both Faust and the Wife rebel against the humdrum and everyday in search of other realms and new experiences. But whereas Faust is allowed, so to speak, to have his cake and eat it too—to seduce, impregnate, and abandon Gretchen and bear responsibility for the deaths of her mother and brother, and then to go on to adventures in the "great world"— Hofmannsthal's Wife only contemplates wrongdoing, which, for her, consists not of activity in the world at large but merely of transgressions of the laws that define her identity as a proper female. Unlike Faust, she returns guiltless—the externalization of her subversive desires having been expelled in the form of the Nurse—to the call of humanity, equivalent here to the call of patriarchy. It is thus fitting that the last lines of Hofmannsthal's libretto, in which the Unborn Children cele-

brate parenthood, are written in the same dactylic meter in
which the closing lines of *Faust II* praise the Eternal Feminine;
the Unborn Children sing:

> Vater, dir drohet nichts,
> siehe, es schwindet schon,
> Mutter, das Ängstliche,
> das euch beirrte.
>
> Wäre denn je ein Fest,
> wären nicht insgeheim
> wir die Geladenen,
> wir auch die Wirte!
>
> Father, nothing threatens you,
> see, already the trouble is vanishing,
> Mother, the fearful trouble
> that perplexed you.
>
> Would there ever be a celebration
> if we were not secretly
> both the guests
> and the hosts!   [III, 16]

Since feminist theoreticians of reading suggest that general-
izations about the activity of reading should be referred to the
experience of actual women,[23] it seems appropriate to conclude
this rereading of *The Woman without a Shadow* by acknowledging
a striking parallel between its plot and an issue of increasing
relevance today. For in its depiction of a woman of wealth and
station using the special powers at her disposal to purchase fertility from a woman of lesser means, Hofmannsthal's libretto
symbolically and unwittingly anticipates the practice of surrogate motherhood, in which a woman unable to have children
herself "leases" the uterus of another woman for this purpose.
The problems that can arise from the practice have received
widespread public attention in recent years through one fiction-

[23]See, e.g., Tania Modleski, "Feminism and the Power of Interpretation: Some
Critical Readings," in *Feminist Studies/Critical Studies*, ed. Teresa de Lauretis
(Bloomington: Indiana Univ. Press, 1986), p. 134.

al treatment, Margaret Atwood's 1985 novel *The Handmaid's Tale*, and one actual instance, the notorious case of "Baby M." Atwood's novel portrays a futuristic dystopia in which healthy young women are enslaved by a totalitarian regime and systematically impregnated by "commanders" with an eye to replenishing the diminished Caucasian population; at birth their babies are turned over to the commanders and their wives, women past childbearing age. As is by now well known, Mary Beth Whitehead, a homemaker and (at the time) wife of a sanitation worker, contracted in return for $10,000 to bear the baby of William Stern, a biochemist whose wife, a pediatrician, was reluctant to undergo pregnancy because of a mild condition of multiple sclerosis. Complications arose when Whitehead changed her mind about giving up the baby and absconded with her after her birth to Florida, where the infant was recovered a few months later. During the controversial hearings called to decide which party should be given custody of "Baby M," Stern was prepared to renounce the child totally if he lost, since he felt that for the girl to see him once a month and eventually be told he was her biological father would not be good for her. Hence the judgment awarding Baby M to the Sterns has been called "Solomonic," favoring as it did the parent who had the child's best interests at heart. In the horrific dictatorship envisioned in *The Handmaid's Tale,* by contrast, the question of the biological mother's right to keep her child does not even arise.

Rereading Hofmannsthal's play in light of these contemporary confrontations with the issue of surrogate motherhood, we can see even more clearly the idealistic nature of its ending. For whereas an analogy to the judgment of Solomon is drawn both in the libretto itself and in Hofmannsthal's comments on it elsewhere, in fact no such judgment is forced. The still intact world view of classical humanism, in which both the Empress and the Dyer's Wife win shadows through renunciation, cannot anticipate the emotional and ethical problems yet to be experienced by actual surrogate mothers and the women and men whose children they contract to bear.

PART V

Motherhood, Power, and Powerlessness

While motherhood has been a major source of women's oppression, as the fictional situations of Ibsen's Hedda Gabler and Hofmannsthal's Dyer's Wife suggest, it has also been the one area of life in which women have typically exercised power, through their authority and control over another human being. Dramatists at the turn of the century, when the cult of the mother met the feminist movement head on, were not only drawn to the theme of women's resistance to maternity but intrigued by the ramifications of maternal power. Two of the most complex of the many mother figures that populated the stage at the time are the title heroine of Bernard Shaw's *Candida* and Laura of August Strindberg's drama *The Father*. It should be immediately apparent that Candida and Laura, in contrast to nearly all the other female protagonists we have encountered so far, are neither ruined nor killed off and even manage to win out in the end. At first glance these two figures seem to represent paradigmatically opposite types, created as they were by an avowed feminist and a vociferous misogynist. And indeed, as early as 1913 Shaw's French translator distinguished between the "benevolent triumph" of the typical Shavian woman and the "evil

triumph" of the Strindbergian heroine.[1] As we shall see, however, careful examination of the female types that Candida and
Laura represent, as well as a closer look at the balance of power
they command, shows this distinction to be too sharply drawn
and reveals the two playwrights' attitudes toward women to be
less far apart than they appear.

[1]Augustin Hamon, *Le Molière du XXe siècle: Bernard Shaw* (Paris: Figuière,
1913), p. 224.

8 The New Woman as Madonna: Shaw's *Candida*

The title heroine of *Candida* (1898), one of the best loved and most frequently performed of Shaw's works, has doubtless had much to do with the play's immense popularity. Her identity is grounded in her role as a mother; as Shaw wrote to William Archer, "Candida . . . is a mother first, a wife twentyseventh, and nothing else."[1] Her children are mentioned twice in the lengthy stage directions describing her home at the beginning of the play, her "characteristic expression" is "an amused maternal indulgence,"[2] and she typically speaks with "wise-hearted maternal humor" (III, 251). By keeping her two actual children off in the country throughout the play, however, Shaw foregrounds her mothering of adults. Most striking is her babying of the eighteen-year-old Marchbanks, whom she refers to variously as a "poor boy" (I, 214), a "dear boy" (I, 215), a "very nice boy" (I, 217), a "great baby" (I, 217), and a "bad boy" (III, 257). She buttons his collar, ties his neckerchief, and arranges his hair just as if he were one of her children; asks Morell for permission for him to stay to lunch "if he promises to be a good boy and help me to lay the table?" (I, 225); and attempts to dismiss him by

[1]Shaw to Archer, 24 January 1900, in Bernard Shaw, *Collected Letters, 1898–1910*, ed. Dan H. Laurence (New York: Dodd, Mead, 1972), p. 137.
[2]Shaw, *Candida*, in *Seven Plays by Bernard Shaw* (New York: Dodd, Mead, 1951), Act I, p. 213; subsequent quotations are identified in the text by act and page number.

telling him to "go off to bed like a good little boy" (III, 261). Her
infantilization of Marchbanks is perhaps most evident in her use
of baby talk when she addresses him: "Poor boy! have I been
cruel! Did I make it slice nasty little red onions?" (II, 244).
Yet Candida's mothering is by no means restricted to
Marchbanks; she is nearly as maternal with the forty-year-old
Morell. Noticing his fatigue, for instance, she remarks, "My boy
is not looking well. Has he been overworking?" (II, 239); similarly, she calls him a "silly boy" and a "dear silly" (II, 240) for
thinking the women in his audiences are roused to enthusiasm
by the content of his sermons, when in fact (she assumes) they
are aroused by the preacher. A further clue to the status of
Marchbanks and Morell vis-à-vis Candida is seen in the fact that
both sit, alternately, in the children's chair next to the fireplace.
In her maternal attitude toward her husband and would-be
lover, Candida echoes the baby-talking Vivie Warren in *Mrs.
Warren's Profession* (1894) and anticipates the title character of
Shaw's *Major Barbara* (1905), who on the last page of the play
refers to her fiancé as her "dear little Dolly boy." These female
figures thus manifest a tendency that Freud considered very
beneficial for a good marriage, as he asserts in "Femininity"
(1933): "A mother is only brought unlimited satisfaction by her
relation to a son; this is altogether the most perfect, the most
free from ambivalence of all human relationships. . . . Even a
marriage is not made secure until the wife has succeeded in
making her husband her child as well and in acting as a mother
to him."[3] That this attitude was widespread at the turn of the
century (though not necessarily new) is suggested by James Op-
penheim's "Bread and Roses," a poem inspired by a slogan carried by women textile workers in the famous strike in Lawrence,
Massachusetts, in 1912, which contains the lines "As we come
marching, marching, we battle too for men, / For they are wom-
en's children, and we mother them again."[4]

[3]Sigmund Freud, "Femininity" ("Die Weiblichkeit"), *SE*, XXII, 133–134.
[4]Quoted in *Feminism: The Essential Historical Writings*, ed. Miriam Schneir (New
York: Vintage, 1972), p. 306.

But because in *Candida*—characterized by its author in a letter to Ellen Terry as "THE Mother Play"[5]—the objects of the title figure's maternal inclinations are not her biological children but grown men, she is linked to the embodiment of ideal mother-hood, the Virgin Mary, with whom she is identified in numerous ways. In another letter Shaw describes *Candida* as "the poetry of the Wife & Mother—the Virgin Mother in the true sense."[6] Indeed, the stage directions preceding Candida's first appear-ance mention a large autotype of the chief figure in Titian's *Assumption of the Virgin* hanging over the fireplace (evidence of Shaw's 1894 trip to Italy to study medieval and renaissance re-ligious art). And following her first entrance the stage directions remark that "a wise-hearted observer, looking at her, would at once guess that whoever had placed the Virgin of the Assump-tion over her hearth did so because he fancied some spiritual resemblance between them" (I, 213). We subsequently learn that the picture was a gift from Marchbanks, and it is he above all who in his poetic imagination sees Candida as a latter-day Madonna. To say her name, he insists, is a "prayer" to her, constituting his happiness, his "heaven" (III, 251). He compares her to an angel and describes his moments with her as time spent on the "summits," with a "sense of the silent glory of life" (III, 254).

More specifically evocative of the Virgin is Marchbanks's cata-logue to Morell of what Candida offered him in Morell's ab-sence: "her shawl, her wings, the wreath of stars on her head, the lilies in her hand, the crescent moon beneath her feet—" (III, 255). Marchbanks's vision of what he would like to give *her* is also relevant: "Not a scrubbing brush, but a boat: a tiny shallop to sail away in, far from the world, where the marble floors are washed by the rain and dried by the sun; where the south wind dusts the

[5]Shaw to Terry, August 1896, in *Ellen Terry and Bernard Shaw: A Correspon-dence*, ed. Christopher St. John (New York: Putnam's, 1932), p. 29, hereafter cited as *Terry–Shaw Correspondence*.
[6]Shaw to R. Golding Bright, 10 June 1896, in *Collected Letters, 1874–1897*, ed. Dan H. Laurence (New York: Dodd, Mead, 1965), p. 632.

beautiful green and purple carpets. Or a chariot! to carry us up into the sky, where the lamps are stars, and don't need to be filled with paraffin oil every day" (II, 236). The parallels between this fantasy and the myth of the Virgin's assumption to heaven are clear: just as the idea of the Assumption originated in the desire to deny the existence of the Virgin's bodily relics, and thus to emphasize the unity of her body and her soul, Marchbanks seems motivated by a desire to deny Candida's physicality. Michael Carroll points out in his recent psychological study of the Virgin Mary, "Mary is quite different from almost all earlier mother goddesses in at least one very important way: she is completely disassociated from sexuality."[7]

Morell is also given to viewing Candida in quasi-religious terms, declaring to his curate, for example, that marriage to a good woman is "a foretaste of what will be best in the Kingdom of Heaven we are trying to establish on earth" (I, 204). In the original manuscript version of the play Morell's secretary, Proserpine, says of Candida, "One would think she was the Queen of Heaven herself. [Morell] is thinking of her half the time when he imagines that he is meditating on the virtues of Our Blessed Lady"; as J. Percy Smith suggests, Shaw's deletion of this passage from the final version of the play was doubtless prompted simply by his concern with public acceptability.[8] Furthermore, Morell's conception of Candida—he tells her, "You are my wife, my mother, my sisters: you are the sum of all loving care to me" (III, 267)—is quite similar to the description of the Virgin Mary offered by Julia Kristeva: "Not only is Mary her son's *mother* and his *daughter*, she is also his *wife*."[9]

With their idealized view of Candida as a Madonna figure, Marchbanks and Morell conform to the pattern of Victorian

[7]Michael P. Carroll, *The Cult of the Virgin Mary: Psychological Origins* (Princeton: Princeton Univ. Press, 1986), p. 5.

[8]J. Percy Smith, "The New Woman and the Old Goddess: The Shaping of Shaw's Mythology," in *Woman in Irish Legend, Life, and Literature*, ed. S. F. Gallagher (Gerrards Cross: Colin Smythe, 1983), p. 80.

[9]Julia Kristeva, "Stabat Mater," 1985; rpt. in *The Female Body in Western Culture: Contemporary Perspectives*, ed. Susan R. Suleiman (Cambridge: Harvard Univ. Press, 1986), p. 105.

masculinity outlined by Freud in "On the Universal Tendency to Debasement in the Sphere of Love" (1912). Proceeding from his theories of the Oedipus complex in men, Freud explains that a portion of a man's sensual feelings can remain attached in the unconscious to incestuous objects, such as the mother, or fixated on incestuous fantasies. The result:

> The sensual current that has remained active seeks only objects which do not recall the incestuous figures forbidden to it; if someone makes an impression that might lead to a high psychical estimation of her, this impression does not find an issue in any sensual excitation but in affection which has no erotic effect. The whole sphere of love in such people remains divided in the two directions personified in art as sacred and profane (or animal) love. Where they love they do not desire and where they desire they cannot love.[10]

My point is not that we should presume in Marchbanks and Morell an unconscious desire for the mother but rather that they, like the male characters in Schnitzler's *La Ronde*, manifest the typical Victorian habit of desexualizing the beloved female. Carol Christ postulates another plausible reason for the creation of the "angel in the house," the ideal of Victorian womanhood celebrated by Coventry Patmore in his poem of that title. Examining works by Patmore and Tennyson, Christ argues that their idealization of female passivity and purity stems from a distaste for male aggressiveness and sexuality.[11] Given Shaw's own discomfort with these qualities in men, it is not surprising to find him endowing Marchbanks and Morell with the tendency to idealize Candida.

But it is important to note that Marchbanks and Morell are not fantasizing when they see Candida as a Madonna; she does

---

[10]Freud, "On the Universal Tendency to Debasement in the Sphere of Love" ("Über die allgemeinste Erniedrigung des Liebeslebens"), *SE*, XI, 182–183. Taking Freudian doctrine as his point of departure, Carroll argues that the entire Virgin Mary cult is based on the son's repressed desire for the mother (*Cult of the Virgin Mary*).

[11]Carol Christ, "Victorian Masculinity and the Angel in the House," in *A Widening Sphere: Changing Roles of Victorian Women*, ed. Martha Vicinus (Bloomington: Indiana Univ. Press, 1977), pp. 146–162.

exhibit characteristics of the Virgin. Candida functions again and again, for instance, as a source of comfort, one of the main virtues associated with the Virgin Mary from the beginnings of the cult through our own day. Even popular culture attests to the significance of this quality as part of the contemporary image of the Madonna, as is evident in the Beatles' invocation of "Mother Mary" in "Let It Be."

Marchbanks's statement that Candida "wants somebody to protect, to help, to work for: . . . Some grown up man who has become as a little child again" (III, 256), the biblical overtones of which are impossible to ignore, is borne out again and again in her treatment of Morell. Her comforting skills are announced even before she comes onstage, when Morell urges his curate to "catch the measles if you can, Lexy: she'll nurse you; and what a piece of luck that will be for you!" (I, 204). Later she insists that he preaches "splendidly" and "beautifully" even while pointing out to him the infatuation of his female listeners (II, 240). After Marchbanks has wreaked havoc in Morell's psyche by undermining his faith in Candida's love for him, she rises to Morell's defense—"My boy shall not be worried: I will protect him"—and "pets" him, insisting that he "musn't be annoyed and made miserable" (III, 256, 257). Similarly, when he is almost overcome by tears over the "auction" of Candida near the end of the play, she "impulsively" goes to comfort him (III, 264). In short, her aim is, as she puts it, to "build a castle of comfort and indulgence and love for him, and stand sentinel always to keep little vulgar cares out" (III, 266–267). These lines inevitably recall Shaw's own appreciation for maternal support and care, which he received in abundance while living with his mother until he married at the age of forty-two.

Another role conventionally associated with the Virgin Mary is that of "merciful dispenser of salvation," a function Candida also performs.[12] She is repeatedly shown to be granting forgive-

---

[12]See Sherry B. Ortner, "Is Female to Male as Nature Is to Culture?" in *Woman, Culture, and Society*, ed. Michelle Z. Rosaldo and Louise Lamphere (Stanford: Stanford Univ. Press, 1974), p. 86.

ness; Marchbanks tells Morell, "Oh, she forgave you [for being a moralist and windbag], just as she forgives me for being a coward, and a weakling, and what you call a snivelling little whelp and all the rest of it" (III, 254). In like manner, when Marchbanks tells her he is "heartbroken" for having made Morell miserable, Candida replies, "Well then, you are forgiven" (III, 261). And the kiss she bestows on the forehead of the kneeling Marchbanks at the end of the play strikes us as a final act of absolution.

Candida's association with the Virgin Mother is further illuminated by recent critical work on Mary's relationship to language. Within a discussion of recurrent literary situations or practices in nineteenth-century British writing by women, Margaret Homans calls attention to the figure of the Virgin Mary, "who gives birth to and is frequently imaged carrying (thus two senses of 'bear') a child who is the Word, the embodiment of the Logos. . . . From Mary . . . comes the repeated figure of a woman who gives birth to or carries a child who represents language."[13] Working along similar lines, Dayton Haskin shows that in Milton's *Paradise Regained* Mary is portrayed as a minister of the word of God. Possessing heightened interpretive powers and privileges, she "bears the word" to Jesus by teaching him about events that are then included in the Gospels, so that she emerges as a mediator of the word to Christ, to the New Testament writers, and ultimately to Christians of every era. As Haskin explains, "Milton concluded that Mary's encounter with God's mysterious word, which began with the announcement of the virginal conception, continued through the course of her life."[14]

Analogously, Candida possesses heightened powers of perception, having, in Marchbanks' words, "divine insight" (III, 254). Fulfilling to the letter Shaw's definition of the creation of

[13]Margaret Homans, *Bearing the Word: Language and Female Experience in Nineteenth-Century Women's Writing* (Chicago: Univ. of Chicago Press, 1986), p. 30; subsequent page references appear in the text.

[14]Dayton Haskin, "Milton's Portrait of Mary as a Bearer of the Word," in *Milton and the Idea of Woman*, ed. Julia M. Walker (Urbana: Univ. of Illinois Press, 1988), p. 177.

comedy as "the manufacture of a misunderstanding,"[15] *Candida* abounds in misperceptions and misunderstandings on the part of Morell and Marchbanks: Morell, who "understand[s] nothing" (II, 243), has misconstrued the appeal of his preaching as well as his role vis-à-vis Candida and is misled by Marchbanks into doubting her devotion to him, and Marchbanks misperceives the dynamics of the Morell marriage. Like the Virgin Mary, Candida acts as a source of enlightenment, educating both men about all these matters. In contrast to Morell and Marchbanks, however, who as parson and poet are steeped in words, Candida, again like the Virgin, functions only as mediator of the word. Homans locates the reason for the mediate role of Madonna figures in their maternal status: "[The] shift from Mary as a girl reading to Mary as a mother holding a book she does not read has important implications for the history of women's relation to the written word, for it gathers in one continuous image much of the ideology of the notion that women can have children or language but not both" (158). Candida's functions as provider of comfort, dispenser of forgiveness, and mediator of the word encourage the male characters to idealize her, and their idealization makes of her something unique, just as the cult of the Virgin, a male creation, renders all earthly women inferior by comparison. As Marina Warner points out, Mary's "freedom from sex, painful delivery, age, death, and all sin exalted her *ipso facto* above ordinary women. . . . She was feminine perfection personified, and no other woman was in her league."[16]

Yet Candida is more than simply a Madonna figure. It is not insignificant that Joseph Molnar's typology of Shaw's female figures does not include her in the type of the "Womanly Woman,"

[15]Shaw, "How to Write a Popular Play," in *Playwrights on Playwriting: The Meaning and Making of Modern Drama from Ibsen to Ionesco,* ed. Toby Cole (New York: Hill & Wang, 1960), p. 53.

[16]Marina Warner, *Alone of All Her Sex: The Myth and the Cult of the Virgin Mary* (New York: Knopf, 1976), pp. 153, 159.

or in any other major type, for that matter.[17] For together with those features that recall the Virgin, Candida possesses qualities of a very different literary type, that of the New Woman. This combination produces a hybrid uncommon not only in Shaw's oeuvre but in turn-of-the-century literature in general. A product of combined forces— notably the drive for female suffrage, the influx of women into factory jobs and other kinds of work, and the example of Ibsen's heroines—the New Woman was less a reality than a creation of fiction and the media. As Carolyn Forrey observes, "journalists seized hold of the term in the 1890's to try to describe the changes which they sensed were taking place among women: changes not so much in women's outward movements as in their outlooks and expectations."[18] A precursor of the New Woman appears in Olive Schreiner's *Story of an African Farm* (1883), but the heyday of the type came in the 1890s, when the New Woman populated novels by George Gissing, Grant Allen, Sarah Grand, George Egerton, Mona Caird, Thomas Hardy, Ménie Muriel Dowie, and others; one of her last appearances was in H. G. Wells's *Ann Veronica* (1909).[19]

One of the primary factors motivating the typical New Woman is rebellion against the "old woman," described by one member of an 1890s women's club as "bounded on the north by servants, on the south by children, on the east by ailments and on the west by clothes."[20] The conventional Victorian woman is accustomed to self-sacrifice; the New Woman pursues self-fulfillment and independence, often choosing to work for a living. She typically strives for equality in her relationships with

---

[17]Joseph Molnar, "Shaw's Four Kinds of Women," *Theatre Arts*, 36 (December 1952), 18–21, 92.

[18]Carolyn Forrey, "The New Woman Revisited," *Women's Studies*, 2 (1974), 38.

[19]On the New Woman in literature see especially Gail Cunningham, *The New Woman and the Victorian Novel* (New York: Harper & Row, 1978), and Leone Scanlon, "The New Woman in the Literature of 1883–1909," *University of Michigan Papers in Women's Studies*, 2, no. 2 (1976), 133–159.

[20]Kate Trimble Stein, "The Art of Selection," *Club Woman*, December 1897, p. 76, quoted in Sandra D. Harmon, "The Club Woman as New Woman: Late Nineteenth-Century Androgynous Images," *Turn-of-the-Century Women*, 1 (Winter 1984), 30.

men, seeking to eliminate the double standard that shaped the sexual mores of the time, and is in general much more frank about sexuality than the old woman.[21] Dismayed by male attitudes or by the difficulty of combining marriage and a career, she often chooses to remain single; concomitantly, she comes to place increasing value on relationships with other women. (This new literary emphasis on female solidarity paralleled the actual growth of women's clubs.)[22] Furthermore, the New Woman tends to be well-educated and to read a great deal. Although not necessarily a woman suffragist, she is likely to be more interested in politics than the conventional woman.[23] Finally, the New Woman is physically vigorous and energetic, preferring comfortable clothes to the restrictive garb usually worn by women of the era. She often has short hair, rides a bicycle, and smokes cigarettes—all considered quite daring for women at the turn of the century. Significantly, however, the ultimate fate of the fictional New Woman is frequently hysteria or some other nervous disorder, physical illness, or even death, often by suicide, her unhappy end reflecting the fact that society was simply not yet ready to accommodate her new ways.

Many of these features—though not the last—characterize the creations of Shaw. He was the first to bring the New Woman to the English stage; indeed, Barbara Bellow Watson calls the Shavian woman "the quintessence of the New Woman."[24] Shaw's

[21]Cf. Livia Z. Wittmann, "Liebe oder Selbstverlust: Die fiktionale Neue Frau im ersten Drittel unseres Jahrhunderts," in *Der Widerspenstigen Zähmung: Studien zur bezwungenen Weiblichkeit in der Literatur vom Mittlealter bis zur Gegenwart,* ed. Sylvia Wallinger and Monika Jonas (Innsbruck: Institut für Germanistik, 1986), pp. 259–280.

[22]Women, of course, still have many of these same concerns today. The August 1987 issue of the magazine *New Woman,* for instance, contains articles on the emotional (and sexual) bond between women and on the difficulty of combining marriage and/or motherhood with a career.

[23]Cf. Keith M. May, *Characters of Women in Narrative Literature* (New York: St. Martin's Press, 1981), p. 116.

[24]Barbara Bellow Watson, "The New Woman and the New Comedy," in *Fabian Feminist: Bernard Shaw and Woman,* ed. Rodelle Weintraub (University Park: Pennsylvania State Univ. Press, 1977), p. 114. Watson's *Shavian Guide to the Intelligent Woman* (London: Chatto & Windus, 1964) was the first full-length study of Shaw and women.

Quintessence of Ibsenism (1891) contains his doctrine of the New Woman in nuce: "If we have come to think that the nursery and the kitchen are the natural sphere of a woman, we have done so exactly as English children come to think that a cage is the natural sphere of a parrot: because they have never seen one anywhere else. . . . The sum of the matter is that unless Woman repudiates her womanliness, her duty to her husband, to her children, to society, to the law, and to everyone but herself, she cannot emancipate herself."[25] These ideas are embodied in such characters as Vivie Warren in *Mrs. Warren's Profession* and Lina Szczepanowska in *Misalliance* (1910), both of whom reject marriage and motherhood in order to pursue a career. Although some critics view these figures as liberated women par excellence,[26] there is undeniably an element of caricature in both Vivie, with her cigars and whiskey and bone-crunching handshake, and Lina, with her men's clothes, aviator's goggles, and acrobat's antics.

As a hybrid type, Candida seems more realistic than such figures as Vivie and Lina. Being a New Woman did not always exclude motherhood, and while Candida clearly does not manifest all the qualities of the New Woman, she does possess some of them. Thus Shaw's portrayal of this fictional woman implicitly anticipates and answers Luce Irigaray's call to actual women some eighty years later to be more than simply mothers.[27] For example, in contrast to the ideal of the Victorian mother and to the Virgin Mary, both conventionally dissociated from sexuality, Candida is presented as a frankly sexual woman. The stage directions describing her first entrance prepare us for this aspect of her character: "Her ways are those of a woman who has found that she can always manage people by engaging their affection,

[25]*Shaw and Ibsen: Bernard Shaw's 'The Quintessence of Ibsenism' and Related Writings*, ed. J. L. Wisenthal (Toronto: Univ. of Toronto Press, 1979), p. 130.
[26]E.g., Gladys M. Crane, "Shaw and Women's Lib," in *Fabian Feminist*, pp. 174–184. On these and other Shavian New Women see also Sonja Lorichs, *The Unwomanly Woman in Bernard Shaw's Drama and Her Social and Political Background* (Uppsala: Universitetsbiblioteket, 1973).
[27]Luce Irigaray, *Le Corps-à-corps avec la mère* (Montréal: Pleine Lune, 1981), pp. 65–66.

and who does so frankly and instinctively without the smallest scruple. So far, she is like any other pretty woman who is just clever enough to make the most of her sexual attractions for trivially selfish ends" (I, 213). Accordingly, she expresses herself with complete openness to Marchbanks, telling him, "I like you ever so much better for being nice to [my father]" (I, 217) and "Now you look so nice that I think you'd better stay to lunch after all" (I, 225). She confides to Morell "with lively interest" that she has grown increasingly fond of Marchbanks and that he is ready to fall madly in love with her; and in expressing concern that, unless Marchbanks learns "what love really is" from a "good" woman rather than a "bad" one, he might not forgive her for not teaching him herself, she reveals that she knows quite a bit more about these matters than the conventional woman of the day was supposed to know (II, 241–242). Similarly, when Morell admits to her, "I thought of your goodness, of your purity. That is what I confide in," she explodes, "What a nasty uncomfortable thing to say to me!" (II, 241)—a reaction that conflicts markedly with her Virgin-like characteristics.

Events in Shaw's own life may have had something to do with his presentation of the sexual side of Candida. Rodelle Weintraub shows that, contrary to the popular notion that Shaw was thoroughly squeamish about sex, he portrays it openly in the plays written before his marriage (which include *Candida*); the fact that sex occurs much less frequently in the later plays reflects the celibacy his wife imposed on their marriage.[28] Weintraub also mentions that Shaw lost his virginity to a woman fifteen years his senior—precisely the age gap between Marchbanks and Candida (41). Whatever the effect of Shaw's personal experience on the characterization of Candida, it is certain he did not sincerely consider her "the Virgin Mother and nobody else," as he wrote to Ellen Terry in 1896.[29] Indeed, in a later letter to Terry he writes of "Candida, with her boy and her

[28]Rodelle Weintraub, "Shaw's Celibate Marriage: Its Impact on His Plays," *Cahiers Victoriens et Edouardiens*, 9/10 (1979), 37–62; subsequent page references appear in the text.
[29]Shaw to Terry, 6 April 1896, in *Terry–Shaw Correspondence*, p. 23.

parson, and her suspicion of trading a little on the softness of
her contours"; and in a letter to James Huneker he refers to
Candida as "that very immoral female," suggests that she got rid
of Morell's former secretary because she was too attractive, and
claims that "Candida is as unscrupulous as Siegfried. . . . She
seduces Eugene just exactly as far as it is worth her while to
seduce him. She is a woman without 'character' in the conventional sense."[30]

Lest these retrospective authorial judgments sound unduly
harsh, it should be noted that much of this vocabulary—"immoral" and "unconventional," for example—is not meant nega-
tively but is the kind of language that Shaw used to describe his
realists.[31] Candida's sexuality goes hand in hand with another
characteristic typical of the New Woman, a sense of self-sufficiency and freedom from concern with convention. When
Marchbanks assures Morell that "Mrs. Morell's quite right"
(about Marchbanks's incompetence in money matters), Candida
says, "Of course she is" (I, 218), demonstrating the self-confidence that later moves her to exclaim to Morell, "How conventional all you unconventional people are!" (II, 243). Her self-
possession is conveyed to the audience most graphically near the
end of the play, when Morell says she must choose between
himself and Marchbanks; she responds, "Oh! I am to choose, am
I? I suppose it is quite settled that I must belong to one or the
other." Marchbanks explains to Morell, "She means that she belongs to herself" (III, 264).

Candida explains to her father that her self-sufficiency "comes
of James teaching me to think for myself, and never to hold back
out of fear of what other people may think of me." Significantly,
however, she goes on to add, "It works beautifully as long as I
think the same things as he does" (II, 243), demonstrating a
critical attitude toward Morell which surfaces several times in

[30]Shaw to Terry, 8 August 1899, in *Terry–Shaw Correspondence*, p. 248; Shaw to
James Huneker, 6 April 1904, in Shaw, *Collected Letters, 1898–1910*, pp. 414–
415.
[31]Cf. Alfred Turco, Jr., *Shaw's Moral Vision: The Self and Salvation* (Ithaca:
Cornell Univ. Press, 1976), p. 104n.

the play. Such independent-minded criticism of her husband
puts Candida at a considerable remove from a conventional Virgin Mother character and further allies her with the type of the
New Woman so prevalent at the time the drama was written. She
does not hesitate, for instance, to give Morell her honest opinion
of his sermons: "Put your trust in my love for you, James; for if
that went, I should care very little for your sermons: mere
phrases that you cheat yourself and others with every day" (II,
242). Similarly, when she urges him shortly thereafter to talk to
her and the others and he replies, echoing her, "*I* can't talk. I can
only preach," she responds, "Well, come and preach" (II, 244).
Her most far-reaching criticism of James and what he represents
appears near the end of the play: "Ask me what it costs to be
James's mother and three sisters and wife and mother to his
children all in one. Ask Prossy and Maria how troublesome the
house is even when we have no visitors to help us to slice the
onions. Ask the tradesmen who want to worry James and spoil
his beautiful sermons who it is that puts them off" (III, 266).

Candida's skepticism about the domestic idyll that she creates
for Morell—an attitude shared by the career-minded New
Woman of contemporary fiction—anticipates Marchbanks's
"disgust" with the Morells' marital contentment at the end of the
play and the much-discussed "secret in the poet's heart" with
which he leaves them. When the members of a school literary
society asked Shaw to reveal the secret, he replied: "The secret is
very obvious after all—provided you know what a poet is. What
business has a man with the great destiny of a poet with the small
beer of domestic comfort and cuddling and petting at the apron-
string of some dear nice woman?"[32] This sense of conventional

---

[32]Shaw to literary society, 8 March 1920, as quoted in *A Casebook on "Candida,"*
ed. Stephen S. Stanton (New York: Crowell, 1962), pp. 168–169. The "secret"
aroused so much curiosity that most consider it the reason for the subtitle that
Shaw gave the play in the standard edition of his works: "A Mystery." Maurice
Valency, however, believes that Shaw had in mind the medieval mystery play as a
prototype of Pre-Raphaelite attitudes in the theater; Valency, *The Cart and the
Trumpet: The Plays of George Bernard Shaw* (New York: Oxford Univ. Press, 1973),
p. 132.

domestic life as a "greasy fool's paradise"[33] for the artist had already been present in Shaw's novel *Love among the Artists* (1881), as is evident in Jack's statement that "it is marriage that kills the heart and keeps it dead."[34] In endowing Candida with a measure of skepticism about the ideal of domestic bliss, Shaw not only reveals his own ambivalence toward this ideal but undermines its embodiment in Candida herself.

And yet, given that marriage and motherhood constitute Candida's world, Shaw depicts her as possessing a great deal of power, an attribute that reinforces her associations with the New Woman. Throughout the play she has absolute authority and control; in fact, her position prompts one critic to compare her with the sphinx: "Like the sphinx, she knows and understands everything, while poor Morell understands nothing. . . . She is entirely and effortlessly autonomous."[35] It is appropriate that at the beginning of the third act Candida wields the poker like a scepter of power. For as Arthur Ganz observes, her subsequent explanation, "I make [James] master here, though he does not know it, and could not tell you a moment ago how it came to be so" (III, 267), is "in fact an insistence, under the very thinnest of disguises, that she is master."[36] Indeed, Shaw's awareness of the power relations in *Candida* inspired him to make the often quoted claim that the play "is a counterblast to Ibsen's *Doll's House,* showing that in the real typical doll's house it is the man who is the doll."[37] This inversion is a particular example of Shaw's general belief in maternal power, which he sums up in *The Intelligent Woman's Guide to Socialism and Capitalism:*

[33]Shaw to Huneker, 6 April 1904, in *Collected Letters, 1898–1910,* p. 415.
[34]Shaw, *Love among the Artists* (Chicago: Stone, 1900), p. 429.
[35]Rhoda B. Nathan, "The Shavian Sphinx," in *Fabian Feminist,* p. 33.
[36]Arthur Ganz, *George Bernard Shaw* (London: Macmillan, 1983), p. 114.
[37]Shaw to Beverley Baxter, 30 November 1944, in *Evening Standard,* as quoted in *A Casebook on "Candida,"* p. 158. For an elaboration of the differences and similarities between Ibsen's play and *Candida,* see Bernard F. Dukore, *Bernard Shaw, Playwright: Aspects of Shavian Drama* (Columbia: Univ. of Missouri Press, 1973), pp. 54–60.

The bearing and rearing of children, including domestic house-
keeping, is woman's natural monopoly. As such, being as it is the
most vital of all the functions of mankind, it gives women a power
and importance that they can attain to in no other profession, and
that man cannot attain to at all. In so far as it is a slavery, it is a
slavery to Nature and not to Man: indeed it is the means by which
women enslave men, and thus create a Man Question which is
called, very inappropriately, the Woman Question.[38]

Drawn both from the timeless myth of the Virgin Mary and
from the turn-of-the-century type of the New Woman, Shaw's
portrayal of Candida moves in the direction of the realistic ap-
praisal of motherhood made some fifty years later by Simone de
Beauvoir: "The distortion begins when the religion of Maternity
proclaims that all mothers are saintly. For while maternal devotion may be perfectly genuine, this, in fact, is rarely the case.
Maternity is usually a strange mixture of narcissism, altruism,
idle daydreaming, sincerity, bad faith, devotion, and cyn-
icism."[39] The similarity of Shaw's views on maternity to those of
the first theorist of the new women's movement is no accident
but rather is typical of his feminism in general. He advocated
equal political rights for the sexes as early as 1884 and came out
in favor of female suffrage when he was invited to run for office
as a Liberal candidate five years later. His support of women's
right to vote was consistent and fervent, manifesting itself in, for
example, the suffrage play *Press Cuttings* (1909). Not surprisingly, his letters and articles in *New Statesman* and *The Times*
were often reprinted in such feminist papers as *Votes for Women*
and *Suffragette*. His opposition to the imprisonment and forcible
feeding of woman suffragists on hunger strikes was adamant, as
is evident in his 1913 speech "Torture by Forcible Feeding is
Illegal"[40] and in the following passage from his letter of 31 Octo-

---

[38]Shaw, *The Intelligent Woman's Guide to Socialism and Capitalism* (New York:
Brentano's, 1928), p. 176.
[39]Simone de Beauvoir, *The Second Sex*, trans. H. M. Parshley (1952; New York:
Vintage, 1974), p. 573.
[40]Rpt. in *Fabian Feminist*, pp. 228–235.

ber 1906 to *The Times:* "As a taxpayer, I object to having to pay for [Mrs. Cobden-Sanderson's] bread and cocoa when her husband is not only ready, but apparently even anxious to provide a more generous diet at home. After all, if Mr. Cobden-Sanderson is not afraid, surely the rest of us may pluck up a little."[41] Similarly, Shaw favored equal opportunities for employment and equal pay for equal work, as well as a number of measures designed to promote marital equality, such as marriage contracts, a wife's right to own property independently and to maintain an income without disclosing it to her husband, and laws permitting divorce with dignity. He also felt that women should be free to bear children outside of marriage and to refuse to bear them within marriage. Moreover, Shaw's description of maternal power should not be taken to indicate that he denied women other kinds of power; he felt that they should always be included in public bodies and should have a part in solving all social problems.

In short, Shaw's goal for relations between the sexes was psychological androgyny. This goal is encapsulated in two of his most frequently quoted statements: "All good women are manly and all good men are womanly" and "The secret of the extraordinary knowledge of women which I show in my plays is that I have always assumed that a woman is a person exactly like myself, and that is how the trick is done."[42] It is important to keep in mind, however, that this goal is an ideal; as Michael Holroyd observes, "Shaw's feminism was Hegelian. He stated as fact what he desired to achieve as an end—that men and women were almost identical. He dreamed of combining their minds to form a higher synthesis of political animal" (32).

Seen against the background of his feminism, the innovative nature of Shaw's depiction of the mother in *Candida* comes even

[41]Quoted in Michael Holroyd, "George Bernard Shaw: Women and the Body Politic," *Critical Inquiry*, 6 (1979), 25. Much of the information in this paragraph is drawn from Holroyd's article; subsequent page references appear in the text.

[42]Quoted by Declan Kiberd, *Men and Feminism in Modern Literature* (London: Macmillan, 1985), pp. 61, 62.

more clearly into relief. Candida, that engaging amalgam of the
Virgin Mary and the New Woman, is a more realistic and con-
vincing representation of maternal power than the idealized
mother figures so common in Victorian literature. And yet from
a historical perspective, Shaw's mixed portrayal is not entirely
innovative, for it accords with male depictions of the mother in
many eras and cultures, depictions whose hallmark has been
ambivalence. Formulations by the major theoreticians of the
mother archetype testify to its duality. Here is Jung:

> The qualities associated with it are maternal solicitude and sym-
> pathy; the magic authority of the female; the wisdom and spir-
> itual exaltation that transcend reason; any helpful instinct or im-
> pulse; all that is benign, all that cherishes and sustains, that fosters
> growth and fertility. . . . On the negative side the mother arche-
> type may connote anything secret, hidden, dark; the abyss, the
> world of the dead, anything that devours, seduces, and poisons,
> that is terrifying and inescapable like fate.[43]

Similarly, Erich Neumann writes of "the ambiguous, that is, life-
giving and death-dealing, fascination of the belly of the Great
Goddess" (the Mother Goddess) and notes that "all this . . . is an
image not only of the Feminine but particularly and specifically
of the Maternal. For in a profound way life and birth are always
bound up with death and destruction. That is why this Terrible
Mother is 'Great.'"[44] And Mary Anne Ferguson, discussing images of women in literature, remarks, "The role of mother is
ambiguous. Myths about woman's dual nature are attempts to
explain primordial reactions to her double role as the giver of
life and death, of pleasure and pain."[45]

Recent feminist work on the archetype has shown the limits of
this conception of the mother archetype, derived as it is pri-

[43]C. G. Jung, *Four Archetypes: Mother/Rebirth/Spirit/Trickster,* trans. R. F. C.
Hull (Princeton: Princeton Univ. Press, 1959), p. 16.
[44]Erich Neumann, *The Great Mother: An Analysis of the Archetype,* trans. Ralph
Manheim, 2d ed. (Princeton: Princeton Univ. Press, 1963), pp. 145, 153.
[45]Mary Anne Ferguson, *Images of Women in Literature* (Boston: Houghton
Mifflin, 1973), p. 12.

marily from works of art produced by men. Through the study
of paintings and sculpture by female artists, Estella Lauter, for
example, moves toward a corrected version of the maternal archetype. She explains, "The mother may be stronger than
Jungians have thought without being 'terrible,' and also more
vulnerable, not just in her relationship to children whom she
must lose one way or another, but in her own body." Lauter also
discovers that "passion has been missing from our descriptions
of the mother."[46] Hélène Cixous wholly refashions the maternal
metaphor in using it to describe feminine writing, defined as the
voice of the mother:

> Text, my body: traversed by lilting flows; listen to me, it is not a
> captivating, clinging "mother"; it is the equivoice that, touching
> you, affects you, pushes you away from your breast to come to
> language, that summons *your* strength; it is the rhyth-me that
> laughs you; the one intimately addressed who makes all meta-
> phors, all body(?)—bodies(?)—possible and desirable, who is no
> more describable than god, soul, or the Other; the part of you
> that puts space between yourself and pushes you to inscribe your
> woman's style in language. Voice: milk that could go on forever.
> Found again. The lost mother/bitter-lost. Eternity: is voice mixed
> with milk.[47]

It seems reasonable to suspect that a female perspective is
necessary for a full and realistic conception of the mother archetype. Indeed, one line in *Candida* intimates that Shaw was dimly
aware of this possibility himself. Conversing with Morell's curate
about Candida, Proserpine comments, "I'm very fond of her,
and can appreciate her real qualities far better than any man
can" (I, 206). Although Prossy is by no means one of the powerful and subversive old maid figures that Nina Auerbach has

[46]Estella Lauter, "Visual Images by Women: A Test Case for the Theory of
Archetypes," in *Feminist Archetypal Theory: Interdisciplinary Re-Visions of Jungian
Thought,* ed. Lauter and Carol S. Rupprecht (Knoxville: Univ. of Tennessee
Press, 1985), pp. 56, 58.
[47]Hélène Cixous and Catherine Clément, *The Newly Born Woman,* trans. Betsy
Wing (Minneapolis: Univ. of Minnesota Press, 1986), p. 93.

discovered in Victorian literature,[48] her remark nevertheless deserves credence, and it suggests the degree to which the male characters' images of Candida are biased by their subjective, sexually colored perceptions. However, just as theater audiences had to wait until Elizabeth Robins's *Votes for Women* (1907) for a realistic portrayal of the New Woman,[49] Shaw and his contemporaries would have to wait until the twentieth century for women to enter the arts in numbers large enough to offer a corrective revision of age-old female archetypes.

[48]Nina Auerbach, *Woman and the Demon: The Life of a Victorian Myth* (Cambridge: Harvard Univ. Press, 1982), pp. 109–149.

[49]See Catherine Wiley, "The Matter with Manners: The New Woman and the Problem Play," in *Women in Theatre*, ed. James M. Redmond (Cambridge: Cambridge Univ. Press, 1989).

9 The Devil in the House?: Strindberg's *The Father*

Eric Bentley finds the ending of *Candida* "much more savage" than that of *A Doll House*. "Only Strindberg could have written a sequel to [*Candida*]. The cruelty of the heroine—merely implicit in the present play—would have to come to the surface in any continuation of the story. Candida has chosen to let her husband discover his shame: she, as well as he, will have to take the consequences. Let the stage manager hold razors and strait jackets in readiness!"[1] In the last sentence Bentley is referring to the final images of August Strindberg's *Miss Julie* (1888) and *The Father* (1887), respectively. *Miss Julie*, having demeaned herself by sleeping with her father's valet, is persuaded by the valet to walk offstage at the play's end with the razor in her hand, leaving the viewer to assume her suicide. *The Father*, sounding the first note of the obsession with uncertain paternity which was to echo in such later works as *A Madman's Defense* (1888) and *The Ghost Sonata* (1907), closes with the Captain paralyzed by a stroke and trussed in a straitjacket, his sanity having been worn away by doubts fanned by his wife's carefully chosen words and his own paranoia.

We can determine the validity of Bentley's assertion by looking at Shaw's drama and Strindberg's side by side. Of the two

[1]Foreword to *Plays by George Bernard Shaw*, ed. Eric Bentley (New York: New American Library, 1960), p. xxiv.

Strindberg dramas to which Bentley alludes, *The Father* is the more appropriately compared with *Candida*, since the mother figure plays a key role in both. The fierceness of the battle between the Captain and his wife, Laura, for control of their daughter gives the drama a sensationalism that has left its mark on audiences throughout the play's stage history. Describing one of the play's first performances to Nietzsche (albeit with characteristic hyperbole), Strindberg writes that "an elderly lady fell down dead . . . , another woman gave birth, and at the sight of the straitjacket three-fourths of the audience rose en masse to leave, yelling madly!"[2]

The shocking quality of *The Father* has no doubt had much to do with audience perceptions of the character of Laura. Much recent literature on the play corroborates the older conception of her as "demonic" or "monstrous," a view that places her at the beginning of a line of monstrous mothers in Strindberg's work.[3] Yet just as reactions to Candida as Madonna must be colored by the features she shares with the New Woman, the perception of Laura as evil must be qualified by a variety of factors. Indeed, as we shall see, several ideas expressed through Strindberg's portrayal of Laura can now be said to have anticipated (if unintentionally) facets of contemporary feminist theory.

Strindberg's mixed depiction of Laura is best illuminated against the background of his ambivalent attitudes toward women and feminism in general. A letter of 1886 to Edvard Brandes reveals that Strindberg considered woman's place to be distinctly different from man's: "Is it really necessary for the unmarried woman to enter the male labor market? After all, she has her own. The unmarried woman can become a maid, a wet nurse, a housekeeper, a teacher, a music teacher, an actress, a dancer, a

---

[2]Strindberg to Nietzsche (in French), 11 December 1888, in *August Strindbergs brev*, ed. Torsten Eklund, VII (Stockholm: Bonniers, 1961), 203.

[3]See, e.g., Gideon Ofrat, "The Structure of Ritual and Mythos in the Naturalistic Plays of August Strindberg," *Theatre Research International*, 4 (1979), 103, 106. In later plays by Strindberg, such as *The Pelican* (1907), the mother, conventionally associated with nourishment, is instead linked with its opposite, vampirism.

singer, a lady in waiting, a queen, an empress, or—in the worst case—a whore. Which latter resource is denied to the male."[4] Strindberg's stance toward the Scandinavian women's movement in the 1880s seems clear from the collection of short stories titled *Married*, which appeared in two volumes in 1884 and 1886. "A Doll House," for example, takes a stab at Strindberg's renowned Norwegian contemporary, telling the story of a sea captain who nearly loses the love of his wife after an unmarried, feminist woman friend encourages her to read Ibsen's *Doll House;* the husband finally wins his wife back by flirting so outrageously with her friend that the wife becomes jealous and throws her out, thus finding her way back to her proper wifely station. It is worth noting that one of the stories in *Married* appeared in the first issue of a Viennese magazine called *Der Frauenfeind* (The misogynist), founded "to counter the exaggerated passion for worshipping women."[5] Similarly, Strindberg's play *Comrades* (1888), a rewritten version of *Marauders*, inverts Ibsen's *Doll House:* two would-be bohemian artists, Bertha and Axel, switch gender roles after Bertha's painting is accepted by the salon and Axel's is refused; Strindberg carries the parody so far as to provide a Spanish woman's costume for Axel. But whereas Shaw's inversion of *A Doll House* ends harmoniously, with Candida "choosing" her husband and sending the interfering young poet off into the night, *Comrades* closes with the breakup of Axel and Bertha and so reveals the ideal of unisexism to be precisely that—an ideal.

Other works that Strindberg wrote during these years demonstrate his attitude toward the women's movement more specifically. In his autobiographical novel *A Madman's Defense* he calls emancipated women "fools" and "half-women,"[6] and he uses the

---

[4]Strindberg to Edvard Brandes, 3 December 1886, in *August Strindbergs brev*, IV (1958), 115. This passage was translated by Barry Jacobs, to whom I am indebted for numerous helpful references and suggestions for this chapter.
[5]Quoted in Michael Meyer, *Strindberg* (New York: Random House, 1985), p. 168.
[6]August Strindberg, *A Madman's Defense*, trans. based on Ellie Schleussner's version, revised and edited by Evert Sprinchorn (Garden City, N.Y.: Doubleday/Anchor, 1967), pp. 251, 258.

latter designation again in the preface to *Miss Julie:* "The half-woman is a type that forces itself on others, selling itself for power, medals, recognition, diplomas, as formerly it sold itself for money. It represents degeneration."[7] Such statements provide an appropriate backdrop for the play itself, in which Julie's waywardness is partially attributed to her upbringing as the daughter of an emancipated woman. Undeniable contradictions, however, cloud our view of Strindberg's opinions about the women's movement. Despite his avowed sentiments on woman's proper place, for example, all three of his wives had careers, one in journalism and two in acting. Although his life would doubtless have been simpler had he married a conventional domestic woman, the prospect evidently had little appeal for him.

Strindberg's feelings about the female sex per se are equally ambivalent. On the one hand, in the preface to *Miss Julie,* in a passage describing theater audiences, he notes that women "still retain a primitive capacity for deceiving themselves and for letting themselves be deceived, that is, for succumbing to illusions and responding hypnotically to the suggestions of the author" (564), and similarly categorical denunciations of women abound in his works of the 1880s. At their extreme his expostulations resemble the views of Otto Weininger, the Viennese Jewish writer who killed himself at the age of twenty-three after publishing the rabidly misogynist *Geschlecht und Charakter* (1903) (*Sex and Character*). Weininger admired Strindberg's works, especially *The Father,* and may have been influenced by them. There are in any case numerous parallels between the thinking of the two men, such as their view of women as nonmoral, lacking in soul and genius, and dominated by sexuality rather than rationality. Strindberg felt that *Sex and Character* had solved the woman problem, and a memorial to Weininger published in *Die Fackel* (The torch) provides him with an appropriate opportunity to

[7]"Preface to *Miss Julie,*" in *Dramatic Theory and Criticism: Greeks to Grotowski,* ed. Bernard F. Dukore (New York: Holt, Rinehart & Winston, 1974), p. 568 (this is the only uncut version of the preface in English); subsequent page references appear in the text.

summarize his views on the subject: "The simple fact that man has created all of culture, spiritual as well as material, demonstrates his position as the superior sex."[8]

On the other hand, Strindberg often claimed that his misogyny was merely theoretical, since he could not do without the company of women. Further, in an article that appeared in *Die Fackel* a few years after the Weininger memorial, Strindberg presents a dialogue between a hypothetical "author" and "interviewer" in which the author points out that he has attacked not woman's attempt to liberate herself from cradle and kitchen but her attempt to liberate herself from bearing children, not woman but contemporary social conditions.[9] This last remark reflects Strindberg's strong feelings about woman's role as mother—feelings similar to those we encountered in Hauptmann's later work—which inspire the author's final exclamation in the interview: "Woman does not need my defense! She is the mother, and therefore she is ruler of the world" (22). And yet, knowing that this is the same writer who on other occasions attributed the decline of patriarchy in his time to man's adulation of the mother,[10] we should perhaps take his glorification of maternity with a grain of salt.

The ambivalence evident in Strindberg's polemical statements is discernible as well in his portrayal of Laura. Although in some ways she is indeed the harridan she has so often been made out to be, her behavior is at least partially explained by her situation. Especially by contrast with the Captain, for instance, she appears relatively uneducated, professing a lack of knowledge about the scientific matters that concern him. Laura's ignorance could in fact be one of the examples to which the "author" alludes in the

[8]Strindberg, "Idolatrie, Gynolatrie: Ein Nachruf von August Strindberg," *Die Fackel*, no. 144 (17 October 1903), p. 1. See also Hugh Salvesen, "The Disappointed Idealist: August Strindberg in Karl Kraus's Periodical *Die Fackel*," *New German Studies*, 9 (1981), 157–179.

[9]Strindberg, "Zur Frauenfrage," *Die Fackel*, nos. 227–228 (10 June 1907), pp. 21–22; subsequent page references appear in the text.

[10]Evert Sprinchorn, *Strindberg as Dramatist* (New Haven: Yale Univ. Press, 1982), p. 47.

interview published in *Die Fackel* twenty years later when he
claims, "I have shown that under present social conditions education has often (not always) turned woman into a stupid creature; I have, in other words—write it down, sir—attacked wom-
en's education" (22).

As the product of an educational system that trains men for
the world and women for the home, Laura is not only ignorant
but socially powerless. Her lack of financial power is evident
early in the play when she has to go to the Captain for household
money and is told she must account for what she has spent. Her
subsequent responses to him are revealing—"If our financial
position is bad, it's not my fault" and "If our tenant doesn't pay,
it's not my fault"[11]—the repeated phrase underlining her lack of
responsibility and thus of authority. Her exclusion from exter-
nal avenues of power is manifest in her wish for her daughter,
Bertha, to stay at home, countered by the Captain's desire for
the girl to study with a freethinker in town, to become an atheist,
to be independent. As Richard Hornby points out, "if Laura
were truly a feminist, she would want these very things for her
daughter."[12] Strindberg's awareness of the difficulties sexual in-
equality caused women in his day is reflected in his definition of
a woman's love as "50 percent ardor and 50 percent hate . . .
because she feels tied to [her lover] and subordinate to him."[13]

Laura's powerlessness and frustration are expressed on the
gestural level as well. When the Captain decides that she can give
him her accounts later, the curtsy with which she "thanks" him
speaks for itself. Similarly, Bertha notes, "She cries so often!" (I,
31)—and her tears of course are a manifestation of anything but
strength and control. Other characters also recognize her impo-

[11]Strindberg, *The Father,* in *Pre-Inferno Plays,* trans. Walter Johnson (Seattle:
Univ. of Washington Press, 1970), Act I, p. 21; subsequent quotations are identified in the text by act and page number.
[12]Richard Hornby, "Man against Nature in Strindberg's *The Father,*" in vol. II
of *All the World: Drama Past and Present,* ed. Karelisa V. Hartigan (Washington:
Univ. Press of America, 1982), p. 34.
[13]Strindberg, "Idolatrie, Gynolatrie," p. 2.

tence and sympathize with it to varying degrees. The Doctor confidentially remarks to her, "You know how one feels in one's innermost being when one's strongest wishes are frustrated, when one's will is thwarted" (II, 35), demonstrating his understanding of her situation. But it is the Nurse, the mother figure par excellence of the play, who puts her finger on the source of Laura's powerlessness—and of her power—when she tells the Captain, "A father has things beside his child, but a mother has only her child" (I, 28). This situation explains Laura's rhetorical question to the Captain in their emotional exchange at the end of the second act: "What has this whole struggle for life or death been about but power?" (44). Lacking power in society and even in the financial management of her home, Laura can exercise it as a mother.

In his attention to the particular combination of maternal power and social powerlessness embodied in Laura, Strindberg, although hardly a feminist himself, can be seen as a precursor of much postwar feminist thinking from its beginnings to the present. As early a commentator as Simone de Beauvoir points out that "the pleasure of feeling absolutely superior—which men feel in regard to women—can be enjoyed by woman only in regard to her children, especially her daughters; she feels frustrated if she has to renounce her privilege, her authority."[14] Sara Ruddick views the conjunction of power and powerlessness as "central to our experience of our mothers and our mothering." She goes on to observe, "In most societies . . . , women are socially powerless in respect to the very reproductive capacities that might make them powerful. . . . Children confront and rely upon a powerful maternal presence only to watch her become the powerless woman in front of the father, the teacher, the doctor, the judge, the landlord—the world."[15] Luce Irigaray provides a historical framework for the dichotomy between

[14]Simone de Beauvoir, *The Second Sex*, trans. H. M. Parshley (1952; New York: Vintage, 1974), p. 579; subsequent page references appear in the text.
[15]Sara Ruddick, "Maternal Thinking," *Feminist Studies*, 6 (1980), 343.

female powerlessness and maternal power by arguing that culture was founded on the murder of the "woman-mother," who had to be disempowered as a woman before male civilization could begin; she claims that women have been valorized only as mothers.[16]

Other writers have come to question the "myth of maternal omnipotence" reflected in the preoccupation with motherhood in so much recent feminist writing. Nancy Chodorow and Susan Contratto, for example, challenge this myth by showing that it "spawns a recurrent tendency to blame the mother on the one hand, and a fantasy of maternal perfectibility on the other."[17] Clearly, Strindberg has not reached this stage of awareness but rather remains under the sway of the myth of maternal omnipotence. Accordingly, Laura's situation is illuminated by Susan Suleiman's explanation of the myth: "Until and unless . . . women can feel that society offers them a trustworthy surrounding in which to pursue both their desire for self-creation and their desire to mother, they will be unwilling to share their child with 'other mothers' and will cling to the fantasy of [maternal omnipotence]. It will appear to them as their only hope."[18]

In keeping with its depiction of maternal omnipotence, *The Father* also reverses the tendency of the traditional, patriarchal belief system to attribute power to beings and relationships that cannot be empirically perceived. The most extensive and influential manifestation of this tendency is of course Christianity, founded on a belief in an invisible divinity. In *Moses and Monotheism* (1939) Freud comments without censure on the role of this tendency in the historical transition from a matriarchal social

[16]Luce Irigaray, *Le Corps-à-corps avec la mère* (Montréal: Pleine Lune, 1981), pp. 15–16, 63. Subsequent page references appear in the text.

[17]Nancy Chodorow and Susan Contratto, "The Fantasy of the Perfect Mother," in *Rethinking the Family: Some Feminist Questions,* ed. Barrie Thorne with Marilyn Yalom (New York: Longman, 1982), p. 55.

[18]Susan R. Suleiman, "The 'Other Mother': On Maternal Splitting (a propos of Mary Gordon's *Men and Angels*)." Forthcoming in *Signs*. In the original manuscript version Suleiman used the phrase "maternal omnipotence"; it is replaced by "ultimate responsibility" in the published article.

order to the patriarchal Mosaic order: "This turning from the mother to the father points in addition to a victory of intellectuality over sensuality—that is, an advance in civilization, since maternity is proved by the evidence of the senses while paternity is a hypothesis, based on an inference and a premiss"—or, as he had written in "Family Romances" (1909), "*'pater semper incertus est'*, while the mother is *'certissima.'*"[19] As Friedrich Engels had shown, the uncertainty of paternity is the basis of the double standard that dictates monogamy for the wife but not for the husband, in order "to make the man supreme in the family and to propagate, as the future heirs to his wealth, children indisputably his own."[20]

In contrast to Engels and Freud, Strindberg, fresh from reading J. J. Bachofen and Paul Lafargue on the original matriarchal order, dares in *The Father* to imagine a world where patriarchy does not automatically reign supreme, where not power but impotence is associated with invisible presences and imperceptible bonds. Hence we find references linking the inability to perceive with the Captain and the ability to perceive with female characters in the play, especially Laura. In his first conversation with his daughter, for instance, the Captain says of the meteoric rocks he examines, "I can study those and tell if they contain the same elements as Earth. *That's all I can see*" (I, 30; emphasis mine). Later, despairing of a man's ability to determine the paternity of his supposed children, he declares, "'My wife's children,' [a father] should say" (II, 40), and "A man never knows anything; he only believes" (III, 54). In light of the drama's emphasis on the Captain's difficulty in perceiving, the fact that the play is presented largely from his perspective appears as an ironic twist.[21]

Having the empirical evidence of maternity on her side, Laura

[19]Freud, *Moses and Monotheism: Three Essays (Der Mann Moses und die monotheistische Religion: Drei Abhandlungen)*, SE, XXIII, 114; "Family Romances" ("Der Familienroman der Neurotiker"), *SE*, IX, 239.

[20]Friedrich Engels, *The Origin of the Family, Private Property, and the State* (1884), based on the translation by Alec West (New York: International Publishers, 1972), p. 128.

[21]Cf. Fritz Paul, *August Strindberg* (Stuttgart: Metzler, 1979), p. 35.

challenges the reasoning behind millennia of Mosaic religion in the guileless question with which she follows the Captain's revelation to her that one cannot know who a child's father is: "That's strange! How can the father have such rights over her child, then?" (I, 23), the "her" standing as a signpost to her unconscious wishes. In like manner, the Doctor, as a partisan of her camp rather than the Captain's, insists that he "must keep to what can be observed" (II, 36). In his demonstration of the tenuousness both of the paternal relation and of patriarchy's corresponding power base, Strindberg implicitly recognizes the compensatory nature of patriarchal social orders—created, that is, in compensation for the unprovability of fatherhood. Jonathan Culler observes, "When we consider that the invisible, omnipotent God is God the Father, not to say God of the Patriarchs, we may well wonder whether, on the contrary, the promotion of the invisible over the visible and of thought and inference over sense perception is not a consequence or effect of the establishment of paternal authority: a consequence of the fact that the paternal relation is invisible."[22] And it is telling that, in *The Father* as in *Rose Bernd* and *Candida*, although perception is associated with the mother figure and the inability to perceive with male characters, the female figures are depicted as functioning outside the privileged sphere of education, knowledge, and, accordingly, language.

In *The Father* the central representation of the mother's power qua mother is the close and yet ambivalent relationship between Laura and Bertha. Precisely these qualities of the mother–daughter bond—closeness and ambivalence—have received a good deal of attention in recent feminist and psychological theory on both sides of the Atlantic. Here again the tone was established by Beauvoir in *The Second Sex:* "In her daughter the mother does not hail a member of the superior caste; in her she seeks a double. She projects upon her daughter all the ambiguity of

---

[22]Jonathan Culler, *On Deconstruction: Theory and Criticism after Structuralism* (Ithaca: Cornell Univ. Press, 1982), p. 59.

her relation with herself; and when the otherness, the alterity, of this *alter ego* comes to be affirmed, the mother feels herself betrayed" (577). Nearly forty years later the psychologists Judith Herman and Helen Lewis wrote: "The power of mothers can be transmitted only to daughters. It is a special kind of power, based not on the ability to kill, but on the ability to create and foster life."[23]

Sensing the special nature of the mother–daughter relationship, Strindberg has the Captain speak enviously to Laura of her "power to change [Bertha's] mind as you wish" (I, 32). Similarly, Bertha's observation that her mother "cries so often" demonstrates Strindberg's intuitive knowledge of the contemporary psychological discovery that "the exploration of the feeling states of the parent, especially the mother, is probably reinforced much more in girls than in boys."[24] Further evidence of Strindberg's awareness of the daughter's special attachment to the mother are Bertha's admonitions to the Captain: "And if you say Mother lies, I'll never believe you again!" (I, 31) and "Don't say anything bad about Mother! You hear?" (III, 56). And of course it is the bond between Laura and Bertha that has the last word of the play, as it were, when Laura's final line—"My child! My own child!"—is followed by the Pastor's "blessing" of the relationship with his pious "Amen!" *The Father* can thus be seen as a preliminary step on the way to Strindberg's *Motherlove* of 1892, a one-act play in which the father is absent from the beginning and the mother has raised her daughter alone, riveting the girl to herself in an attempt to turn her against men.

Strindberg's recognition that the mother–daughter link is in part a reaction against the authority of the father unwittingly prefigures a central tenet of contemporary feminist theory.

[23]Judith L. Herman and Helen B. Lewis, "Anger in the Mother–Daughter Relationship," in *The Psychology of Today's Woman: New Psychoanalytic Visions*, ed. Toni Bernay and Dorothy W. Cantor (Hillsdale, N.J.: Analytic Press, 1986), p. 139.
[24]Judith V. Jordan and Janet L. Surrey, "The Self-in-Relation: Empathy and the Mother–Daughter Relationship," in *Psychology of Today's Woman*, p. 89.

Irigaray, for example, writes in *Le Corps-à-corps avec la mère* of the
need for daughters and mothers to form a reciprocal relationship in order to work toward their mutual emancipation: "[This
relationship] is indispensable for our emancipation from the
authority of the fathers. The relation mother/daughter, daugh-
ter/mother constitutes an extremely explosive nucleus in our
societies" (86). Yet Irigaray is aware too of the profound ambivalence of the mother–daughter relationship, an ambivalence nowhere more graphically expressed than in her lyrical piece "And
the One Doesn't Stir without the Other." Written in the daughter's voice, it is pervaded with the imagery of ambivalence, con-
veying the daughter's simultaneous feelings of suffocation by
and love for the mother: "With your milk, Mother, I swallowed
ice. And here I am now, my insides frozen. And I walk with even
more difficulty than you do, and I move even less. You flowed
into me, and that hot liquid became poison, paralyzing me. . . .
And I can no longer race toward what I love. And the more I
love, the more I become captive, held back by a weightiness that
immobilizes me."[25]

Strindberg also demonstrates considerable insight into mother–daughter ambivalence, for Bertha's protectiveness toward
Laura is countered by feelings of resentment and entrapment.
"How I'd like to get to town, away from here, anywhere at all!"
(I, 31), she exclaims to her father, and goes on to complain that
her mother "doesn't listen to me!" (I, 31). Her response to the
Captain's pressure on her to conform to his will—"I want to be
myself" (III, 56)—points to the motivation for her rebellion
against Laura as well. The dramatization of mother–daughter
ambivalence is not limited to the relationship between Laura and
Bertha, however, since Laura is presented not only as a mother
but as a daughter herself. Although Laura's mother never ap-

[25]Irigaray, "And the One Doesn't Stir without the Other," trans. Hélène V.
Wenzel, *Signs*, 7 (1981), 60. See also Eléanor H. Kuykendall, "Toward an Ethic of
Nurturance: Luce Irigaray on Mothering and Power," in *Mothering: Essays in
Feminist Theory*, ed. Joyce Trebilcot (Towota, N.J.: Rowman & Allanheld, 1983),
pp. 263–274.

pears on stage, she is referred to often, and her presence seems
to hover over the action like a dark cloud; indeed, for Harry
Carlson she is the "secret heart of the play, hidden and mysterious," a modern incarnation of the Terrible Mother archetype.[26] Significantly, the one time she speaks is to ask Laura
whether her tea is ready, and the dutiful daughter replies that
she will "bring it very soon" (I, 24). Yet Laura is by no means a
wholly subservient daughter. That she maintains some distance
between herself and her mother becomes evident when she tells
the Nurse, "My mother musn't know anything about all this [her
efforts to have the Captain committed]. Do you hear that?" (III,
49). Laura's attitude toward her own mother suggests that she is
not terribly sanguine about the mother–daughter bond. And in
general her treatment of Bertha suggests that she is not committed to motherhood for its own sake but rather because of the
power it affords her—the only kind of power she can have. This
aspect of *The Father* anticipates Strindberg's one-act play *The
Bond* (1892), in which a divorcing couple claim that their child is
the focus of their concerns but in fact use him as a tool to justify
their own respective selfish causes.

An illuminating commentary on Laura as mother is provided
by Strindberg's younger contemporary Emma Goldman, the
American anarchist and feminist. Viewing *The Father* as a portrayal of "motherhood, as it really is," she argues that "motherhood, much praised, poetized, and hailed as a wonderful thing,
is in reality very often the greatest deterrent influence in the life
of the child. . . . The average mother is like the hen with her
brood, forever fretting about her chicks if they venture a step
away from the coop. . . . Woman must grow to understand that
the father is as vital a factor in the life of the child as is the
mother. Such a realization would help very much to minimize
the conflict between the sexes."[27] This argument that the father

[26]Harry G. Carlson, *Strindberg and the Poetry of Myth* (Berkeley: Univ. of
California Press, 1982), pp. 51, 53.
[27]Emma Goldman, *The Social Significance of the Modern Drama* (Boston: Badger,
1914), pp. 48, 50.

should play a greater role in parenting surfaces in *The Father* in the relationship between the Captain and Bertha, a relationship portrayed with moments of genuine poignancy. It is to her father that Bertha runs screaming when she thinks that her grandmother wants to hurt her. She burns the midnight oil to work at sewing her father's Christmas gift. And the image with which she describes his arrival home is a beautiful expression of happiness and relief: "It's always so heavy, so terrible in there as if it were a winter night, but when you come, Dad, it's as if we were taking out the double windows on a spring morning!" (I, 31).

Just as the career women Strindberg himself married failed to conform to his expressed ideal of womanhood, the Captain's explanation for his wish that Bertha become a teacher appears to contradict the playwright's avowed sexism in delimiting woman's proper sphere: "I don't want to be my daughter's pimp and bring her up for marriage alone. If she doesn't marry, she'll have a hard time" (I, 19). His interest in Bertha's education is a nurturing influence, as we can see in the horticultural image he uses to describe his sense of having lost her: "I grafted my right arm, half my brain, half the marrow in my backbone to another, because I believed they could grow into one and become a more perfect tree, and then someone came along with a knife and cut everything off just below the graft, and now I'm only half a tree" (III, 55); he tells the Nurse, "It isn't enough for me to have given life to the child—I want to give her my soul, too" (I, 28).

Strindberg's criticism of maternal omnipotence and his corresponding suggestion that the father should have a role in raising children foreshadow the argument voiced in our own day by Dorothy Dinnerstein and Nancy Chodorow. Dinnerstein shows how female-dominated child care guarantees the perpetuation of the sexual double standard that generates so much discord between men and women, how it furthers age-old antagonisms toward woman, including "a deeply ingrained conviction that she is intellectually and spiritually defective; fear that she is untrustworthy and malevolent . . . [and] a sense of primitive outrage at meeting her in any position of worldly authority."[28] Similarly, Chodorow—who, unlike Freud, focuses on the preoedipal phase of development—argues that women's mothering is responsible for crucial and problematic differences in the feminine and the masculine personality: "From the retention of preoedipal attachments to their mother, growing girls come to define and experience themselves as continuous with others; their experience of self contains more flexible or permeable ego boundaries. Boys come to define themselves as more separate and distinct, with a greater sense of rigid ego boundaries and differentiation. The basic feminine sense of self is connected to the world, the basic masculine sense of self is separate."[29] Both Dinnerstein and Chodorow advocate that the father and mother participate equally in child-raising from the beginning of the baby's life, since only this kind of double exposure will prevent the child from reproducing conventional gender distinctions. The non-feminist Strindberg's belief in and censure of maternal omnipotence illuminate the characteristics of the myth as well as its analysis by Suleiman, Dinnerstein, Chodorow, and other contemporary feminist thinkers.

The Captain's wish to play a greater role in raising Bertha, if forward-looking in its implied criticism of maternal omnipotence, is motivated also by two selfish considerations: his desire for a sense of immortality and his need to counteract the strong female influence in the house. In pursuing the second of these concerns he goes too far in his demands: he asserts that "children are to be brought up in their father's faith, according to the law" (I, 22), and that a mother has no rights over her child at all, thereby inciting Laura to battle. The Captain's stance is reminiscent of Strindberg's own as he expressed it in two letters written in January and February 1887: in the first letter he praises

[28]Dorothy Dinnerstein, *The Mermaid and the Minotaur: Sexual Arrangements and Human Malaise* (New York: Harper & Row, 1976), pp. 36–37.

[29]Nancy Chodorow, *The Reproduction of Mothering: Psychoanalysis and the Sociology of Gender* (Berkeley: Univ. of California Press, 1978), p. 169.

Bismarck's Germany, "where patriarchy and virile member are still revered"; in the second he instructs Edvard Brandes to "have a penis of red sandstone erected on my grave."[30] Yet as John Ward points out, by putting such autocratic and obviously unreasonable opinions in the Captain's mouth, "Strindberg is able to criticise the man and to condemn those bourgeois notions of marriage for which he felt both contempt and intense longing."[31]

The conventional view of Laura as evil mother is further undermined by the play's intimation that on a metaphoric level she is scarcely a mother at all, since she appears as hardly feminine. Like Shaw's depiction of Candida, Strindberg's portrayal of Laura flies in the face of the Victorian ideal of the angel in the house; she is hardly the woman envisioned by Patmore and described by Gilbert and Gubar as the "girl whose unselfish grace, gentleness, simplicity, and nobility reveal that she is not only a pattern Victorian lady but almost literally an angel on earth."[32] Laura's divergence from the typically feminine is suggested by her repeated expressions of anger, an emotion traditionally characterized as unwomanly. As Jean Baker Miller has written, "women generally have been led to believe that their identity, as women, is that of persons who should be almost totally without anger and without the *need* for anger. Therefore, anger feels like a threat to women's central sense of identity, which has been called *femininity*."[33] Marianne Hirsch observes of the mother's anger specifically: "Anger . . . stands in a paradoxical relation to the maternal as culture has defined it. In fact, the term 'mater-

[30]Strindberg to Brandes, 19 January and 19 February 1887, in *August Strindbergs brev*, IV (1958), 145, 168; cited in Egil Törnqvist, *Strindbergian Drama: Themes and Structure* (Stockholm: Almqvist & Wiksell, 1982), p. 243n.

[31]John Ward, *The Social and Religious Plays of Strindberg* (London: Athlone, 1980), p. 49.

[32]Sandra M. Gilbert and Susan Gubar, *The Madwoman in the Attic: The Woman Writer and the Nineteenth-Century Literary Imagination* (New Haven: Yale Univ. Press, 1979), p. 22.

[33]Jean Baker Miller, "The Construction of Anger in Women and Men," *Work in Progress* (Wellesley: Stone Center for Developmental Services and Studies, 1983), p. 3.

nal anger' is itself something of an oxymoron. . . . A mother cannot articulate anger *as a mother;* she must step out of a culturally circumscribed role which commands mothers to be caring and nurturing to others, even at the expense of themselves."[34]

Laura's anger is not the only indication of her nonfemininity. After she has had the Captain locked away in an upstairs room, the Pastor indirectly compares her to Lady Macbeth, asking, "May I look at your hand?—Not a spot of blood to give you away, not a trace of the treacherous poison!" (III, 51). Just as Lady Macbeth rejects feminine weakness in her plea to the "spirits" to "unsex me here," Laura gains strength as she sheds femininity. The analogy between Laura and Lady Macbeth has not gone unnoticed by critics of the play, but guided by Janet Adelman's observations on *Macbeth*, we can take its implications even further. Adelman argues that the source of Lady Macbeth's power over Macbeth is her attack on his virility, and that she acquires that power in part because she can make him imagine himself as an infant vulnerable to her: "As [Lady Macbeth] progresses from questioning Macbeth's masculinity to imagining herself dashing out the brains of her infant son, she articulates a fantasy in which to be less than a man is to become interchangeably a woman or a baby."[35] From this moment, Adelman argues, stems the play's central fantasy of escape from woman, manifested first in Macbeth's envisioning his wife as the all-male mother of invulnerable infants ("Bring forth men-children only! / For thy undaunted mettle should compose / Nothing but males") and then in the witches' prophecy: "None of woman born / Shall harm Macbeth."

In *The Father,* the equivalent of Lady Macbeth's attack on her husband's virility is Laura's questioning of the Captain's paternity, a process similarly bound up with the male's fantasies of

[34]Marianne Hirsch, *Speaking for Her: Mothers, Daughters, and Narrative* (Bloomington: Indiana Univ. Press). Forthcoming.

[35]Janet Adelman, "'Born of Woman': Fantasies of Maternal Power in *Macbeth,*" in *Cannibals, Witches, and Divorce: Estranging the Renaissance,* ed. Marjorie Garber (Baltimore: Johns Hopkins Univ. Press, 1987), p. 102.

being a child or a woman. It is as a child that the Captain begs Laura for mercy: "Don't you see I'm as helpless as a child? Don't you hear I'm asking for pity as from a mother?" (II, 45). Like Candida, Laura slips into the maternal role vis-à-vis her husband: "Weep, my child; then you'll have your mother with you again. Do you remember it was as your second mother I first came into your life? . . . I loved you as my child. But, you know, every time your feelings changed nature and you came as my lover, I was ashamed, and your embrace was a joy that was followed by pangs of conscience as if I had committed incest" (II, 46). Particularly in view of the Captain's later remark to the Nurse that "it's a delight to fall asleep on a woman's breast—a mother's or a mistress', but most delightful one's mother's!" (III, 61), it seems that Laura's inability to reconcile her maternal feelings for her husband with his erotic desires for her represents a male projection of this problem onto her. Thus in contrast to Freud's claim in "Femininity" (1933) that a wife's assumption of a maternal posture toward her husband will strengthen their marriage—a belief anticipated by Shaw's numerous portrayals of women who infantilize their husbands or lovers—Strindberg's drama acknowledges the conflict between men's filial and sexual feelings toward women, a conflict Freud himself had described in his earlier paper "On the Universal Tendency to Debasement in the Sphere of Love" (1912).[36]

Whereas Shaw sustains his desexualized presentation of wife as mother and of husband as son throughout *Candida*, Strindberg contrasts the mother–son relationship idealized by both the Captain and Laura with the reality of male–female sexual relations, fraught with tension and hostility. Here the Captain's fantasy of his womanhood comes to the fore: the more masculine

[36]Axel Johan Uppvall regards all of the mother-son references in *The Father* as proof of Strindberg's incestuous fixation on his mother; see Uppvall, *August Strindberg: A Psychoanalytic Study with Special Reference to the Oedipus Complex* (Boston: Badger, 1920). While Strindberg may indeed have been close to his mother, to reduce his treatment of the issue to a version of his own family constellation seems unnecessarily limiting and obscures the larger significance of this conflict for men at the time.

Laura becomes, thus following in the footsteps of the "unsexed" Lady Macbeth, the more feminine he imagines himself to be. This gender reversal reflects Strindberg's belief that "the emancipation of women necessarily leads to the effeminization of men."[37] Laura symbolically expresses her appropriation of her husband's male power by having all the bullets removed from his guns and bags, a gesture that calls to mind the actress's requesting that the count unbuckle his saber in Schnitzler's *La Ronde*. The Captain's obsession with gender reversal pervades his language in the latter part of the play: "When women get old and have ceased to be women, they get beards on their chins. I wonder what men get when they become old and have ceased being men?" (II, 47). And he envisions Laura as Omphale, the Lydian queen to whom Hercules was sent as a slave, who amused herself by making him dress up as a woman and do woman's work. "Omphale!" the Captain exclaims. "Now you're playing with the club while Hercules spins your wool!" (III, 58). The Captain displays a similar sense of gender slippage in suggesting that the ruler over life is "the god of strife then! Or the goddess nowadays!" (III, 60). In contrast to the situation in *Macbeth*, however, in *The Father* it is not the female but the male presence that is ultimately eliminated from the play. This outcome represents not a male wish-fulfillment fantasy but rather Strindberg's horrific anxiety dream of a female assumption of power.

In Strindberg's oeuvre the idea that each gender possesses aspects of the other is by no means limited to *The Father*. The switching of gender roles in *Comrades* has been mentioned; the title character of *Miss Julie* tells her father's valet that in growing up she learned everything a boy learns and was dressed like a boy, and that on the estate of her emancipated mother, the men were given the women's jobs and vice versa. Similarly, in the one-act play *Creditors* (1888) Adolf describes a sense of identity between himself and his wife, admitting that when she gave

[37] Barry Jacobs, "'Psychic Murder' and Characterization in Strindberg's 'The Father,'" *Scandinavica*, 8 (1969), 26.

birth to their child, he too felt labor pains. The preoccupation
with gender duality, with masculinity in women and femininity
in men, appears in the post-Inferno Strindberg as well, as Stephen Mitchell points out in his analysis of *Easter* (1901).[38] Indeed, Declan Kiberd calls Strindberg "the first modern writer to
make androgyny *the* central issue in his accounts of sexual relations."[39]

When we recognize the importance of androgyny in Strindberg's work, we are inevitably reminded of the equally large role
it plays in Shaw's; and when we compare their work we are led to
a rather surprising conclusion. For Shaw, androgyny is an ideal,
but for all his attempts to present men and women as equal and
alike, as in *Candida,* he succeeds only in perpetuating sexual
stereotypes that underline the *differences* between the sexes.
Strindberg, by contrast, repeatedly emphasizes sexual difference, often scandalizing audiences by the vituperation of his
misogyny, yet his male and female characters are governed by
the same passions and driven by the same rages; his men and
women, in the last analysis, are very much alike. These para-
doxes epitomize the complexities of the European drama created by male writers at the turn of the century, a period in which
conflicting currents of thought about women inevitably created
an atmosphere of confusion and yet excitement, perplexity and
yet hope.

[38]Stephen A. Mitchell, "The Path from *Inferno* to the Chamber Plays: *Easter*
and Swedenborg," *Modern Drama,* 29 (1986), 163.
[39]Declan Kiberd, *Men and Feminism in Modern Literature* (London: Macmillan,
1985), p. 34.

Index

Bovenschen, Silvia, 81
Bowlby, Rachel, 97n
Brandes, Edvard, 208, 222
Brecht, Bertolt, 79–80
Breuer, Horst, 108n
Breuer, Josef, 8–9, 136n
Brooks, Louise, 92–93
Brown, Janet, 18n
Brownstein, Rachel, 17n
Burke, Carolyn, 14n
Butler, Josephine, 140

Caird, Mona, 195
Cakmur, Belma, 167n
Campbell, Mrs. Patrick, 17
Carlson, Harry, 219
Carlson, Susan L., 121n
Carpenter, Andrew, 106
Carpenter, Edward, 2, 13, 67
Carroll, Michael P., 190, 191n
Case, Sue-Ellen, 19n
Cauer, Minna, 140
Chamisso, Adelbert von: "Strange Story of Peter Schlemihl," 166
Champsaur, Félicien: Lulu, Une Clownesse danseuse, 80
Charcot, Jean M., 9, 27
Chekhov, Anton, 15
Chodorow, Nancy, 146–47, 214, 220–21
Christ, Carol, 191
Cixous, Hélène, 8, 18, 159n, 162, 180n, 205
Clément, Catherine, 8, 159–62, 180, 205n
Cohen, Ed, 65n
Collett, Camilla, 150
Collins, Michael, 118
Colum, Padraic, 115
Comedy, 193–94; and gender roles, 112, 120–21
Contratto, Susan, 146, 214
Cook, Ellen Piel, 68n
Coss, Clare, 19n
Couch, Lotte S., 43n
Cowen, Roy C., 144n
Cranach, Lucas, 55
Crane, Gladys M., 197n
Culler, Jonathan, 20, 216
Cunningham, Gail, 195n

Dacre, Kathleen, 156n
Dandy, 68
Décaudin, Michel, 56n
Dickens, Charles: Old Curiosity Shop, 89
Dijkstra, Bram, 52n
Dinnerstein, Dorothy, 147, 220–21
"Dora" (Ida Bauer), 10, 126, 161, 164
Douglas, Lord Alfred, 58
Dowie, Ménie Muriel, 195
Dowling, Linda, 68n, 69n
Downs, Brian, 159n
Dukore, Bernard F., 201
Dumont, Louise, 17
Duse, Eleonora, 17

Egerton, George, 195
Ehrenreich, Barbara, 7–8, 180n
Ellenberger, Henri F., 29n
Ellis, Havelock, 14n
Ellis, Sarah S., 4n
Elsaesser, Thomas, 93n
Emrich, Wilhelm, 81n
Engels, Friedrich, 100, 215
English, Deirdre, 7–8, 180n
Erikson, Erik H., 126n
Evans, Richard J., 4n, 5n, 140n
Eve, 53
Eysoldt, Gertrud, 81n

Farr, Florence, 17
Father–daughter relationship, 15; in Hedda Gabler, 156; in Lulu plays, 82–87; in Playboy of the Western World, 103, 106–14, 119, 123–26, 129–30; in Rose Bernd, 103, 123–26, 129–31, 144; in Salomé, 61–62, 82, 84–85
Fay, Frank, 115
Fay, William, 115
Fechter, Paul, 127
Felman, Shoshana, 16
Female sexuality: Freud on, 10–14, 32–35, 139; 19th-century myths of, 3–4; post-Freud views on, 32n; Schnitzler on, 29, 35–50; Wedekind on, 101
Feminism, contemporary, 6n, 126, 146–47